For ten years, **Amelia Dalton** owned a small ship running cruises to the remote island chains of Scotland's stunning West Coast. She worked closely with The National Trust for Scotland, and gained her commercial qualifications as a Captain. Amelia advises for individual clients on river and ocean cruises and runs her own travel company, Amelia Dalton Travel.

Also by this author

Mistress and Commander:
High jinks, high seas and Highlanders

PAGES
from my
PASSPORT

AMELIA DALTON

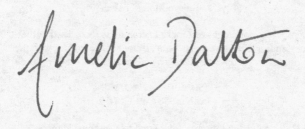

SANDSTONE PRESS

First published in Great Britain in 2023 by
Sandstone Press Ltd
PO Box 41
Muir of Ord
IV6 7YX
Scotland

www.sandstonepress.com

ISBN: 978-1-913207-78-6
ISBNe: 978-1-913207-79-3

Sandstone Press is committed to a sustainable future.
This book is made from Forest Stewardship Council ® certified paper.

Cover design by Nathan Burton
Typeset by Iolaire, Newtonmore
Printed and bound by CPI Group (UK) Ltd, Croydon, CR0 4YY

To my talented, resourceful and entertaining son Hugo.
Without him, I might not be here.

Contents

Acknowledgements

I owe many, many thanks to those who enabled me to flex the Pages of my Passport.

Firstly, to the *Hebridean Spirit* team. Together we created a stylish ship to voyage in many seas visiting secret corners and remote islands. Particular thanks go to Andrew Quarrie who gave me a chance, to Michael Fenton for his faith in my abilities and to the ship's captains and crew who took on the challenges of unknown anchorages and uncharted waters. You all sewed the *Pages* together.

To Lee Durrell, who has embraced and been a vital element of so many of my adventures from Madagascar to Borneo, to Alexander McCall Smith, whose company and talks were such an inspiration at the Tobermory Book Festival and to Moira at Sandstone Press, who again has wrestled with my wayward prose and to Peter Hughes for his advice and encouragement.

Bjarkøya

Lofoten Isles

FINLAND

Utvær

Sognefjord

Helsinki

Stockholm

Bergen

St. Petersburg

RUSSIA

NORWAY
& THE BALTICS

GREECE

GREECE & THE CYCLADES

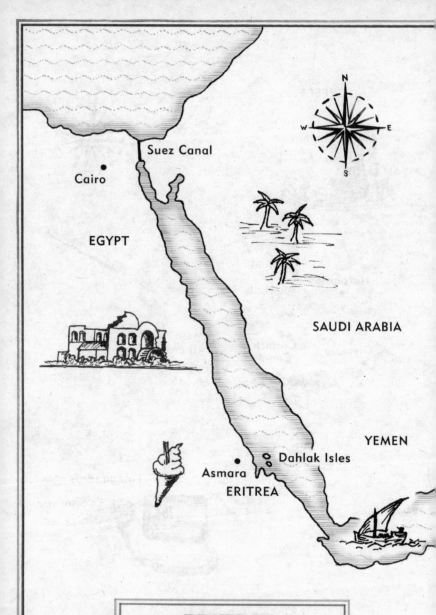

ERITREA
& THE RED SEA

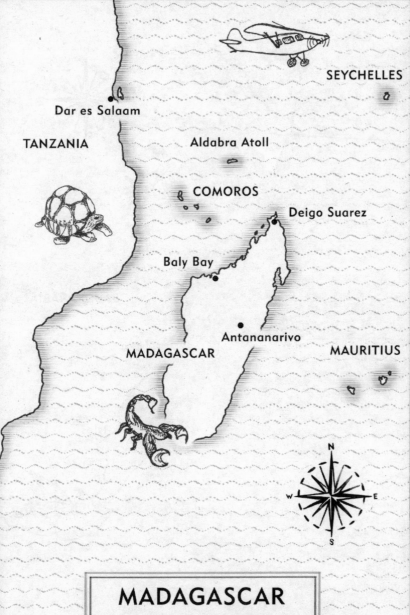

SEYCHELLES

Dar es Salaam

TANZANIA

Aldabra Atoll

COMOROS

Deigo Suarez

Baly Bay

Antananarivo

MADAGASCAR

MAURITIUS

N
W   E
S

MADAGASCAR & THE COMOROS

The Story So Far

I decided on a whim, in my thirties, when I should have known better, to plunge into the salty, men-only business of ship-owning, taking everyone by surprise, not least myself. I was born into Yorkshire county life and lived like a butterfly, dining and dancing in great country houses. A care-free life of hunt balls, shooting parties and idyllic family seaside holidays in Scotland, on a small boat. A boat that changed my life.

After the sudden death of my treasured younger son, Digby, at the age of eight, I decided to set up an expedition cruise business to support a Scottish skipper. Together we found a boat in Denmark, *Monaco*, a sturdy eighty-five-foot Arctic trawler, built of solid oak. It was about as far from whimsy as a boat could be. My first book, *Mistress and Commander,* charts the years of crises amongst Scotland's coastal communities, the chauvinism, adventures and quirky passengers that followed.

My raffish Skipper schooled me in seamanship; in turn, I tutored him in Scotland's wildflowers and fauna, until one day he disappeared. A succession of skippers followed, one incontinent, others randy, none permanent. The only solution was for me to take on the officials and to achieve a commercial skipper's ticket.

Eventually, the Scottish escapade came to an end. But I needed a job – and I longed to be back at sea. So I dusted off my passport...

1

At Last! We Go to Sea

'Amelia, did you get the memo?'

Michael watched me bound up the gangway two treads at a time, enthusiasm lending impetus to my legs. I knew I was cutting it fine, but it had been worth it.

I had needed to see him, just one more time.

'What memo?' I asked breathlessly. Michael Fenton was keen on memos.

'The one about Marigolds? Did you bring them? Pink or yellow?' he asked, his voice fizzing with excitement.

'Oh, rubber gloves! Yellow, more nautical than pink, I reckoned,' I replied, thankful I had remembered them. Do I smell of stale pub, smoke and booze, I wondered?

It was a big day. There would be champagne, marbled Highland beef, Scottish prawns, Tobermory Cheddar, lobster and Colonsay oysters. All far more appealing than rubber gloves. Only the very top-quality west coast produce had been carefully loaded on board, and I was relieved I had missed the bustle of vans, lorries and tradesmen. The two vessels lay quietly alongside the quay, almost smugly, waiting for the off while Oban's small fishing fleet of battered trawlers, tangled with clam dredges, masts and radar aerials, provided a stark contrast to the two navy-blue hulls, glossy and immaculate. The bridge, cabin windows, davits and rails all sparkled with fresh paint, white and crisp in the morning light. The two ships occupied most of the pier and had even succeeded in taking over the space reserved for the CalMac inter-island ferries. Their air of glamour, prosperity and elegance was palpable and striking. The 'new' ship, *Hebridean Spirit,* lay astern of the elderly lady *Hebridean Princess,* and Scotland's cruise line, now grown from one to two sleek vessels, brought an air of modernity and glamour to the grey granite of Oban.

Today was both an end – the end of extensive refurbishment – and a beginning. Today, three years' worth of dreams were to become a reality, and a large portion of the buck, or the millions of bucks, stopped with me. Soon, well-heeled passengers with sky-high expectations would saunter up the gangway, be presented with canapés and bubbly and introduced to their 'staterooms'. They were not mere cabins on this fancy ship. Even the gangway, enlivened with bunches of daisies and silver thistles, had a marine blue carpet. From the moment of arrival on the quay, there was to be no doubt that this, the world's newest small cruise ship, would also be the most exclusive. Stylish and elegant, she would lead the world in chic expeditionary travel.

There was no hiding. I was responsible: responsible for the captain knowing where he was to go and where he should anchor; responsible for the crew knowing at which jetty to land our precious passengers. Once ashore, I was responsible for the passengers' entertainment; after all, they were the *raison d'être.* From churches to museums, dancing to wine tasting, beach barbecues to concerts, bird watching to snorkelling, every element was my responsibility. Three years of searching, exploring remote coasts and islands, of recces and inspections were about to become frighteningly real. Until this moment, the passengers had been virtual. But now, after all the years of planning, my itineraries would run, be tested and operated. Would my far-flung schedules live up to my colourful brochure descriptions? Had I succeeded in replicating the romance of Scotland's lonely islands in other parts of the world? Had I found the St Kilda, Rum or Jura of far-flung countries? Would the Med, Indian Ocean and Baltic prove as enticing as the charms of the Outer Hebrides, Skye and Mull?

Any moment now the new ship, with a full complement to test the systems, would be off on her 'shake-down cruise' from Oban to Leith where she would be officially 'Named', followed immediately by her first real cruise, with real passengers. It was fully booked.

Finally, *Hebridean Spirit* was ready.

Well, kind of.

Oban was bustling, the waterfront thronging with visitors impeding my path to the pub. I had just enough time to see him. But holidaymakers, many elderly and white-haired, doddered along, making good use of sticks and walking frames, whiling away their day. It was the usual, low-spend, inactive bunch that Oban seemed to attract. I pressed on, trying to weave my way through without barging into anyone. But I was determined. I had to see him. For so many years Cubby MacKinnon had exasperated, amused and annoyed me, and had almost ruled my life. It was seven years since I had last seen him but being back in Oban presented an opportunity – one I had long wondered about and did not want to miss.

The moment I ducked through the low doorway into the Oban Arms, I knew he was there. His smooth, sexy voice, laden with *double entendres*, was unmistakable. From the wheelhouse high above the water, Cubby's quips, tall stories and blether had entertained islanders, passengers, the Coast Guard and fishing communities. For the years when he was Skipper of 'my' boat, *Monaco,* the Arctic trawler we had found together in Denmark, he had been a powerful presence. I had bought *Monaco* for him to operate and together we had battled with storms, daft passengers, dodgy finances and crippling bureaucracy.

Naturally, he was propping up the bar, regaling anyone who would listen to his seadog tales, denouncing the scourge of fish farms or proclaiming which island grew the best Golden Wonder potatoes. He spotted me as I came in but there was not the slightest hesitation in his story, just a knowing wink. It was a tale I knew well, a good one, the one about hiding in the bracken on Jura, tickling trout and escaping from the Laird.

'Aye, well, I'll be leaving you all just now.' He straightened up and moved across the floor to a table by the window. Carefully setting down his partially drunk pint and whisky chaser, he turned and looked directly at me.

'So, it's yourself . . . Let me see you now. It's been that long, you'll be a wee bit heavier!'

'Cubby – what cheek! You're a wee bit greyer yourself!' I retaliated. Really, despite a little grey in his beard and moustache, and at his temples, he looked just the same, and with the same mocking twinkle in those 'sea' eyes.

'You'll have time for a wee sensation?' he asked. I remembered his father asking the same question many years ago, in a life before I knew anything of the sea, before I had been sucked into the charms, vagaries and complications of the west coast.

'But of course. And I want to hear all about what you've been up to.' I had heard about the new boat a shipyard was converting for him to operate cruises to St Kilda.

'Aye, and what have you been up to?' he asked. 'Have you a new boyfriend?' He had always been perceptive.

'No, Cubby, I have not.' But maybe I had. His question flipped my thoughts away, away to the man I thought of as HH. Was he married, had he a girlfriend? Where did he live? As yet I had no idea; HH had given nothing away.

'Och, well there's hope still for me, then?' the warmth in Cubby's voice, welcoming as ever, brought me back to the harbourside pub.

'Cubby, there's always hope for you!' I lied, smiling at him with affection.

'Aye, so you say, but I can see I'm too late, you've a wee look in your eyes that tells me otherwise.' He glanced out of the window. 'And I can see you've moved up in the world.' He nodded towards the two sleek vessels beside the quay.

'Well, I've got to earn my living somehow! They look smart, don't you think?'

'Aye, smart enough,' he agreed, almost reluctantly. 'And you've plenty of potential out there.' He waved the almost-empty whisky glass towards the esplanade. 'If they've a stick or Zimmer, you just smile and give them a brochure.'

'Cubby, that's shocking! Anyway, the new ship is an expedition ship with beach landings on islands all over the place. Norway, Russia, Egypt, Eritrea, Oman, India, you name it.' I hoped it sounded grand.

'They'll be needing plenty of spondulicks too, then.'

'Mmmm, it's not cheap, but it will be great value,' I replied loyally. 'And we're upping the "adventure" element for *Princess* too.'

'You've done well to be ready on time.' He was fishing for a story to regale the pub with later.

'Not much choice. The ship's got to get round to Leith for the Naming Ceremony with Princess Anne. She won't be able to change her diary, so we have to be on time. But there'll be no paying passengers in the cabins until after that. They will come on board immediately after the ceremony for the first cruise to Norway, but we've lunches, teas and dinners every day till Leith.'

'So where are you going to be for all these fancy meals?' he asked, teasing out a line of tobacco and positioning it neatly along a Rizzla paper.

'Oh, all the way round. Douglas, Liverpool, Dublin, you name it, and I've got her into the Pool of London for three nights,' I said. 'It seems opening Tower Bridge is free, and I love the idea of stopping all the rush hour city traffic. Watching the bridge open from the water will be fun.' I was smiling at the thought.

'Och, have you no sense of economy, girl? The bridge may be free, but what about all the charges once you're through? Lightermen and all. It'll be a closed shop, everything tightly controlled.'

Since I had last seen him, I had travelled from the Arctic to the Tropics while Cubby stayed in his home patch among the Scottish islands, fishing and boating. Yet he still knew more about the whole business than I did.

'Cubby, I've got to go. You're the one who taught me the importance of being on time. I'd be in real trouble if they left without me.' He picked up his whisky, drained the final drop and set the empty glass down on the ring-marked tabletop.

'Aye, aye. Well, it's been grand to see you.' He looked

almost sad and somehow smaller. Seeing him had stirred up a lot of buried feelings. His warmth, piercing sexy gaze and playful humour were still as attractive. But through his charms crept the same hint of unpredictability. Our disputes resulting in a tribunal were long gone, yet that old sinking feeling of constant worry, of dodgy finances and frightening accountability came welling up. Now, I was responsible again, but this time there was a whole raft of other people to share the load, a fancy ship and a well-founded company for support.

Being late now would be much worse.

'You've only just made it.' Michael's rebuke brought me back to the present.

'Are we leaving now?' I asked, still trying to catch my breath and shake off the memories of Cubby – and my feelings.

'In precisely six minutes. Both ships will sail together down the sound. *Princess* first of course, then we'll follow. The chopper for the video should be here any minute. We'll have a management meeting in a couple of hours once we're down by Jura, so I hope you're ready.' He scanned the waters looking across the harbour.

I suddenly remembered his question. 'So, why the Marigolds?'

'A few things still to be done,' came his economical reply.

'Things that need Marigolds?'

'One or two of the bathrooms, and possibly the heads, seem to be giving trouble. Hopefully, the engineers can fix them, and with any luck, you won't need them.'

I jumped as gurgles and squeals like a sick pig burst out from above. Then, across the bay, above the finger of the Hutcheson Memorial, a dark spot grew, clattering towards us above the yachts on moorings in the Kerrera marina, coming to hover by the cardinal buoy marking the channel south, past Kerrera. The chopper had arrived. Now the piper had his pig under control and 'Scotland the Brave' skirled around the ship. As if by divine command, the clouds parted and the sun burst through, illuminating the whole harbour. *Hebridean Princess* gave two short toots and, belying her age, pulled smartly away from the quay, her bow swung round to head down the sound. On board *Hebridean Spirit*, the whole ship seemed to be holding its breath. We waited. A little tremor shook the decks as life and her identity swept up from her keel. *Hebridean Spirit* became a living ship. Like all ships, she would have a character, and we would have no choice but to get to know her.

The two vessels, both a rich marine blue with a red water-line and white superstructure, sailed together for the first time.

Kerrera, its low hills green with mid-summer bracken dotted with sheep, slid past to starboard. To port, on the mainland side, knots of on-lookers stood outside the few white houses scattered along the coast road. The people of Oban watched and waved from among billows of blue and pink hydrangeas.

Scotland's cruise line sailed serenely past. The crew, none of whom I knew, grinned. Everyone grinned. The air of excitement was universal.

We had just one day left before our first potential passengers came on board to look round, so for the moment the manifest comprised shipyard lads and a bunch of Andrew the purser's friends. He had told them what they were in for. They were on board to clean. This was not a jolly. I fought my way along the passageway where rolls of carpet lay idly like giant Swiss rolls, pictures leant nonchalantly against the walls, cardboard boxes huddled together. There was plenty still to be completed.

'Anyone seen Andrew?' a voice shouted above the general hubbub in Reception.

As the romantically named archipelago 'the Isles of the Sea' drew abeam, *Princess* gave a blast of her horn and turned a few degrees west heading towards Iona. Her decks were lined with waving, cheering passengers, on their cruise to the Barra and beyond. *Spirit* replied, and we headed south towards the Isle of Man and our first 'show-off' port.

Lacking an official job on board, I slipped up to the top deck to enjoy the surroundings. These were waters I knew well with deep-sea lochs and secret anchorages which Cubby had introduced me to, where he had anchored *Monaco* in golden evenings or tucked her away from winter storms. We had dropped off our passengers ashore to walk and revel in the seclusion and peace on many different islands. Once I had had a happy married life with two little boys and a springer spaniel. A life before death and Scotland had changed me.

There, to port, between the islands of Scarba and Jura lay the infamous Corryvreckan, '*the cauldron of the speckled sea*'. The turbulent waters looked benign at neap tide in the afternoon sun but playing the eddies and tidal currents had been Cubby's 'thing', another aspect of his practical seamanship. Through him, in the good times, I had managed to achieve my marine qualifications, but would that experience and knowledge be adequate now? Was I sufficiently experienced to create a complete passenger programme for this new ship? The responsibility was now inescapable. As soon as HRH had named her, the passengers would come on board and my itineraries would be put to the test.

The 'Show Off Tour' with stops at Douglas, Liverpool, Dartmouth, Plymouth and Dover slipped by in a frenzy of entertaining. Mounds of vol au vents, canapés and copious champagne, each day an endless succession of greeting, smiling and also pride as the inhabitants of each port came to look over the ship and, we hoped, choose their future cabin. Mornings were for coffee with eclairs and croissants. Lunches were lavish buffets and tea, waist-threatening with tarts and scones. Dinners were of Scotland's best: scallops and Colonsay oysters, wild salmon and prawns, haggis and marbled beef preceded cranachan, rich with oatmeal, cream and raspberries. Each day we grew fatter and increasingly exhausted. The moment a meal was done, and the passengers had ambled down the gangway, we returned to join the shipyard lads working in shifts to finalise another cabin. My Marigolds were wearing thin. There was a hole in the right thumb, not an appealing thought should I have to unblock one of the heads.

From the outer entrance of the estuary, the Thames is tricky. All the way upstream, from Canvey Island, past the porticoes of Greenwich, the rows of warehouses, right through Tower Bridge and until we tied up alongside HMS Belfast, the captain would have to be on his toes, but for me, with no responsibilities, it would be the passage of a lifetime.

'What time will we be entering the Thames?' I asked, determined not to miss a moment whatever time of day or night it might be.

'The bridge lift is scheduled for eight thirty tomorrow morning,' the captain replied, a glint of satisfaction in his eye. Raising the roadway during the morning rush hour would create a jam. The traffic had to be stopped while the bascules slowly lifted apart to allow us through.

'How did you swing that one?' I asked, enjoying the pun.

He shrugged. 'Just depends on the tide. Anyway, with the amount we're paying, I reckon they can open it whenever we want.'

'But it's free! That's why I put the Pool of London into the schedule,' I said, afraid that, at the very start of my planning, I had missed something.

'Yes, sorry, you're right. It's not the bridge that's costly, but once we're through we're a sitting duck. Thank God we don't need a tug to get alongside Belfast.'

Cubby had been right. The need for a tug had not even occurred to me. Unhappily, I left, pushing through the heavy steel door. I had anticipated the manoeuvring would be tricky but neither the captain nor the marine department had made any objection. Increasingly I felt overwhelmed by nerves. Would the itineraries I had constructed so carefully for so many years, work? Were they actually operable? Had I thought of every aspect? Landing fees, Customs clearances? What else had I missed? I had studied depths, anchorages and wind patterns for so many seas and ports.

My brief from Michael had been to replicate the intimate cruises *Hebridean Princess* had been making so successfully around Scotland's convoluted coasts. I was to find the equivalent of the west coast worldwide. Archipelagos, islands, lochs, castles and communities that echoed those so-successful Scottish voyages taking people to visit the remote and inaccessible. For three years, I had not stopped. I had created sequences of voyages ranging from northern Norway east to India. I had found distant islands, tiny ports with colourful histories and small museums rich with local interest.

Immediately the bottle had been smashed, *Spirit* would be off. She would set sail for Bergen with all the staterooms filled. Every passenger would be anticipating an unforgettable experience as they cruised among the unknown Norwegian islands and remoter fjords in this elegant small ship. Some had booked more than two years ago. Expectations ran high and my job was to turn their expectations into reality.

Would my plans work? What had I forgotten? I felt, unusually, slightly seasick.

Rain, relentless and drenching, forced me back under the steel overhang. I knew better than to seek cover on the bridge: navigating in the narrow waters of the tidal Thames required non-stop concentration, even in good visibility. But the estuary was wider than I had anticipated. Muddy water stretched away to port and starboard, muddy and dirty compared with the clear waters we had left behind in Scotland. Sea and sky merged into grey nothingness. Surrounded by mud flats and low land, the crew would be relying on the navigational equipment as *Hebridean Spirit* made her way carefully upstream.

06.45 on the twenty-fifth of June. How could the weather be like this? June should be sunshine, roses, frocks and fancy hats, strawberries and cream. And this evening we had our biggest, most prestigious party.

> The Chairman & Directors
> **AT HOME**
> Champagne & Canapés on the Aft Deck
> *Monday 25th June 2001*
> R.S.V.P.   18.30
> *Hebridean Spirit*   Black Tie

These invitations had amused me. How could the Directors be 'At Home' on the ship? They all lived in Yorkshire.

'Amelia! Amelia!' My name was being called urgently over the Tannoy. 'Please come to Reception.' Giving myself a shake to remove as much of the rain as I could, I pushed through the weathertight door. At last, the carpet in Reception was going down.

'Are, there you are.' Michael looked frazzled, his glasses were smeared and his hair was in need of a comb. He fired questions at me. 'What are the plans for tonight? Will we be tied alongside *Belfast*? She'll be closed to the public by then. Are people allowed to cross her? How will the Chairman get on board?'

I tried to be reassuring 'I'm sure Andrew or the first officer will have sorted the ship's arrangements out. We have a couple of launches hired to ferry people across the river from Tower Pier as the tenders aren't here yet.'

Immediately I mentioned the tenders I realised it was a mistake. The tenders were being specially designed and built in Orkney. They were entirely Michael's babies. But they were not on board, we did not have them and with every day I became increasingly terrified they would not be ready. By now there had been several terse conversations about this.

'Amelia, don't worry, they'll be waiting, ready for us in Leith. I know how critical they are.' Did he realise they would be needed several times every day, all through the Norwegian fjords and islands to get passengers ashore? Without tenders my carefully designed itineraries were inoperable.

Hoping to divert him, I said, 'The Watermen wouldn't let us use our own tenders, anyway.'

He turned towards the door. 'Come up to the bridge.' He disappeared up the stairs, but I knew this was not a good moment to interrupt the deck officers.

No one even stirred as the Managing Director entered. Tension filled the air. No chat, no scanning for dolphins or sipping of coffee. Just concentration. I slipped through the portside door onto the bridge wing to be out of the way. We were just passing the looming UFO of the Millennium Dome. Visibility was improving. Slowly the ship turned a corner, following the river as it snaked inland. Weak rays of yellow morning light began to squeeze through the rain clouds.

'Nearly there,' said Michael, oblivious to the tension. White colonnades and pepper pots of the Old Naval College, elegant reminders of Greenwich's long maritime history, rolled slowly past on the port side. A few more twists and turns, north then west until a distant sound of sirens floated towards us over the muddy water. Tower Bridge, all gables, turrets, walkways and Victorian charm, looped across the river ahead barring the ship's progress. *Hebridean Spirit* swept nearer as a little crack appeared and slowly, smoothly, it grew. Steadily and surprisingly quickly the bascules pivoted, the road lifted and parted. Just visible above the blue and white railings were vans, trucks and lorries, queuing in the morning rush.

Smoothly, *Hebridean Spirit* slipped between the piers and under the high walkway. Pale faces peered, staring over the balustrades at the smart navy blue and white ship. Engines revved impatiently. Almost before the stern was through the sirens wailed again and the road quickly descended, returning to its place providing passage across the river. Close by on the port shoulder lay HMS *Belfast*. Heaving lines snaked out from *Spirit* crossing the few yards of turbulent water. Fat ropes followed, hauled over the gap. Black fenders, like taut, giant aubergines became gently squeezed as *Spirit* snuggled up to *Belfast*. Smoothly she came alongside. The captain grinned.

The stacks of boxes in Reception were lower, the piles of logo'd fleeces still in their tissue paper had diminished. Fluffy bath robes, neatly folded on pristine bed covers, now graced their appropriate staterooms. By degrees the ship was becoming an entity, not exactly 'a well-oiled machine', but the crew were slicker and smarter by the day.

Fresh from a shower and in evening clothes, Michael looked a little more relaxed. He asked me to go ashore to meet the Chairman and his party, as he still had plenty to do on board.

'Of course I will, a pleasure. Pity about the rain, but we can show off the new brollies. I'll take a clutch with me.' I grasped an armful from the polished brass stand.

With the wash from every passing boat, the slight wooden pier rocked. Minutes stretched out as I waited. Despite the rain, the Thames bustled with boats. Disco lights pulsed, flashes of electric pink and blue danced in slithering patterns across the water. Michael Jackson's world drowned out the roar of City traffic. To my left the Tower, still a formidable bulk, exuded menace, lurking grey and grim in the mist. Where on earth were the Chairman and his party?

'Amelia. Amelia.' The VHF clipped to my lifejacket burst into life. 'Amelia, this is *Hebridean Spirit*. Channel 73.'

'Channel 73.' I twisted the little knob.

'Have they arrived?' The captain was curt. 'I can't see anyone through the binoculars. Anyone with you on the pontoon?'

'No, 'fraid it's still just me.'

'Rats! No one at all?' His irritation crackled through the air.

'Nope, sorry.'

'Blast! Well, they've missed their party. The launch has had to go off now, they won't extend their hours. Pity we don't have the tenders, but there's nothing I can do.'

'Oh no! Does Michael know?'

'No, he seems to have disappeared, probably in one of the cabins fixing something. Will you be Ok?'

'Yes, no problem for me. I'll just go home. But all that food and drink, what a waste and the galley's been working for hours!'

'Good evening.' From behind me came a gentle, educated voice. I turned to see an elegant man in a grey suit walking onto the wooden boards, his long face creased into a rather strained smile.

'Are you anything to do with *Hebridean Spirit*?' Behind him, teetering in high heels, cowering under brollies and swathed in macs, came a gaggle of flimsy dresses, accompanied by dark-suited men. Tentatively they stepped onto the bouncing jetty.

'Hello! Good evening. Yes, I'm Amelia.' I held out my hand.

'I do apologise we're so late. There was a hold up on the embankment and then the minibus didn't seem to know how to find this pier.'

'Just a moment, please. I'll give the ship a shout.' I walked out of earshot to the end of the pier. '*Hebridean Spirit, Hebridean Spirit,* this is Amelia. Captain, they're here now. What do you think? Any chance you can whistle up that launch?'

'No, afraid not. As I said it's gone off until the end of the evening. It will be back then to return people ashore. Nothing we can do, I'm afraid.' Was it relief in his voice?

I turned, wondering how to break the news, my gaze

sweeping across the ruffled rain-spattered waters. The disco boats had all disappeared down river, taking their parties of dancing revellers on to different sodden views. There was no good way to tell the chairman and shareholders I was unable to get them onto their ship.

Then, in the distance, under the central arch of London Bridge, I saw a small tug chugging rapidly towards me, borne swiftly downstream on the ebbing tide. I twirled the VHF to Channel 67.

'Tug under London Bridge. Tug under London Bridge. This is Amelia.' Silence. He would be past me soon. I had to make him stop.

'Vessel under London Bridge! Vessel under London Bridge! This is Amelia.'

'Amelia. This is Dougie. Channel 77.'

'Dougie, hello, thanks for responding. I can tell you're a Scotsman. Could I beg your help, please? Can you help that wee Scottish ship over there, *Hebridean Spirit*?' I didn't give him time to reply. 'I'm on Tower Pier, abeam of you now and I've a few folks here with me. I really need to get them on board *Spirit*. Do you think you could give them a quick lift across, please? Our launch has done a bunk and we're really stuck.'

The current was fast, any moment now he would be too far downstream and be gone.

'Och, it's time for my tea. Johnny's just away down to the galley to fetch it. Would it be Ok in half an hour? I'll take my tea and then I'll be back to take you over.'

Would he come back? The Chairman and his guests would not be happy waiting in the cold and rain on a windy pier.

'Not really,' I said. 'They're VIPs. Now, if you were to pop them over you could tie alongside. You and the lads can have your tea on board. Tea with a wee dram of course.' Water swirled at the stern of the tug as he put on the brakes and began to turn.

'*Hebridean Spirit, Hebridean Spirit,* this is Amelia.'

'Go ahead, Amelia.'

'Please tell Michael and Andrew the chairman's party will be on board in a moment. And ask the galley to get a good tea ready for the Skipper and crew of this tug, with a dram or two. And maybe you'd like to give a bottle of the ship's whisky to the skipper?'

It was the lack of movement that woke me. Jumping out of bed, I pulled back the curtains. Below the window stretched the concrete quay of Leith. An incongruous line of brass stanchions stood to attention, linked by blue cord, resplendent with gold tassels. We had arrived.

How could I have overslept this morning, of all mornings? Quickly, I dressed, tugging on jeans. The new white dress, hanging in the cupboard, waited. It had been waiting for several years.

The ship was strangely still and silent. After the constant hustle of the past days when an average of three hundred people had dined, wined, peered and poked their way round, it seemed delightfully quiet and empty. Even on the bridge.

'Morning. Any sign of the tenders?' They had been promised at every port where we had docked.

The watch gulped his tea. 'No. All quiet. Dougie's touching up a few chips in the paint, so it'll have time to dry.' He waved his mug at the open foredeck where the anchor winch and bits were all painted an unassuming dove grey. 'Do you think we'll be needing them for Norway?'

'Need them?' I took a deep breath, but I was unable to

control the exasperation in my voice. 'From the moment you leave Bergen, you'll need them!'

I explained that villages in the fjords generally had only one jetty, and that, as in Scotland, it would be reserved for the local ferry. The ship would be standing off and using the tenders twice or even three times every day. They had been scheduled to arrive in Oban to allow time to test them and practise handling the jet drives.

I descended the wide stairs into an unusually calm Reception and asked for Michael. Only the whirr of a hoover broke the silence. Maria, standing behind the desk, was almost hidden by a luxuriant display of blue delphiniums.

'Well, when I last saw him he was running downstairs with a drill in his hand, so maybe one of the cabins on Castle Deck?'

A faint buzzing led me to 'Brodick Castle' where Michael, in a clean boiler suit, knelt on the bed, drilling above the bedhead.

'Ah, Amelia. Hold this, would you? Down a bit, get it straight! Ok, that's better.' He screwed the frame into place. A view of a golden Korčula, palm trees, castellations and belfries, one of my photos taken during the Croatia recce, now graced the wall.

'She might want to see one of the cheaper cabins, you never know.' He clambered off the bed. 'She asked for a full tour, so we'd better be ready everywhere. Get a dustpan, could you?'

'Sure, but maybe Housekeeping should do a proper dust again? Don't the passengers come on board immediately after Princess Anne leaves?'

'Oh. Of course. Quite right, thanks.'

I waited, making sure I had his full attention, 'Michael, please tell me where the tenders are? There are only four hours now until the ceremony and if they don't arrive soon, then what? We can't load them while Princess Anne is here.'

'Don't be such a fusspot, Amelia. They'll be here, go to the Mess, have a biscuit and a coffee. Calm down. I expect they'll be here by the time you've finished.' I felt like a child, and a difficult, impatient one. But it couldn't wait any longer, I knew I must make the phone call, and I wanted to do so without being overheard. I punched in the Bergen number.

'Amelia. 'ello, this is Gunna. How are you? How is the new ship? All ready?'

'Fine, thanks. Princess Anne will be here soon. But I have a problem.'

'Vat can I do?' Gunna's flat Norwegian tones came soothingly across the North Sea.

'Gunna, there's no point in wrapping this up, we have no tenders.' Silence, just the sound of his breathing.

'Vat do you mean you 'ave no tenders? A joke, ya?'

'No, Gunna, I'm afraid it is not a joke. What do you think you can do?'

'You mean this? Ya?'

'I'm sorry but I do.'

'This is not good. I call you later.'

Here, up on the top deck, everything was ready and immaculate. From the smooth varnished handrails, newly laid wooden deck, teak tables and steamer chairs, everything waited for passengers. But at the stern was an empty space. An empty space where the tenders should be stowed. An empty space where they should be neatly one above the other. Coiled, waiting to uncurl like a sun-warmed reptile, the launching davit waited. Everything waited.

I knew I too was waiting. Had I really made use of the time since the '*Monaco*' years? Those years, now long past, had been formative, crucial to what I was doing now, but I knew I was still waiting. I was haunted by that meeting in the dark at the Southampton marina that had promised much, but those middle-of-the night visits had taken place over three years ago and still I had no conclusion.

2

Ocean Village, Southampton
Of Bilges and A Man

A massive belch ripped out across the silent waters.

I was hoping the darkness would provide cover, but the boom reverberated around the marina. Metal masts, halyards and rigging buzzed. The noise had never seemed to matter before when the power of *Monaco's* huge engine had been disguised by clattering fishing boats or ferry whistles, but now among the silent yachts, the noise was totally out of place. It was dark though, the hulls and boats still in shadow, so perhaps with luck, it was possible no one would know where the boom had come from.

A deep, steady throb thudded through the waters as *Monaco's* diesel engine came fully to life. Ducking out of the low engine room door, I stood on the deck peering over the gunwale, relieved to see the spout of cooling water splashing onto the pontoon. Like a panting dragon, *Monaco* was ready, longing to be out of her lair, away to open waters and free from the confines of a marina.

There was no disguising the noise or penetrating throb. No disguising there was now someone on board this ugly duckling of a trawler. Surrounded by neat little holiday toys, *Monaco* seemed vast and powerful. She loomed high, shadowing the neighbouring yachts. Once she had been an industrial fishing trawler, unromantic but purposeful, designed to thrust aside chunks of ice, impervious to searing cold and freezing Arctic waters. She was capable of rebuffing huge seas, keeping her crew safe to return home with her cavernous hold crammed with lucrative cod. Icebergs could batter her hull, stormy seas could break over her bow, but her steep decks would simply shake them off while the red dragon of her engine purred smoothly on. But in this effete marina her attributes seemed irrelevant. I felt guilty. I had let her down. The least I could do as she languished, waiting for a buyer, was ensure she was not neglected. A hint of warmth began to steal through the engine room as the dragon breathed again, warming its lair, waiting.

As I shone my torch from the top walkway of the engine room down below, the light slid over the sheen of oil covering the five cylinders stretching underneath me away into the shadows. I climbed down the little ladder to stand on the metal floor plates and shone the beam into the darkness beneath my feet. Inches under the lattice of the floor lay oily black water. Smooth, catching the light, the viscous surface shook slightly with the beat of the engine. There was no avoiding it, there was far too much water inside the boat. After all, this was why I was here, the reason I had left London at midnight on a wet December night. I knew I would need the cover of darkness. Parking as quietly as possible on the scrunchy gravel, I had reversed the Discovery against the wall, surreptitiously hiding the incriminating spare wheel with its cheerful cover emblazoned with the logo: a ship's wheel encircled with '*M V MONACO Cruising, Diving*' and my phone number, would be best hidden.

In the faint light, I had crept through the avenue of shiny tucked-up yachts, making my way along the pontoon to where *Monaco* waited silently at the far end. The pontoon moved and each delicate boat, carefully put to bed for the winter, bobbed on either side. Thin fibreglass hulls were protected from banging against the pontoon by three or four little sausage-shaped white fenders but as they did their work ripples started to slap noisily against hulls. But now, as *Monaco's* engine boomed into the quietness, I felt foolish to have bothered to creep.

Did anyone sleep on their yacht here on the south coast in December? Unlikely, in this affluent suburb of Southampton. Had it been a Scottish marina, there would be a community of hardy liveaboards waiting out the winter. But here, all seemed empty and I could get on with it. I knew exactly what I needed to do now the initial booming start of the engine had changed to a regular thump. The bilge water must go.

With luck, when I pushed up the inoffensive little switch controlling the electric pump, it too would burst into life, and the water would spew out of the side of *Monaco's* hull in a solid jet. Oily, black and greasy, the Jabsco pump would empty the bilges. It had to be done or *Monaco* would fill with water and eventually sink.

I pushed the switch and ducked out, relieved to see the filthy jet as greasy water gushed and crashed unnecessarily noisily onto the pontoon. Like an incoming tide, a slick of oil began sneaking its way between tidy yachts. Would it leave a black mark on these immaculate white hulls? It was a powerful pump so I knew it would not take long. As the jet diminished, I ducked back into the now-warm, friendly engine room and relieved, job done, flipped off the switch. I returned to the depths, clambering down the ladder to make the other necessary checks to the lubricator, oil pressure and cylinder temperatures. Now it had warmed up, the dragon would be happy in its lair for a while. Silence settled over the boat again. *Monaco* and her complicated machinery went back to sleep. In a couple of weeks, I would have to come and do it all again but for now I could sneak off quickly, escaping before anyone saw me. I had only been on board for forty minutes. Of course I could stay, sleeping on board, but I had no wish to linger in what had once been my cabin, or in the passenger accommodation. Even in the wheelhouse, I felt uncomfortable. The memories were too fresh and the bleak emptiness of my life now too great a contrast. Better to get going. The drive back to London at least would occupy me.

'Hello there!'

I jumped, banging my head against a hydraulic pipe as a voice penetrated my thoughts and the engine room. Stooping, I bent to peer out of the low doorway and found myself face to face with a man. Standing on the pontoon, he was looking over the gunwale, his face barely a foot from mine.

'Hello,' I said cheerily, 'Are you looking for me?' It was two-thirty in the morning so it seemed unlikely.

'I don't think I'm actually looking for 'you' in person.' Deep brown eyes glared at me. 'But at this ungodly hour, you seem to be the person in charge of this hellish noise, so who else would I be looking for?' Now that *Monaco's* engine no longer boomed, the chill quiet of a December night fell over us.

'I'm really sorry to have disturbed you... But she's not really made for this kind of place, and I can't just let her sink.' Unable to resist, I added, 'You must admit she's quite a boaty!'

Our faces were inches apart and even in the faint light, I

could see he had those eyes. Sea Eyes. The eyes I have always found irresistible with their searching gaze.

Suddenly aware of how scruffy I must look, I said, 'Next time I'm here, would you like a look round? She's an amazing machine.' He stood below me on the pontoon, a padded yellow Helly Hanson jacket keeping his top half warm while his bottom half was swathed in a thick stripy towel. Bare legs, adequately hairy, ended in neat feet squarely planted on the chilly wooden planks. He was not, I noticed, standing on the oily, greasy patch where the bilge water had bounced onto the slats. Behind him, the oily slick was rapidly diminishing, sneaking silently away between the boats. I kept talking, hoping he wouldn't turn and see the shiny remnants.

'I'd love to show you round a real boat,' I said cheekily. 'Just give me a ring.' Delving into my jeans, I held a card out over the bulwark. After all, I was almost a free woman now, barely still married, and the cards were newly printed. 'Here, my mobile's on this card.'

He had the confident air of someone at ease with being in charge, but he seemed more amused than annoyed, and I felt confident he would not report me. Wordlessly he took the card and turned to stroll back into the shadows, stepping neatly over the grease on the pontoon. I wished I had asked his name but for now, I decided 'Helly Handsome' seemed to fit.

Returning to the job, I gave the greasy pontoon a scrub, watching the bubbles of washing-up liquid bob across the water. They too seemed incriminating. I locked the engine room door, wheelhouse too and said goodbye to my boaty. No matter how much she had once ruled my life, I knew I must get free of her, move on from this old life and find a new, different one. Driving for four hours in the middle of the night every two weeks to pump out oily bilges was not fun. It was now more than a year since I had resigned as the managing director, responsible for all aspects of the business as well as *Monaco*. My resignation had not been popular: none of the Board, especially my almost-ex-husband, had been pleased. But to my relief and surprise one of the directors, a tiresome drip from the Midlands who had always been a thorn in my flesh and who had always wanted to get rid of me, elected to take on the eighty-foot solid oak trawler and a business with dodgy finances. I was free simply to walk away but I still felt responsible.

Walk away to what? I was ill prepared for anything. After twenty-three years of happy family life, I had no marriage, no home, no dog and soon, no boat. But I did still have one precious boy. I pushed back the memories of my other little boy, Digby. Driving in the dark, thinking of Diggers, his jokes and fun, would lead to tears and driving while crying was a bad idea. The memories refused to go away, they remained bright and clear. I liked to remember him locking his thin little arm round my neck, pulling me in tightly when I bent to kiss him goodnight. 'Mummy! Mummy. You're not leaving me. You're spending the night here, with me,' he would say.

I needed a job.

'Top End Travel, Good morning. Can I help you?' asked a crisp, no-nonsense voice.

'Good morning.' My response sounded less assured than I had expected. 'Please could I speak to Rosemary?'

'There are two Rosemarys here. Which would you like?'

To this day, I have no idea what had inspired me to pick up the phone. I had only met Rosemary a couple of times during the last ten years. She was the girlfriend of a distant and much older Dalton relation and I remembered her as frighteningly efficient and slightly aloof. But she had teased and played with Diggers and that had been good enough for me.

I scrambled around in my head trying to remember her surname. 'I'm afraid I can't remember. What are the options?'

'Stevens or Willoughby,' was the chilly response.

'Willoughby, please. Could you say it's Amelia Dalton calling?' I wondered whether she would remember me. Would she know about the divorce? Technically she was on the 'Dalton side', so possibly unwilling to speak to me, but she was the only girl I knew with a proper job.

'How very nice to hear from you, it's been such a long time.' She sounded as if she actually might mean it. 'How are you? And how is that boat of yours? I really must come and see her when I'm next in Scotland. I'll be up later in the year for the annual fishing party.'

Encouraged, I plunged in, explaining that sadly *Monaco* was no longer operating and I needed a job. I would not let life trickle away with no purpose. I had no house to run, no one to cook for and unknown income. A job was imperative, the divorce lawyer's words a constant theme in my head. Hugo had enrolled at Central St Martin's to do an art foundation course where I hoped he would make new friends and launch a career. London with new friends would be just what he needed. Having a motherly reminder of how much his life had changed was unnecessary, and I feared I would not be good at disguising how empty and lost I felt.

'Well, I don't think I can help much,' Rosemary said, 'but you could send your CV to these people.' Quickly she reeled off the names and addresses of three companies and the appropriate contacts. 'You never know, something might come of it. Tell them I suggested you should.' I scribbled as she talked, hoping I was getting the information down correctly.

'Good luck and do let me know if you're ever in London.' I quailed at the idea, lacking the courage to say I was just a mile away in a rented flat.

Send my CV. I had never had one. I had never needed one. What should I put on it? What were the required elements of a CV? Dispirited I gazed out at the communal London square, dull in the flat morning light. Outside the window, a grey squirrel worked its way face-first down a tree trunk as I began to embroider my Scottish life into an irresistible CV. *Monaco* became an 'expedition ship' – more glamorous than an 'Arctic trawler'. Our contract with the National Trust for Scotland had an air of respectability and I had good handwriting. Italic, regular but with a curl or two to add style. By mid-afternoon I had finished and pushed three envelopes into a post box in Fulham Road. The moment I heard them drop, I knew I had compiled it far too quickly. Had I checked for spelling mistakes? Was the CV too long? Too short? I could have wrestled over the contents for weeks, losing my nerve. I consoled myself thinking that at least I had sent them.

I waited in hope, but there were no responses, no acknowledgements. After three weeks there was still not a squeak, nothing was forthcoming. I needed a purpose; even a drinks party would be better than emptiness. A little party would tell the few people I knew in London that I was here. I would ask everyone I knew living south of Birmingham, so a heap of envelopes lay on the desk by my elbow, waiting for stamps. The heap vibrated. Envelopes cascaded onto the floor, shaken off the desk by a new treat I had allowed myself. The Blackberry buzzed, shaking the pile into life.

'Yes, this is Amelia.' I held my breath.

'Good morning, this is Gladstone & Sussex.'

One of Rosemary's contacts wanted to meet me. They had a group of twenty-five Americans booked for a tour entitled '*Castles and Gardens of Bohemia*'. It was a chance to become a tour leader in the Czech Republic.

In all *Monaco's* ten years, there had been only one group of Americans who had heard of us through the National Trust. *Monaco*, they had been told, was just the boat for St Kilda. We had taken them out into the wild Atlantic, forty miles beyond the Outer Hebrides to the remote loneliness of St Kilda. For the ten days of island visits, walks, food and chatter, they remained in blissful ignorance. They never knew our regular skipper had done a bunk and their lives were in the hands of a temporary man who had first set foot on board shortly after they themselves had embarked. They never knew not one of us had known how to start the big red dragon of an engine, had no idea how to decipher the spaghetti-like knots of electric wires or the tangles of hydraulic pipes threading round the engine room. While the Americans were welcomed and deflected by shortbread and tea, Bill, our engineer, had instructed me over the phone on how to get *Monaco* moving. Every morning after that initial call, with the shouts of the fish auction echoing down the line, he had told me what to grease, where to oil and how to maintain the complicated machinery. We had been lucky. The June sun had shone for the party, there had been little wind or swell, and we had carried it off.

Now I needed courage again.

I firmed up my voice. 'Yes, I've been taking Americans around Scotland for about ten years.' It was more of an embroidery than a complete lie. 'Tomorrow? In the Cotswolds, Stow. Yes, that's fine for me. I'll be there.'

3

Czech Republic
Castles & Pugs

The Land Rover trundled me through the limestone folds of the Cotswolds. It was a dull car. So dull I had not even found it a name, though every other car I had buzzed around in had been a person and named, from the topless Flying Tomato XR3i to the bouncy little Fiat Uno named the Bluebottle. But the Disco was a relic of my Scottish life and it gave me a sense of stability.

I took a deep breath, stepped up the worn stone steps and pushed open the glass door etched with the company's logo of a range of stylized hills complete with rising sun – or possibly moon. Underneath were the words *'Gladstone & Sussex'*. When I closed the door behind me, the cheerful buzz of the market town fell away to a deep hush. Neat, hair pulled back behind velvet bands, pearls nestling against cashmere jerseys, two girls looked up. Sitting at desks, adorned with typewriters, staplers and notepads, they were calmly in control. Instantly I felt scruffy. I had never lived a 'pearls and twinset' kind of life. Should I want to, I wondered?

'Hello. Do come in.' Superficially welcoming, but with a faint frost, sufficient to make it clear this was their patch.

'Good morning, I'm Amelia. I have a meeting with Gregory Cox.'

I settled on a wicker sofa. It creaked loudly. On a low glass coffee table were stacked copies of Country Life, The Field and Architectural Digest. I picked up The Digest, flipping the pages to study elegant and expensive houses.

'Yes?' A curt voice burst from a box on one of the desks.

'Amelia Dalton is in Reception; shall I send her in?'

'No. Ask her to wait. I'll be out in a minute. She's early.' I had made sure to be early, only five minutes. My mother had instilled in me that early equalled respect. I flipped the glossy pages, seeing nothing and trying to suppress the butterflies taking flight in my stomach.

Soon a tall man, slim, in his early forties, appeared. He oozed the self-assured confidence of good looks. The sheen of his immaculate grey suit demanded to be stroked and curly hair cried out to be ruffled. Both girls gazed longingly.

'Good morning, I'm Gregory.' A gold signet ring winked on his little finger as he proffered a bronzed hand. 'I run the Escorted Tours. Let's go round the corner, the Angel will give us a bite and we can have a chat.'

He held open the glass door for me. Did he have any boating connections? He would look good on a sleek super yacht, lounging among cushions in his bathers and shades. But he would look good almost anywhere, as he knew. I followed him into the low-ceilinged bar wondering if my experience with seasick passengers and greasing a mighty engine would be of any use in his world of wealthy Americans.

'Here we are.' The waitress set down two bowls. 'Your usual, the curried parsnip soup, Mr Cox.'

As he broke his bread roll, Gregory Cox began to describe what he needed. His American clients were to think I was one of the regular G&S Tour Leaders and that I had worked for them for years.

'It's vital also that no one knows this Czech-gardens tour

is a new itinerary. No one must suspect it hasn't been operated before. Is that clear?'

I dispatched some soup, playing for time to assess the implications of operating an unknown itinerary combined with appearing to be a 'regular'.

'That's Ok, but I think it would be sensible for me to have a look round Prague at least before your clients arrive. I have been there but in the depths of a snowy winter. Also—' taking my courage in both hands '—if I'm asked a direct question I am not prepared to lie. I will *imply* I am a regular Tour Leader for you, and I know your properties in Africa, so that will help. I hope that will be Ok?'

He leant back, studying his now empty soup bowl, and rearranged his napkin on his knees. 'I think that will be all right. This is an important group with at least six of our VIP repeat clients. Their tour of Germany with Ronald Greaves, the ex-ambassador, ends in Prague, then they will join you.'

It seemed I had passed the soup test. I had not slurped or eaten with my mouth open, and I had used my napkin. Thoughtfully, I returned to London, two weighty ring-back files wedged on the back seat.

Settling at the table in the window of my rented flat, I opened the files. How could so much paperwork be necessary? The thickest file was labelled 'Tour Leader' and the other 'Operations'. 'Tour Leader' first. Four different coloured tabs divided the contents, each tab with a neatly typed heading:

1.	GREEN:	Dress Code & Manners
2.	RED:	Cash
3.	PURPLE:	Lecture Topics
4.	YELLOW:	Dos & Don'ts

The grey squirrel raced down the flaking trunk of a plane tree head-first. Seed heads like Christmas tree baubles danced gently in the breeze. A slight haze of green from new unfurling leaves gave a hint of spring. Time for a new start for me too, even if it felt like climbing a mountain. So where exactly in Europe was the Czech Republic?

Lectures. They were likely to be the most frightening part. My school history had been exclusively English, not even including Scotland, and European history limited to a few toga-wearing Romans and William the Conqueror. And what about *Monaco*? She would need a pump out before I left. If I did it at the last minute, she would probably last the three weeks before the water level in her bilges became critical. If I went during the day Helly Handsome perhaps might be there. I wanted to see him, accidentally, naturally. But pumping oily fetid, bilge water would be more notice-able in daylight. Late evening would be best. His presence at that one momentary meeting, half-dressed, in the dark on the pontoon had made an unforgettable impression, his eyes assessing me with the hint of a smile that was almost mocking and unquestionably sexy.

This time the bilge-pumping mission had a new focus and quickly I completed the necessary jobs before swinging the Discovery out of the marina through the chain-link gates. Pulling up, I jumped down to close them behind me, taking a last look across the maze of yachts. *Monaco's* great bulk, so out of place among the holiday boats, loomed solid and dark in the fading light. She would be fine now until I came back from Europe, with dry bilges and tucked away out of the weather. The security lights flickered on, casting long shadows, silhou-etting the sleeping yachts and reflecting on the oily sheen spreading across the water among the white hulls.

No sign of Helly Handsome. I tried to persuade myself that was a good thing; after all, he had seen the oil previously. The dual carriageway reeled out behind me as I passed Southampton heading back to London. No Phil Collins crooning from the dashboard for this drive, I needed to think. I had never given a talk or lecture in my life. Would I have to use a microphone? A yellow light flashed on the dashboard – diesel.

Clambering back behind the wheel after filling up, I glanced at my friend the Blackberry, my slick new toy, the latest model and now, with a job, a justifiable expense. This new, small, upgraded model had clever little flashing lights: green to confirm it was connected to the world and red for a missed call or message. I was yet to receive a call on it. There were no calls for *Monaco* bookings and Hugo was busy. The light flashed red. *Red*! I must have missed a call. Someone wanted me. While I was pumping diesel in, rather than out, someone had rung and left a message. Whoever it was, they were not in my Contacts, as there was no name.

'I see you've been visiting again. Let me know next time.'

That was the whole message. A deep voice with just the hint of an accent. A suspicion of... what? I tried to pin it down. It could only be him, Helly Handsome. I had been out of the car for just a few minutes, and I had missed him. Could I pretend I hadn't picked up the message? Why didn't he leave his name? I pressed Call Back and held my breath.

'Yes?'

'Someone rang this number a moment ago and I missed the call.' I tried to sound curious, as though I had no idea who it might be. 'Who am I speaking to?' Even to my own ears, this sounded lame.

'I saw you from the Clubhouse,' was the unsettling reply.

'You should have come up. G&T in the evening sun, the view's good up there. You can see right out to sea.'

'What a lovely idea, but maybe next time?' A whiff of diesel and bilge water pervaded the Land Rover. I was certainly not turning round, even though I could have been back there in ten minutes.

From the moment *Monaco* had gingerly made her way to the selling agent's slot alongside the pontoon, she had dominated her surroundings. Even as I had tidied away the charts in the wheelhouse, clearing up biscuit crumbs and coffee mugs accumulated during her final voyage from the Scillies, I had been aware I was being watched. She was tied up immediately adjacent to the Clubhouse so *Monaco's* wheelhouse, standing twenty feet above deck level, was level with the windows of the Members' Bar. Any yachtie member, relaxing by the window, pink gin in hand, would have an unimpeded view straight into *Monaco's* wheelhouse. Helly Handsome must have been there. He must have seen me ducking in and out of the engine room. But the jet of filthy, greasy bilge water bouncing off the slats of the pontoon would have been out of sight on the far side of *Monaco's* substantial oak hull.

'It seems you always visit in poor light.' Maybe he *had* noticed the oily water. Were there black lines on the hulls of the dainty yachts? Was he going to report me? What about his own boat, whichever one it was? Was that mucky too? Surely, he would have done or said something by now if he was going to.

'I can tell when you've been,' he went on. I held my breath. 'You're the only person who ever scrubs that pontoon.' A long breath escaped me.

'I can't make it during the daytime, unfortunately. It's called Work,' I lied.

'And what's the work, then, Mistress Monaco?' Was it a tease or patronising?

'Travel. I'm off to Prague to see some of the castles and gardens in the country round there. A couple of weeks and then I'll be down again.' I hoped I sounded interesting.

'Give me a call before you come next time. I'd like to take a look round that tub of yours, and you can tell me about Prague.'

'Tub? What cheek! She's an Arctic trawler, solid oak and a fantastic machine. Tub indeed!' The banter was cheering. Was looking round *Monaco* an excuse or was he really interested more in the boat than in me?

'When are you usually at the marina?' I asked, wanting to prolong the conversation but trying to sound casual, rather than inquisitive. I was curious, what was he doing there at night? Surely, he had somewhere better to sleep, but then I had no idea what kind of yacht he had. He would suit one of the huge ocean-going yachts in the expensive berths in the high-security area, at a distance from *Monaco's* 'For Sale' section.

'Most nights I'm here. I like sleeping on board. Usually, it's quiet.' There was heavy emphasis on 'usually'. 'I get space, time to think, in peace, uninterrupted.' No wonder the boom of *Monaco's* starting engine had upset him. 'Just give me a call the day before you're coming. Have fun.'

Click, and he was gone. What did he mean 'think'? Was he a writer? He seemed energetic, fit and clearly self-contained. Grinning, I punched the CD button and Phil Collins crooned out of the dashboard.

Three days later, hesitantly, I walked out of the Customs Hall to find a small squat man holding up a crisp sheet of paper with 'Emilia Dalton' printed on it.

'Hello. You must be Vladimir?'

Folding the paper, he tucked it carefully into his jacket pocket and held out a hand.

'Yes. I am Vladimir Svoboda.' He bowed formally over my hand. 'I welcome you to the Czech Republic. I am pleased you arrive on time. We drive now into the city.'

Having wrung the few extra days out of G&S, I was determined to make the most of my time with the local guide to acquaint myself with as much of the itinerary as time would allow. Vladimir was to drive me around, and in five days he would show me the majority of what our Americans would see in sixteen. He was to be my guide now and for the whole tour. Twenty-one days together. We needed to get on and, as it turned out, that was the easiest part. Vladimir was knowledgeable, attentive, safe and likeable and, in the coming years, we worked happily together several times. He was unflappable and had an old-fashioned sense of duty combined with quiet charm and an occasional twinkle of humour.

I knew Vladimir's main job was as a history professor at Prague University. Maybe he could give the lectures. Confidently, he swung the Skoda about the road avoiding puddles, potholes and skinny dogs. There was little traffic to dodge as we headed into town, and I had my introduction to featureless communist buildings. This was May 1996 and Prague was still working on its rehabilitation; the Velvet Revolution had been several years earlier but everywhere looked grey.

'We go to the Palace Hotel; this is close to Wenceslas Square. You know about this square?' The Palace Hotel, I knew from studying my guidebook, was considered the best in Prague and it would be where the group would stay.

Wenceslas Square was a significant place for the newly liberated country.

All around the buildings looked drab and depressing. There was no bustle, no traffic and almost no people. Shops were boarded up. An occasional trestle table, guarded by a comfortable-looking woman, lurked in a doorway. Arranged in carefully balanced mounds were giant cabbages, neatly trimmed, yellow turnips and pit-prop like leeks. Industrial-sized vegetables it seemed were all there was for sale.

The Skoda slowed to a halt as Vladimir parked almost casually across a corner. We had arrived at the Palace Hotel. Above the entrance was a canopy, an intricate design of Art Nouveau flowers and leaves, gold and blue wrought iron and enamel, entwined overhead. This ebullience was in striking contrast to the dreary surroundings. But no liveried flunky was waiting. No one appeared, no porter, no one eager to take my bag or provide a smiling welcome. The Americans would not appreciate that.

After checking in, and without wasting time to look round the bedroom, I left my bag and clutching an already well-thumbed guidebook, I ventured out. Providing I did not get lost, I reckoned I might find the Old Town Square in time to see one of the city's attractions, the ancient astronomical clock. Its saintly figures were crowned with tiny halos and processed past the clock's little windows every hour. I wanted to see the skeleton of time bang his golden bell. It had to be this evening as my instructions from Vladimir were for an early start to the country next morning.

'Prague is easy,' he had told me. 'The programme is busy, and I will do the talking, but the country, that, I think is what you need to know.'

So early next morning Vladimir and I set off to cover the

G&S *Castle and Gardens of Bohemia* in four days. He drove with care, concentrating on finding the patches of smoother tarmac, avoiding the worst of the potholes to preserve the Skoda's suspension. I knew I should begin a conversation, but my head buzzed, crammed with too many thoughts. Vlad hummed gently.

'Kesky Krumlov,' I said at last. 'Is that how I pronounce it? Is that where we're going first?'

'Ya. Česȳ Krumloff,' came the reply. My pronunciation hadn't been a bad attempt. Vladimir outlined the basics – a small castle on a bend in the river, gable-roofed buildings, cobbles and surprisingly a beer-brewing widow. It was a charming little town, colourful with window boxes of red geraniums, and a welcome contrast to the grim outskirts of Prague. The beer slipped down easily too.

Next, would be Telč, deeper in the country, a three-hour drive. Telč did not appear in my guidebook, but the G&S tour description had it down as a 'glorious little Renaissance town'.

'We are here now,' Vladimir said with a sigh. I could tell he was tired after the demanding pothole-hopping drive. The dim sweep of light from the Skoda's headlights was just strong enough to illuminate more faceless housing blocks with grubby windows. We drew up at a featureless concrete façade. This time there was no Art Nouveau riot, only a stark electric-blue neon sign proclaiming, 'Hotel Pangea'. Telč seemed far from its enticing description.

'Vladimir, I expect you could manage a beer after all that driving. Should we meet in the bar and then check out the hotel's restaurant? We've two vegetarians to look after so we had better eat here and see what it's like.'

'Ya. Good idea. We meet again in fifteen minutes?'

I tried not to be affected by the depressing surroundings as I carried my small bag up the stairs, each tread edged with a utilitarian strip of aluminium. The bedroom was stark and chilly. Apart from a single bed with a thin blanket, there was no other furniture, no bedside table, lamp or chair. Nothing was inviting, nothing encouraging, nothing to make anyone want to linger. The bathroom had a fig-leaf sized towel hanging from a chrome hook above the bath, and the floor was cold with shiny green ceramic tiles. I gave up waiting for the hot water to arrive and splashed my face with cold before I went downstairs.

'Hello.'

The man behind the reception desk looked up from his paper.

'Would it be possible to have a bathplug, please?'

'Ne. No, you bring your own. We have none.' English it seemed was not a problem, even if bath plugs were.

'Ah, Ok. I'm here to see about the group coming to stay with you in a few days' time. We have a dinner here and there will be two vegetarians. May I see a menu, please?'

He shuffled papers under the desk without saying a word and then disappeared through a swing door. Back then only Americans had food 'issues'. The door swung creakily while I studied the empty room. There were no sofas, chairs or tables gracing this reception.

'Ya, ya. Here you are.' He proffered a plastic-backed ring folder. 'This is menu.'

Inside the grimy plastic was one crumpled sheet of paper. The corners were curled and the edges torn, but the heading, carefully centred and in faint, but legible type read:

'FLESHLESS F●●D'.

The letter 'o' was solid black. It must have been fifteen years since I had seen the dirty type from a machine in need of a new ribbon and a clean. The menu had two choices: 'pie cheese' or 'pie pea' and both could be 'joined with Onion Wheels'.

'Good morning. It is nice to be in this lovely place.'

I tried not to be irritated by Vladimir's cheerful greeting. I had been too cold to sleep and everything about Telč seemed far from encouraging. Why had G&S included this dreary hotel, and how could well-heeled Americans enjoy coming here?

'I will show you the town after we have breakfast.' Vladimir continued brightly as we went into the dining room. On a side table, covered by a plastic tablecloth, were two milky-white melamine bowls, a pile of plates and some melamine mugs. Flaccid grapefruit segments lay in a Pyrex bowl, next to a mini log cabin of individual Weetabix packets. There were thin, almost wet, slices of white bread and a plate of tiny foil packets of 'spread'. Maybe the Fleshless Food would be more luxurious. Again, I wondered how this miserable hotel, in what had seemed to be an equally discouraging town, life-less and grey, be a Renaissance joy? How could it be the kind of place the Americans were anticipating?

After breakfast, we walked through the empty streets, avoiding broken drain covers. Vladimir, walking smartly ahead, turned and disappeared round a corner, and I trailed after him into a huge empty square. It was breathtakingly beautiful. Silent and devoid of life. The unspoilt Renaissance square of Telč was simply glorious. Unbroken pastel façades were topped with crested gables, ornate wrought-iron signs hung from the elegant buildings, their gold symbols proclaiming the type of shop or service offered. The square was entirely quiet, no traffic lumbered through to disturb the peace. Once it must have hummed with life as the cobbles were shiny, worn smooth with the passage of feet, hooves and carriage wheels. Looking at the glorious architecture around me, I felt ashamed of my ignorance. I had never seen anywhere like it.

In the opposite corner two old women dressed in black pottered slowly into view, baskets looped over their arms and their heads close together. The gentle murmur of their gossiping drifted across the square. A horse, scruffy, workmanlike and ungroomed, trotted in pulling a steaming cart. It clattered over the cobbles; one or two clods of dung bounced out to fall with fat plops. Had I slipped back a century or two – or perhaps I had dropped into a movie set?

Vladimir had designed the programme and made all the necessary arrangements for the group, apart from the next place, Omlovice. This would be a G&S special, the ultimate *piece de resistance:* Gregory had made this very clear.

'We are in the business of meeting expectations, Amelia. It will be up to you to ensure no one is disappointed.' He paused. 'Omlovice…' He looked at me, making sure I grasped the importance of what he was saying. 'Omlovice… is critical. Things must go smoothly. It will be the first time 'outsiders' rather than friends or family will have stayed at the castle. We're lucky to have permission to take our group there, and you'll be the vanguard. We're hoping, if all goes well, to send lots of G&S clients to stay there.'

He had left me in no doubt that the visit must be seamless. The lady owner of the chateau was sceptical and possibly slightly unwilling. It seemed Gregory had charmed and persuaded her into the visit when they had met in New York. But that was in America, and he had not been fortunate enough to visit her castle, so it was up to me to ensure everything went smoothly.

Like so many of her neighbours with grand houses, Lady Dobřenšti's parents had fled at the beginning of the war. Eventually, the family had arrived in America, where she had grown up in comfort and married a wealthy New Yorker. Tall, talented and lively, after the early death of her husband, she had become a much sought-after interior designer. When the Velvet Revolution transferred power to Václav Havel, she had returned, retrieving ownership of the Renaissance chateau. The German occupation had left its mark, but with a fortune to lavish and using her skills, she had restored the castle. Re-wiring, new plumbing, fresh furnishings as well as a rose garden and game park had all been accomplished. Now it was complete. My visit must reassure her the G&S clients would be suitable and maybe even desirable. Our stay at the chateau was described as the highlight of the tour but were I to put a foot out of place, the visit would be cancelled. Then there would be no 'privileged access', no staying as her guests or dinner with local aristos.

Part of my role, as laid out in the *Guide Manual,* was to allocate bedrooms appropriately, with G&S regulars top of the list. At the chateau each room was different, I knew. Some quirky, some classical, some chintzy. I would need to meet my group before I could decide which couple would fit where.

Vladimir seemed nervous as we drove up the avenue and along a strikingly pothole-free drive to the chateau. The heavy front door swung open and four pugs burst out. Yapping loudly, they hurtled across the wide flagstone doorway and scuffled around my ankles. I hate pugs. I can never decide which end is which: the only clue is the horrible snuffling and string of dribble which hopefully comes from the nose end.

'Hello little dogs!' I exclaimed, bending down to pat each in turn. A pair of brown brogues appeared at eye level. It could have been my mother-in-law: the same height, hauteur and air of command, but she lacked an English county tweed skirt. Her head was topped by a swirl of blonde hair, curled into a neat French roll. There was nothing English about her; she looked far too chic.

'Welcome. Welcome. Here you are.' She turned to Vladimir. 'Just carry on.' Bracelets jangled as she waved airily across the rose beds. 'Go round the corner of the house and down the drive, the stables are over there, across the park. Not so many horses these days, so there is space for your car. I'll give Bohdan a ring so he's expecting you.' She smiled at me, then turned back to Vladimir. 'We'll be finished by about ten tomorrow morning, so come back then, will you, to collect Amelia?'

I opened my mouth in horror but Vladimir, bowing slightly, seemed unsurprised and perfectly happy. He jumped back into the driving seat and set off, careful not to create grooves in the deep gravel.

'Come along, my dear.' I followed as obediently as Vladimir and was led through the archway to an inner court-yard where a central fountain splashed into a generous basin. Painted frescoes of horses, musical instruments and flowers danced along on the top of the walls and down between the windows. Everywhere was warm, sunny and welcoming in soft pink terracotta. This was the stuff for Americans, for anyone really. Who could not love the billowing roses and opulence of this castle? The pugs clustered round my feet, snuffling and dribbling. I tried not to kick one as Lady Dobřenšti opened an ornate door. Stretching ahead was the most beautiful floor I had ever seen. Intricate, golden parquet floors, I was to learn, were a feature of Bohemian grand houses; this was simpler than many but perfect in its simplicity. Zigzag patterns created by blocks of wood in differing shades of gold and rich brown, spread ahead down the long, glazed loggia. Jardinières, bursting with luxuriant geraniums, stood to attention between the windows, and from above Lady Dobřenšti's ancestors looked down serenely gazing from ornate gold frames, a striking contrast to the russet pink walls.

'What wonderful scented geraniums!' I silently thanked my granny who had always placed bowls of these at the foot of the stairs in her little Harrogate semi. Each time someone passed, touching a leaf, the heady scent would waft about the hall. It was a smell I loved, and Lady Dobřenšti looked pleased. Round One negotiated.

A girl waited at the bottom of the stairs, her uniform a green and white striped dress complete with elasticated buckled belt and crisp white apron.

'Ah, here you are Anna. Kindly show Amelia to her room.' She turned to me, 'Do come down when you're ready, you'll find me in the drawing room.' I followed Anna's ample backside up the wide shallow stairs which curled around the walls of the hall. Sunlight bounced off the wooden floor below reflecting warmth on to the gold frames of yet more ancestors.

Anna opened a door and stood back for me to enter. It was an enormous room with a huge four-poster. Staring out from between the damask drapes of the bed were six or seven pairs of fierce dark eyes. Pugs. They lounged smugly on the damask bedspread. To my surprise, as I drew closer they remained motionless – eventually revealing themselves to be a heap of tapestry cushions. On the right of the bed was the turret. Matching curtains were looped back by heavy golden ropes. The turret windows, reaching from floor to ceiling, were mullioned and gave clear views of the Park. Sunk into the middle of the turret was the bath. Marble steps with a curved golden handrail, carved to look like a sea snake, led into the soapy depths. The bather, whose head would be flush with the floor, could luxuriate in style, gazing across the park where a herd of fallow deer were just visible. Not all the other nine bedrooms were quite so idiosyncratic, but each had its individual style and colour scheme. Most had four-posters and one had a roll-topped bath at its foot. Anna showed me them in turn as I made careful notes of the differences and quirks.

Lady Dobřenšti, although dauntingly elegant, was easy to like and seemed interested in my life in London. I didn't mention *Monaco* or bilge water, but I felt confident G&S would be happy.

The five hectic days with Vladimir were encouraging, and at the end I felt excited, ready to get going. The tour was no longer an unknown quantity. Now I knew places, but better still, Vlad and I were friends. There were of course the lectures, which should be 'talks', I decided, a nuance which I hoped would not be lost on the Americans. European history I now realised was horribly complicated. Far too many people seemed to have tramped across or fought over the rivers, cities and rolling plains. Vladimir was the professor; he was the historian, and I knew he would be excellent at elaborating as we travelled on the bus, vividly bringing local events, like Napoleon's great victory, to life. When we had driven through the gently rolling hills of Austerliz, he had pointed out where the Russians and Austrian troops had been stationed.

After the Renaissance delights of Omlovice, Brno, an industrial textile town – the Manchester of the Czech Republic, seemed charmless. Again, there was no Art Nouveau gem, instead we had a Best Western Hotel, the 'best' or at least the most modern hotel for miles around, our base for the next set of visits to other country castles. Again, the streets were grey but inside, the eight floors of the hotel, a modern high-rise block, came as a shock. Between each window was a shocking pink plastic panel. Inside, the receptionist and every other member of the staff were similarly colour co-ordinated. Satin trousers, belted jackets, short skirts and big blouses, all were bright pink. The whole hotel was a riot of pink. Even the bellboy in the lift wore a tight-fitting pink suit and a furry pink fedora. Brno, recently released from drab communism, was embracing colour.

During the long drives over uneven, bumpy pot-holed roads, I had felt it was my duty to entertain Vladimir as much as I could. Huge lorries, belching smoke and exhaust fumes, occupied most of the roads, and I was also keen he stayed awake. The countryside had not been helpful. Unlike England with little villages, rivers, pubs and churches popping up frequently, here the landscape was empty. Mile after mile of arable land with an occasional dense, gloomy forest stretched in every direction, and I struggled to find amusing topics. But as yet another thick forest closed around the dead straight road, inspiration dawned.

'Vladimir, what is the position about shooting in your country?' I asked. 'There must be deer, wild boar and game living in these forests. Do people go hunting?'

Vladimir stared through the windscreen at the road reeling out ahead, but I persisted, 'Can anyone go hunting? Do you need a permit?' I asked, knowing how carefully controlled *la chasse* was in France. Here there were no signs on the trees proclaiming 'Chasse Gardée'.

'Shooting,' he pondered, 'Ya, ya. Many people do this. It is carefully controlled, but very expensive. You must have a licence and also a permit, and then there is the gun and ammunition. Ya. It is very expensive.' He paused and by now I knew him well enough to know more would follow. He turned, whispering conspiratorially even though he and I were the only occupants of the car. He grinned. 'But when I was younger, I used to go out poking.'

I managed to suppress a grin. Poaching was rather different from 'poking', but it would not do for me to embarrass the strait-laced, super-correct Vladimir.

My instructions in the G&S guide manual were that I must invite the group for a 'Meet the Guide' drink on the first evening. Rules were strict. No spirits and only one glass of wine. How could I prevent an American who had paid thousand dollars for his holiday from having a 'scotch'? (This rule was the first I would ignore.) I should introduce myself formally, tell them my background and provide a participants' list covering formal names and, as they were American, nicknames too. A Charles might be a Chuck; it would all be matey, I could tell. For those who were members of the regular clients' club, I had to buy gifts, and again there was a strict protocol on cost and type. Amongst the group of twenty-five was the special party of eight Gregory had mentioned who would be finishing their tour of Germany and would join me. Naturally, it would be wise to meet their Tour Leader, the ex-ambassador who was a regular leader for G&S: he was, I had been told, one of their top tour leaders.

As the lift in the Palace Hotel descended, I needed to summon up every bit of courage. At ease in a wing-backed chair was an elegant man; it could only be him. I walked firmly towards him, holding out a hand.

'Good evening, you must be Ronald. I'm Amelia.' He uncoiled himself. Greying hair, charcoal grey suit and a clubby-striped tie. His handshake was firm, of course.

'How do you do?' He had a slightly drawling, deceptively lazy voice, one you know disguises an astute mind. He looked me up and down. 'Good to have this opportunity to go over a few things.' There was to be no friendly introductory chat. 'Don't think I've come across you before, have I? Are you new? Done many of these tours before?'

'None, actually. This is my first.'

'First tour, eh!? That is a surprise. Gregory must have had difficulty finding someone. He usually breaks people in.'

We sat down and the silence dragged out as he waited for me to speak but I had nothing to say.

'Ok, let's get on with it, then. I have a dinner to get to.'

'Please could you tell me about the clients I'm taking over this evening?'

'Actually… the ones carrying on with you are quite demanding.'

I did my best to look attentive and to take it all in as he talked at me but instead, I found myself wondering if he had bored the clients as much as me. Eventually, I stood up. It seemed the only way to interrupt his complacent monologue.

'Forgive me, I have some paperwork to do before the tour leader drinks. I hope you have an enjoyable farewell dinner and maybe we'll meet in the morning.' I almost ran to the lift. Empty and calm, the mirrored panels, etched with scrolling art-nouveau flowers, were soothing as it whisked me up and away to the safety of my eaves room on the third floor.

For the fifth time I read through the list of names, trying

to get them fixed in my head. I checked the mirror. I looked all right. I would do. I would have to do.

With the yellow and brown G&S 'Tour Manager' badge pinned to my blue dress, I took care it was straight, and the lift returned me to the ground floor. I hoped Ronald would have gone to his dinner by now, but no, he was in the bar surrounded by a little group of adoring acolytes. As one they turned to look at me.

A man in his sixties, suave in an expensive suit, with a war-painted woman attached to his arm, detached themselves from Ronald's side. They headed towards me with a determined air.

'Hi, I'm Chuck Reynolds and this is my wife Sissy.' Before I could reply he continued. 'This hotel is frankly, not suitable. We would like our money back. Now.'

4

Czech Republic
Candles and Cakes

Money back, now!

Had anyone else heard? What about the super-confident Ronald, had he heard?

'Oh dear, that seems a pity.' I tried to play for time, searching for something to say. 'I can certainly look into it for you, but I see from my notes you are *Christopher Columbus Club* members, so frequent G&S travellers.' I smiled sweetly at Chuck, who continued to assess me.

'Don't you agree,' I carried on swiftly, 'travelling is all about variety, different cultures and experiences? Otherwise, we would simply stay at home, wouldn't we?' I tried another smile. 'Shall we see how it goes? Wait a few days?' He was hesitating, perhaps not wanting to make a scene in the bar. 'And of course, if you're still unhappy, then naturally, I will take it up with G&S.' He glared, temporarily bereft of words. Seizing the moment, I went on. 'It would be such a pity if you were to miss out on the glamorous places we will be visiting. Prague you can take in anytime, but the chateaux and castles outside the city are wonderful, truly memorable.' Regaling their friends in Florida was likely to be high on the agenda after their return.

Chuck bent towards his wife, saying loudly, 'Come on Sissy, let's go. We've Ronald's dinner to attend.'

'I'll send the bellboy up to collect your luggage at eight thirty – I do hope that will suit you.' But already they were across the room and out of earshot.

Very quickly I discovered the benefits of being 'English'. The G&S Americans loved my voice and what I began to learn were my 'old-fashioned expressions'. When the ladies asked about suitable dress for the opera, my reply had mystified them.

'Well, I think I'll wear some smart trousers and a pretty top, but I'm sure whatever you wear will look lovely – you all have such great taste,' I said, thinking of the preppy golfing clothes which instantly identified them as Americans on holiday.

'Thank you, honey.' I was also getting used to being called 'honey'. 'But what are 'smart trousers?'

'Well, not jeans, neat trousers – evening ones, perhaps?'

They chuckled. 'Oh, she means dressy pants.'

Vladimir was universally popular and together we made a good team, showing them castles and gardens, explaining the nuances of the statues, paintings and gushing fountains. We strolled the cobbled streets passing gabled buildings with their elaborate gilded signs, proclaiming the trades of the shop below. Chuck and Sissy were full of questions, obviously enjoying themselves and there was no further reference to leaving. But Brad and Stacey Powell were different.

People dynamics during *Monaco's* cruises had taught me much about groups, in particular that having an odd-ball couple frequently cemented the others, providing they were not over tiresome. Curiously, the misfits never realised. Brad was techno-mad and flourished the most high spec and undoubtedly the newest camcorder. He never missed a moment. His aim for each day was to impress everyone with just how expensive it was, how envious they should be and how clever he was to own such a smart piece of kit. Nowhere went unrecorded and once back on the bus, anyone within range of where he sat was regaled remorselessly with footage of what they too had seen only minutes earlier. Stacey did not hold back either. Generously proportioned, she was an unrelenting and indiscriminate shopper. Her whole being focused on 'stores'. She needed to shop at least every day and preferably every hour. Today, having left Prague two hours earlier she pounced at the country service station when the bus pulled off the road for 'a comfort break'. After the austerity of communism, colour was popular, and these garage owners had chosen purple. We entered a mauve world. The petrol pumps, the tarmac surrounding them – everywhere was a rich mauve. While waiting in line for the loo, Stacey had spotted a display case. There, among the gee-gaws, lay a string of giant pearlized purple beads. She had been deprived so far today, but now she perked up. Parting with a ridiculously large number of dollars she slipped the 'pink pearls' over her head where they lay resplendent on the shelf of her bosom. They bounced energetically with each step.

This was our first day outside Prague, and I emphasised it would be the first of many memorable ones. The sun shone as we completed our first visit at Karlova Koruna, a glorious castle of baroque swirls and curls.

'Horses!' declared Sissy as we strolled down the avenue of oak trees lining the drive, leaving Karlova Koruna behind on the top of the hill.

'That place had horses everywhere. Far too many paintings of horses. Count Kinsky was clearly obsessed. And the horses all had such huge butts!' She turned to me. 'Amelia, dear, why do they have such huge butts? No horse could move with a butt like those!'

Horses were not my thing either, but my father had taught me always to have an answer. Inspiration dawned.

'Yes, they were huge weren't they. I think the Count wanted to show off how strong his horses were and how likely to win races. His friends were keen on a bet, I expect.' It sounded plausible and Sissy was content with the answer. I was learning. We strolled on under the white castellated arch in the warm October sun. As people climbed into the bus, I counted them in. Two short. Two people were missing. Brad and Stacey.

'Vladimir, have you seen the Powells?'

'I think Mrs Powell is looking for a shop,' Vladimir said. The shopping and filming were inexplicable to him, and he was sick of them too. Together we quickly returned up the drive.

'You go to the shop at the entrance,' panted Vladimir. 'I will go back into the castle. It will be easier for me to get in than you.'

'Good idea, I'll see you back at the bus.'

The shop was empty. Hoping Vladimir had found them, I ran back down the drive. As I neared the bus the faint beat of a slow hand clap reached me. There they were, Stacey near the front and Brad towards the back, as far apart as it was possible to be. Vlad outlined his enthusiasm for our next stop, Omlovice, as the bus moved off. I weaved between the seats, counting as I went to be one hundred per cent sure. Brad stood up, blocking my way, his face an inch from mine.

'You don't know what it's like!' Angrily he jabbed his finger into my chest. 'To be left in a country where you don't speak the language!' He sat down with a thump. I did. I knew exactly what it was like. I could not speak Czech either and Karlova Koruna had not been part of my earlier recce. The one piece of advice Gregory had given me sprang to mind, 'Remember, Amelia, it's only an issue if you make it an issue.' I returned to my seat, biting my tongue.

Crunching on the copious gravel, the bus swept up to the wide stone steps of Omlovice where Lady Dobřenšti appeared in a flurry of pugs.

'My dear girl, how simply lovely to see you again.' She kissed me on both cheeks. The warmth of her greeting was clear to all. Brad was still scowling as he stepped down from the bus, and he was also filming. Lady Dobřenšti spotted the camcorder instantly. Stepping towards him, she took hold of his arm.

'Do please come along in, it's a joy to have you all here. No filming please. Branislav has tea ready in the Orangery.'

Brad smiled ingratiatingly and pocketed his machine. Stacey, purple pearls bouncing, stomped grumpily after him.

'I trust our valises will be in our rooms.' She had elevated her vocabulary to suit the occasion.

'Yes of course,' I tried a conciliatory smile. 'The bellboy has the rooming list.'

Part of the G&S style was our own travelling 'bellboy'. Resplendent in green and gold, a Harrods doorman on the move, he was in charge of suitcases, and from the very first day a guest need never touch their bags. He whisked them from hotel to hotel, room to room, assuming I gave him the correct information and none of the cases had been left behind. His duty was to arrive ahead of us and ensure the correct cases were waiting in each room. So far it had worked and while we had our afternoon tea, I hoped he was working his magic.

Sunlight poured through the stained-glass crest in the tall window as I made my way up the wide stairs. Vermillion and emerald reflections glinted on the polished surface. Outside, the park stretched into the distance, peaceful in the golden warmth. A herd of fallow deer, spread like a crumpled, spotty handkerchief, lay together in the deep shadows of an oak tree. This was not a hotel, there were no telephones in the rooms or housekeeping available at the flick of a switch. We were privileged guests but even so, I should check, knock on each bedroom door in turn to see everyone had their luggage, understood about dinner and was happy.

'Amelia, this is simply divine.' Sissy drawled. They had the most beautiful room and I smiled, happy there had been no more reference to leaving. At each room came more ecstatic comments. People were impressed by the rich 'drapes', loved the old-fashioned 'faucets', it was all 'so elegant'.

Finally, I came to the door for the Powells' bedroom. Aware of Rosemary's advice, given when I had thanked her for the introduction to G&S, I had followed it unwaveringly. The Powells had what I felt was the least attractive room.

'Amelia,' Rosemary had advised, 'there is always someone tiresome. Always one annoying couple, so if you have to allocate rooms, give them the worst. They will complain anyway, so they might as well have a bad one. Of course, if you can move them, you'll score a few points.'

The thought of knocking on their door filled me with dread. Inevitably there would be something amiss. The rooms, not being regular hotel rooms, were quirky in nature and unlikely to fit with Brad's conventional views. I did not want his aggressive voice shattering the calm of the chateau, and there was no alternative room to offer. I could just miss them out. They would never know. But a little voice nagged in my head – *we've only had three days. Things will get worse if you start avoiding them.*

I tapped smartly on the mahogany door. Almost instantly, Stacey opened the door. She glared, taken aback to find it was me. Behind her stood Brad, a suitcase open on the ottoman at the foot of the four-poster.

'Apologies for disturbing you, but there are no telephones in the rooms, so I just wanted to make sure you're Ok and that you have your luggage.' Brad straightened up and came towards me across the floral swags of the Aubusson carpet.

'Young Lady,' he drawled, 'I owe you an apology. This is a beautiful room. Thank you, we are fine.' Another lesson learned. He had had an opportunity to apologise privately, and without losing face.

Dinner was excruciating. Lady Dobřenšti had invited a clutch of her neighbouring castle dwellers but there was little common ground, no mutually easy topics of conversation. My wealthy and strangely naïve Americans were obsequious, while the Czech aristos, with their perfect English, were jolly, educated and unimpressed by American materialism. We ground through six delicious courses, each presented by white-gloved staff. Silver shone, crystal wine glasses sparkled and were continuously refilled. For me, the porcelain was the star. Every plate was different. Around the rim ran a pattern like a necklace of golden pearls encircling a perfect botanical painting. There were bunches of scarlet poppies, delicate pink daisies, arching ferns and nodding bluebells. Each design filled the centre of a plate and had a halo of attendant buzzing bees, blue-winged butterflies or ladybirds. And every plate, dish and tureen was a work of art in itself.

'Forgive my curiosity, Lady Dobřenšti, but this is the most

beautiful china. It's utterly breath-taking.' I was longing to pick up a side plate and look at the mark underneath.

'I am so pleased someone has noticed!' she smiled across the crisp white lace tablecloth. 'We are using the *Flora Danica*, the Royal Copenhagen dinner service made in the late eighteenth century. Long ago, the service was a present to my family. It is beautiful, isn't it? I only use it occasionally.'

'What an honour, thank you. It really is superb.'

She gazed at me slightly wistfully. 'You know, I've always wanted a daughter. Maybe even one a little like you.'

I shall never forget the two short days at Omlovice. They confirmed I had been right. Right to leave the *Monaco*. The winter storms, entangling bureaucracy and dodgy finances were no match for this world of glamour and castles.

There remained one more hurdle for Vladimir and me to jump. Chuck had a 'significant birthday'. Sissy, the G&S folder informed me, had made arrangements to follow on from the main tour. Sixty of their closest friends were coming from the States, flown in by private jet. Chuck was not in the know, but the State Dining Room of Prague Castle had been reserved for the party. There, surrounded by glitter and gold, candle sconces and chandeliers, with their friends in tuxes and tiaras, they would all dine in style. Sissy's greatest friend Mavis would sing and a massive cake would appear.

Vladimir seemed totally unconcerned about this event, and I feared he had not fully appreciated the significance of the occasion. As the days of the tour ticked by, the logistics assumed more and more mountainous proportions – not least because Sissy was a vegetarian. She had been amused by the Fleshless Food and Onion Wheels of Telč but Prague was a capital city and tasteless wooden carrots or tree-trunk leeks would not be acceptable. Money was not a consideration, and I had free rein to fix cars, champagne and differing menus. Everything had to be organised by our return to the city. With no mobile phone network, fax machines in dark cupboards and corners became my friends. Sissy's friend was also a concern. Was Mavis a diva, difficult to please and temperamental? I had grown to like Chuck and Sissy, they were always interested in the places we visited and were unfailingly courteous to me and others, so I was anxious there would be no hitches.

The Birthday Dinner was at last in full swing. Vladimir wriggled uncomfortably in his rented tux. We watched, peeping through the slits of an ornate panel. I wondered how many riotous parties over the centuries had been squinted at by curious servants through this very panel. So far all was going well.

'Amelia,' Vladimir whispered, though there was no need, the high-ceilinged room buzzed with chatter. 'It is so very nice to see this.' He paused, looking at the seated throng. 'This is like it should be, here, in this room. People dressed appropriately. This is what this room and the castle was for.'

He was right. The elegant room with its highly polished parquet floor was lit by huge crystal chandeliers sparkling in the soft light from candles in gold sconces, high on the walls between each of the arched windows. Seated at long tables the party too sparkled, the ladies bright with serious jewellery – tiaras, necklaces, earrings and chokers – and the men equally well-groomed. Not a hair was out of place.

The moment for cake and singing drew near. Unexpectedly a slip of paper popped through our viewing slit. Opening the note I read, 'Amelia, dear. Could we have the lights down for the cake?' Mavis, in a mauve sequined evening dress with a small train, swished across the parquet to the piano. She twirled aside the heavy fabric and sat down to play.

'What do they want?' asked Vladimir.

'They would like to have the lights dimmed when the cake comes in. We'll have to hurry, but let's turn off the big chandeliers and leave the candles burning in the wall sconces.'

I could see the golden wheeled trolley resplendent with the cake blocking the doorway. A waiter bent towards the many candles.

'Quick, Vladimir. I'll catch the waiter before he lights the candles. Would you turn off the chandeliers, please?'

Vladimir disappeared. I grabbed the matches from a surprised waiter. The minutes ticked by while Mavis tinkled through another tune at the piano, looking over her shoulder, assessing when to burst into song. Suddenly with no notice, the chandeliers went off and only the candles in the curving wall sconces flickered. A soft golden light lit the Castle's grand State Dining Room. A hush descended, broken by an ominous creaking as the cake appeared, its gold chariot wobbling dangerously on account of a dicey wheel. Mavis, with perfect timing, burst into 'Happy Birthday to you!' Chuck stood up grinning with delight, took three giant breaths and blew out his seventy candles. It was perfect.

Immediately, the chandeliers burst back into life. Crystals sparkled, light glittered and bounced off silverware and glasses, jewellery and glossy heads. Watching Chuck to ensure he was happy, I saw him waving a hand, beckoning to me. I crossed the floor, weaving between the gold chairs, confident all was well.

'Congratulations, Chuck! That was lovely.'

'It was great, just great, thank you. But it's a little bright now. Too bright. Could you please get those chandeliers turned off again? It will be more intimate for the dancing.'

'Ok, fine.' I replied. There was always something more. 'I'll get onto it right away.' I weaved away again through the chairs, looking for Vladimir. There he was, standing discreetly in a doorway mopping his forehead with a large handkerchief.

'Well done, Vladimir! Perfect. He was delighted, thank you.' He smiled, visibly relaxing. 'But,' I said, 'Chuck would like the chandeliers turned off again now, for the dancing. Tell me where the switch is, and I'll do it this time.'

'That will not be possible, Amelia.'

'Not possible! Why, what's the problem?' Vladimir had never said 'no' before. Not once had he refused to do anything I had asked for.

He smiled deprecatingly and blew his nose. 'Well, Amelia. It's like this.' He bent closer, whispering confidentially. 'To make the darkness necessitated a discussion, a discussion with the supervisor of the city's main power station. He had to be persuaded it was important. I impressed upon him the need to have darkness for the singing. There is no switch for this part of the castle, it is either lit or not. So, to turn off the chandeliers, he had to cut the power for the whole central city. There were no lights throughout the city, complete blackout, but I cannot ask him again.'

5

Norway

Beset by Trolls

Leaning against each other like drunks in Oban on a Friday night, the russet-coloured warehouses of Bergen's waterfront swept past the bow as the hydrofoil turned out of the harbour to face the sea. A gaggle of ferries and two huge cruise ships slid astern as we picked up speed. Two white jets of water curved high in an arc of shimmering droplets, and I felt the lift of the swell. I should go and chat, get to know this new group of Americans. It was the first day, and there were nineteen to come on this tour of the Baltic.

Even on a hydrofoil, the same excitement washed over me: the thrill of leaving a harbour, of shaking off the land, a sense of freedom with who knew what adventures ahead. I waited a moment longer to savour the space, knowing I really ought to go and tell them about the Sognefjord, Kaiser Wilhelm II and our day ahead. The hydrofoil turned north, the starboard side dipping until the deck became steeply raked as she swung round the coast to enter the dark waters of the fjord slicing deep into the hills.

Suddenly, I remembered. The wheelchair. Might it go careering across the deck and tip over the railings? I pushed through the chattering tourists thronging the bar, through the metal doors and out onto the aft deck. A Viking, blond, tall and with obligatory bushy beard, braced himself against the railings, casually holding the wheelchair. Still comfortably seated, Deborah gazed serenely at the fjord.

'Wonderful, isn't it? You can tell it's deep, look at the colour of the water!' Seeing me she turned. 'Amelia! This delightful man has just saved me from going over the side. You must have forgotten to put the brakes on.' She smiled coyly at her fair Viking rescuer.

'I'm so sorry, thank goodness you're in such safe hands. Silly of me, but I'm afraid I had no idea wheelchairs had brakes.'

'Ja, ja. Of course! All chairs do.' said the Viking. He gave the lever a reassuring little push before ambling along the deck to disappear through a door marked 'Crew Only'.

This was my second tour for G&S, and again I had an untested itinerary, but this time there was no reassuring Vladimir. Our first three days were to be in Norway, followed by three in Stockholm before a short luxury cruise of the Baltic. Everywhere would be new to me. It was a glamorous itinerary and, as my twenty-six Americans all knew each other and regularly holidayed together, there had been none of the initial checking each other out reminiscent of dogs. Deborah, who was a spindly six foot and could barely stand, was accompanied by her husband Dick, unmistakeably a golfer. Every item of his American clothes, from brogues to cap, sported golfing logos. He even had a pair of clubs embroidered in gold on his jacket. In his late seventies and sunburnt from life on courses, he was wiry, but the medieval cobbles of Bergen had defeated him. It seemed pushing Deborah was added to my duties. With Greg and Maisie came their son, Rad. Nineteen-year-old Rad was fed up with everything already. Sullen, spotty and spoilt, he oozed boredom.

It was going to be a long three weeks, and I was annoyed G&S had not mentioned the wheelchair. But I would be seeing new places. Sognefjord, so deep the water was almost black, snaked ahead, cutting a route through green hillsides. Occasionally a white church spire surrounded by red ochre houses zipped past as we zoomed inland. The group was cheerfully chatting, bunched together on blue plastic seats in the shelter of the aft deck as they caught up on their lives and news. Today was designed as a relaxing, easy start and travelling through the powerful fjord scenery was glorious. A typical Norwegian lunch, my notes told me, would be waiting for us at Flåm, the village nestling at the head of the fjord. This would be followed by a trip on the famous Flåmsbana, the train up into the mountains, before a short ride on the main line would return us to Bergen in time for tea. The programme was carefully timed and, providing lunch ran on time, it should be an easy day for me.

'We're nearly a hundred miles inland now,' I said as I joined them, feeling I should engage as their guide. The hydrofoil slowed, turning into Balestrand to collect more passengers.

'We're following in the wake of Kaiser Wilhelm; he stayed at that hotel.' I pointed at the ornate white façade of the Kviknes Hotel, its columns and balconies reflected in the water, wavering in the ripples created by the hydrofoil as it slowed, dropping low in the water. Tourists disembarked in the bright sunlight to be replaced by more; it was a popular scenic route.

As we came into Flåm, I asked, 'Deborah, would you mind if I pushed you quickly to the hotel? I need to go and collect the train tickets. There's only one train a day so we can't afford to miss it.'

'Honey, that's just fine. You go ahead and do whatever you need to do, don't mind me.' She was what her American friends referred to as 'gracious'.

The 'typically Norwegian' lunch, a slab of poached, pastel pink salmon accompanied by straw colour boiled potatoes sprinkled with dill, was pallid, but it was delicious and, with no choice, to my relief, turned out to be efficient and quick.

'Ok everyone? Yes, lunch was good, you're right. We've fifteen minutes before the train goes, so please use the restrooms here, there are none on the train. I'll wait for you all outside.'

Sparkling clean, the seven green carriages waited behind the small engine that would pull us high into the mountains. According to my notes, this was 'one of the world's most beautiful train journeys.'

'Deborah, do you think you would you be able to pull yourself up into the train if I push you close to the doorway?' With no platform, no steps and no hunky Vikings here to help, I suggested I go round, get the chair in through another door and meet Deborah on the inside.

'Sure, dear. I'll have a go. Dick'll help me.' She could barely stand but she was game.

Back then virtually nothing was organised for people in wheelchairs. They were expected to stay at home, I assume. However, G&S should have prepared me: it had come as a total surprise that one of the party was in a wheelchair. How would I manage on the ship? What about all the walking tours and marble stairs of the Hermitage? I would just have to work it out on the hoof, but I wished I had been to some of the places before.

'Please sit on the right side,' I instructed, thanking the Rough Guide that I could sound knowledgeable. 'You'll get the best view. It's only forty-five minutes so make the most of it.'

The train pulled smoothly away from the cluster of painted wooden houses and began trundling up the valley, gaining height by the moment. The single track snaked along the course of the river twisting and turning as hot July air blew in through the open windows. Occasionally the track looped round and the deep waters of Sognefjord were visible, shining below. We wound on up the mountainside, the views growing wider. Conifer plantations gave way to scrubby birch trees, their trunks shining white in the bright sun. The views became increasingly spectacular, and a contented post-prandial lassitude crept over the group.

The train jolted. Shuddered. We drew to a halt.

'Ah, we must have reached the passing place, where the drivers pass the baton across. Up train to down train,' I said. 'It's single track all the way, apart from this passing place.'

'Oh, that's so quaint.'

The minutes ticked by, heads nodded again.

'Takes quite a while, dear,' said Macey, who had stuck her head out of the window.

It was unexpectedly peaceful in the heat of the afternoon, with bees buzzing loudly among the rosebay willowherb lining the track; the whole world seemed to be dozing.

Suddenly a shrill bell rang through the carriage, shattering the peace. Everyone jerked awake as a loud voice burst out of the speaker above our heads.

'Ladies and Gentlemen,' announced a lugubrious voice, we wait here. You understand, we have to wait here. Today, weather is too hot. The rails have grown and the train cannot move. We wait for cool down.'

To my surprise, no one complained, no one muttered. I

was lucky to have such an easy-going lot, they simply settled back to snoozing the wait away.

An hour later, restlessness began to seep through the carriage. It was hot, very hot. Brochures and hats flapped, creating little currents, barely cooling but better than nothing in the oppressive July heat. People were beginning to wriggle. It was now over two hours since lunch, so I needed to find them a loo. If I clambered down to find one the train would probably lurch off without me, but their increasing need could not be ignored.

'If anyone needs a... restroom this might be a good moment. I'm going to try and find out how much longer they expect to wait.'

I scrunched along the gravel at the side of the train towards the engine. Subdued voices came from the other carriages, doors began to open, and people climbed hesitantly onto the track. There was not a single, green-uniformed official to be seen. I returned unhappily.

'What's the news?' asked Greg. Dick stood in the carriage doorway, but everyone else except Deborah was on the track.

'Well, the guards are away, getting help.' I replied, trying to sound positive.

'Amelia,' Dick murmured, 'Deborah needs a restroom.'

'Right, yes of course.' For a moment I considered an empty bottle.

'Ladies, if we get Deborah down, do you think we can make a screen? We can stand close together.' Squeezing up tightly, they linked arms, closed up and corralled the wheelchair.

Mission accomplished with surprisingly easy decorum, we dragged the chair and Deborah back across the hardcore towards the train and Deborah hauled herself up just as two breathy, imperious toots made us jump.

With a third cheerful toot, a slight backwards jerk, the train resumed its slow chug up the track. It was a relief to be moving after the long hot wait. Again, we peered out of the windows at the passing scenery, trees and glimpses of the widening fjord shimmering below. Jagged mountains began to crowd closer as the gradient grew steeper. Patches of grass dotted with alpine flowers and sleepy brown cows relieved the harsh mountain terrain.

The loudspeaker crackled again. Nervously, we looked at each other. More crackles.

'Ladies and Gentlemen, please to look on left side. We see highlight...gushing waterfall. Rjoandefossen.'

Close to the track, a sheet of blue-green snow water thundered over a granite ledge crashing into a pool many feet below. The train battled on up the steep gradient as the air cooled and the sun disappeared, sliding behind towering clouds. The carriage became dark and quickly the chill spread through the carriage. Heavy drops of rain clattered violently on the tin roof. The air fizzed and crackled as lightning cracked off the surrounding peaks. Thunder burst out, immediately above. The summer thunderstorm seemed dramatic and exciting rather than frightening here among the high peaks.

'Well,' I began, aiming for reassurance. 'I don't expect you were anticipating such an exciting day, when you woke up this morning?' I had to shout to be heard above the noise of the rain on the tin roof. Thunder rolled louder round the mountains, bouncing from peak to peak. Wet rocks were lit by flashes of lightning that illuminated the now gloomy carriage. Then the train stopped. Everyone turned expectantly to me, but no one spoke as, again, we waited.

'Hello. We need electrician. Do we have on board the train? Electrician?' asked the same doleful voice.

'Don't worry, I'm sure it'll be Ok,' I said. We sat in the gloom, waiting. People began to hunt for jerseys as the chill seeped in.

'I'll go and see what I can find out.' Adding, with a grin, 'Don't let them go without me!'

Uphill, towards the engine, I could see two figures who seemed to be looking at a coupling between the engine and the carriages.

'Hello! What's the problem?'

'Ja, we have no power. Sorry. The storm has got the train.'

'I've a group here, and we should have been in Myrdal two hours ago. We need to catch the train back to Bergen.'

'Ok, no problem. Replacement come. Please, you just wait.' There was not much choice, stuck there in the mountains. I hoisted myself back into the green carriage.

We had no alternative but to wait – there were no roads nearby.

Cold air from the mountain tops slipped downhill between the dripping tree trunks, invading the carriage. The loudspeaker crackled into life again.

'Ja! Ja! Hello, hello. Please now get out. Take track on the right. Replacement cannot come right here. Just short walk.' Doors clanked as the passengers jumped down, stamping their feet to warm up, and a multi-coloured crocodile began to wind along a track disappearing up the hill and through the trees. Deborah, aided by Dick, pulled herself out of the train and collapsed into the chair. He tried to push it over the rubble.

'Amelia, I'm not sure about this.' He panted with exertion. 'The chair is not made for rough terrain.' I joined him, each of us taking a handle. The small front wheels dug into the jagged lumps of hard core.

'Oh dear. Unfortunately, we've not much alternative, but they said it's only a short way to the replacement train.' Dick, worried and embarrassed at his own lack of strength, made tutting noises and released his handle.

'Let's try like this, maybe backwards will be better, the little wheels at the front dig in.' Determinedly I dragged it backwards over the stones while a silent Deborah bounced about in the seat.

'How are you doing, down there, Deborah? Are you Ok?'

'You're doing a great job, honey. I'm so sorry, but don't you mind about me, I'm just fine.'

'Out of the way, old chap.' One of the younger husbands joined me, taking one of the handles and easing the weight on one of the wheels. 'Let me get a look in here! Come on Pete, you're strong with all that gym training you do,' he said over his shoulder to Pete who came to join him. I lifted the back and they each took a wheel as the three of us began to walk backwards. With the chair almost completely off the ground, we carried Deborah, chair and all, up the track. The young Rad made no move to help.

Dick walked beside us, chatting to Deborah as we staggered on. Reaching a small crest, we stopped for a breather and could see below the brightly clad passengers spread out like a patchwork rug in the little clearing, as they waited for the replacement train. Cautiously and slowly, trying not to bounce poor Deborah too much, we slithered down to join them, as from between the dripping conifers a little green engine appeared. Like Percy in *Thomas the Tank Engine*, it gave a cheeky toot. But there were no welcoming carriages. Percy pulled just a flatbed with a crane curled at one end. Immediately, the picnic rug came to life. Like colourful ants the passengers flowed towards the engine, pushing and clambering onto the flatbed to find a space.

'Oh my!' Doreen exclaimed nervously, eyeing up the mob. 'Do we have to get on that? Is that for us?'

'No.' I said firmly. 'That is not for us. Let me go and see what I can do. That doesn't look very safe to me.'

Breaking the G&S rules about staying with the group, I left the clutch of elderly Americans and frail lady in a wheelchair and ran downhill. As I neared Percy the Engine, he gave a triumphant toot and moved off, shunting off between the trees. Quiet fell on the clearing. Everyone had gone; there was no one left but my amazed Americans. A watery sun broke through the clouds and the woods begin to steam. Little puffs of midges appeared and began to dance in the sunbeams. Biting and whining they buzzed round our heads.

'Amelia!' Chuck flapped his arms at the midges. 'Look! Look! There's someone coming. There, through the trees.' A lean figure loped up the slope with ease, a coil of climbing rope slung casually over one shoulder. He strolled into the clearing; he looked muscled and fit in his camouflage trousers.

'What are you doing here?' He sounded annoyed, rather than curious. 'You are not supposed to get off the train.'

'Yes, we know that,' I snapped. 'The train broke down in the thunderstorm and the replacement was dangerous. Could you help us get to Myrdal, please?

'Myrdal! There is no road to Myrdal or anywhere else from here. The train is the only way.' He seemed almost triumphant. 'But there is a track. That will take you to Myrdal. I'm not going that way.' He strode on, adding casually over the rope, as he disappeared, 'The path goes up and down a bit, but don't follow the railway – that is a long, long way round. The path is shorter – it's about an hour to Myrdal.'

In silence, we resumed our positions; there was nothing to say. Chuck and Pete each took a wheel and I lifted again the handles at the back.

He was right, the track rose and fell a lot as it snaked through the mountains. Mostly it was wide enough for Pete and Chuck to walk beside the chair, but it was slow going. The gradients were steep and poor embarrassed Deborah was no lightweight. Soon we were far behind the rest of the group; brief glimpses of colour showed them trudging far ahead.

'Let's stop here. Catch our breath . . . admire the view.' The sunlight softened, encouraging relentless clouds of midges. Dick was panting, finding even the walk a challenge, Chuck was breathing hard, but Pete seemed to be holding up well.

'These damn "no-seeums"!' Chuck groaned, flapping at the clouds of midges. He was tired, and we were all becoming increasingly exhausted. The soft summer light so far north was misleading, but I was aware it was taking us a long time. We had no option but to plod on determinedly along the ever-rising track.

Eventually, high above us sunlight glinted, flashing on windows and, looking up, I saw a long, low building, its green roof blending with the surroundings. Myrdal station at last. We had taken almost four hours but with the end in sight, we struggled the remaining yards breathlessly, finally settling Deborah onto a reassuringly flat platform. I put on the brake.

'Well done! Have a seat here,' Maisie called. She was sitting with the others on a bench, a row of swallows waiting to migrate. After a moment to catch my breath, I went into the station office.

'Ah. So. You have made it,' said a young man. 'We have

been watching you. We have very good view from here. Good view of you coming up the track.' Three hunks of solid, strapping Norwegian muscle lolled, totally at ease in their padded swivel chairs.

'What time,' I growled, 'is the next train to Bergen?'

'Oh, well, Ja. Ja, you have just missed one.' He glanced at the big clock. 'But of course, there'll be another. In two hours now.'

'Is there a Waiting Room, with some proper chairs and a toilet, please?' I asked, taking a deep breath to control my anger.

'Nei, we have nothing here, but you are welcome to wait on the platform.' Restraining my desire to say I understood that was what platforms were for, I pulled my phone from my pocket, relieved to see five bars of signal. I called the hotel to ask if they could provide a bus to collect us, but it turned out that would take two hours by road. We might as well wait for the train. However, they did assure me there would be food waiting for us when we finally got there.

Three hours later, at exactly one thirty in the morning, I held open the plate glass doors and my weary, dishevelled bunch walked creakily into the brightly lit foyer. Like uncertain ducklings, they straggled ahead of me into the welcoming warmth.

'Hello, welcome!' cried the uniformed night porter. 'We have a smorgasbord of smoked salmon with dill, herrings in mustard sauce, rye bread, cheese and oat biscuits for you. I hope that will that be suitable. The kitchen is closed, of course.'

We descended like locusts with no energy to spare for conversation.

Next morning everyone chattered loudly as we waited for

our plane. Having survived their adventure without a scratch, they were all fired up with relief. It was only a short hop to Stockholm, followed by two days to explore the Swedish capital before we were to embark, right in the middle of town, on our sleek cruise vessel. This was the moment I had been longing for. I had never been on a smart, cruise ship and, much as I loved my sturdy *Monaco,* I hoped there would be little in common. No pumping out stinking bilges, no greasing hinges on deck hatches, no cranking up generators. What sort of cabin would I get? I knew I would be allocated whatever was free, so it would be potluck, no choice.

The plane banked and turned to land at Arlanda airport; beneath lay silvery sea. A group of islands were woven together like a spider's web by the wake of boats buzzing and crossing the stretches of water between them.

I felt confident my ration of disasters was complete. Stockholm, and the Grand Hotel, would be a delight: the guidebook told me it was 'truly grand'.

As the group made their way to the airport exit, I thought I'd better check the luggage for the bellboy.

'There's just one more to come,' said the Swedish lad, again resplendent in Harrods green and gold, as he referred to the list pinned to his clipboard. Pete had two cases, but only one had arrived. Pete was a calm, unflappable fellow and even the rigours of the mountain trail had not ruffled his composure. In Bergen, he had worn a different jacket each evening, all immaculate, well cut and different colours.

'Pete,' I said, 'I'm afraid it looks as if one of your suitcases hasn't made it but there are lots of flights each day so don't worry, I'm sure it will be here this afternoon. The bellboy will track it down and bring it to the hotel.' A heavy frown darkened Pete's face, but his wife intervened.

'Darling, it's not a problem. Bergen is only a short hop away. Amelia will get it here later today, so don't you fret. You have your other bag, it's Ok.'

'What's the timing?' he asked, straining to be polite.

'Sir, it'll definitely be here by tomorrow morning at the latest, I'm sure,' said the Bellboy. 'I'll come back straight after I've delivered the rest of the luggage. There are many flights from Bergen, don't you worry, sir.' His confidence was encouraging, although Pete still looked unhappy.

The Grand Hotel was as smart a hotel as I had ever seen and certainly the most glamorous I had ever stayed in. Built to be one of the great hotels of Europe, it was unquestionably grand. From the green roof, pierced by round windows and topped with flags, to the balconies sporting red geraniums, the late nineteenth century façade stretched along one side of the harbour. Window after window, each shaded by an arched coral-coloured awning, gave uninterrupted views across the water to the Royal Palace where the fresh waters of Lake Mälaren gushed into the harbour. White ferry boats, neat and elegant with small funnels, were tied in rows at the piers and jetties immediately outside the hotel. The burgers of Stockholm strolled along the quays enjoying the traffic-free cobbled space.

Breakfast was appropriately hushed next morning. No raised voices or raucous noises interrupted the gentle murmur of breakfasting guests who politely manoeuvred around the lavish buffet. Herrings naturally. Herrings in tomato sauce. Herrings with pickled onions. Herrings with mustard seeds. Rolled herrings, soused herrings or just plain pickled herrings. Thirteen bowls, each brimming with a different type of herring. I helped myself to berries and yoghurt.

'Good morning, Pete. I hope you slept well. I'm so sorry but it seems your suitcase has not yet arrived, I've just checked.' Pete, wearing yesterday's slightly too bright brown jacket, looked disconsolate. I added quickly, 'I've asked the bellboy to stay at the airport until he has it. Such a nuisance, but I'm sure it will be here when we come back this afternoon, I'll remind the Concierge before we leave for the museum.'

The Concierge leant over his desk towards me. 'Good morning, Miss Amelia. Are you here to enquire about the missing suitcase? I will tell you this, but in confidence.' Conspiratorially, I leant closer to his gold frogging.

Looking around to see if anyone might hear, he licked his lips and leaned further over the high, polished desk, uncomfortably close.

'The SAS have a special room,' he whispered. Spittle dribbled from his bottom lip onto the crested note pad. 'It is a security policy. Sometimes, at random you understand, they take a bag to the "Special Room".' He nodded at me, smugly satisfied he knew every aspect of the SAS systems.

'What do you mean "Special Room"?'

'Sssh! SAS, they have a special "holding" room.' He was loving the drama. 'A "Special Room" for cases to explode. My friend has told me.'

'Explode!' I tried not to explode myself. I moved back a little, enough to be out of range of the spittle spray.

He glanced around. 'One might hold a bomb. When they feel like it, you understand, they put a suitcase in the "Special Room" for twenty-four hours.' He shrugged. 'If it doesn't explode, they release it. It takes only twenty-four hours, and then he will get his suitcase for sure.'

'Mm. We leave the hotel at midday tomorrow, so perhaps you'd tell your friend we need it here this evening. It would be unfortunate if it has not arrived by then, as I wouldn't be able to thank you properly. We're off on a cruise around the Baltic, so who knows when I might be back. Years.'

The focus of the day was a visit to what remains one of my favourite museums, The Vasa. A brief boat ride took us across the harbour to the soaring boat-shaped building that gave no clue to the smells and delights inside. Air blew into my face as I pushed open the huge oak door. Cool and fragrant, it smelt strongly of the sea, of tar, pitch, twine, hemp ropes and wood. Strategically directed shafts of light were just sufficient to illuminate a huge shape that rose high up into the rafters, the shape of a magnificent ship, but a tragic one. It dated from the mid-seventeenth century and had been designed by the then young King Gustavus Adolphus. He had assembled a remarkable array of foreign guests, dignitaries, ambassadors as well as the good people of Sweden to witness the spectacle of his great warship's first outing, sailing in the harbour by his Palace.

As the great crowd watched, a puff of wind, unexpectedly strong had simply rolled her over, and she sank into the mud and dirty water of the harbour. Top-heavy and unstable, she was saved by this immediate sinking to be preserved for centuries in the airless sludge, a perfect, ornate example of a seventeenth-century war machine. Now, the richly carved hull loomed high above us, cannons poking from gun ports on the sides, while carved figures stood to attention around the stern. Every inch was deeply carved and decorated.

Next morning, Pete, at last resplendent in a Sherwood Green jacket, beamed as he worked round the bowls of herrings at breakfast. The suitcase had been waiting when we returned from the Vasa, so it was an entirely cheerful and expectant party that ascended the carpeted gangway ahead of me to board our luxurious cruise ship, *Renaissance V.* The ship's foyer bustled. Blue hydrangeas frothed in shiny brass pots, tightly rolled umbrellas stood to attention in groups. Trays of steaming hand towels reminiscent of spring rolls were presented as we entered.

It was an encouraging beginning. Clutching flutes of champagne, each couple was swept along the hushed corridor to be introduced to their suite. Dutifully, I followed my usher, wondering. Walking along the rosewood panelled passageway carpeted in deep blue with gold swirls, we reached a door inlaid with marquetry flowers. Suite 12 would be my home for the coming two weeks. With a flourish, he flung open the door.

'Madame, welcome to your suite. My name is Michael, I will be your Suite Butler. I hope you will be comfortable here. You can ask me for anything.' Suppressing a grin at the thought of 'asking him for anything', I stepped into the capacious cabin and gasped. In a mirror-lined alcove nestled an enormous bed topped by a heap of cushions. Paddling serenely across the pale blue bed cover, fringed with navy and gold bobbles, was a swan. Created from rolled white towels it was clearly at home. Michael swept open the floor-to-ceiling windows.

'Here is Madame's private balcony.' Teak furniture, a hexagonal table and two steamer chairs with gold piped cushions occupied only half the space. The table held a tray with two glasses and an ice bucket with a bottle of champagne.

Next, he showed me the bathroom. It was a cavern of pale grey marble, lightly veined with charcoal, holding both a shower and a neat bath. At the foot of the bath was a large window. I would be able to lie in the bath to watch the river Neva, Helsinki's Esplandi and the towers of Tallin slipping past. Gold racks and shelves held shampoos, body lotion and conditioner secure and, naturally, the taps were gold dolphins.

'Will Madame be comfortable here? Is there anything Madame would like now?' I gazed round overwhelmed by the opulence. Helly Handsome instantly came to mind. Pity. I felt sure he was the kind of fellow who would enjoy this glamour and privacy. This must be more akin to his yacht than the industrial strengths of *Monaco*. But he was not here, and I was alone. A waste.

6

Russia

St Petersburg, Bombs and Shards

Islands slipped by granite mounds with fuzzy topknots of purple heather. Rowans, branches covered with mopheads of white flowers, and dainty silver birches grew beside pebbly beaches. It could have been Scotland.

A familiar sense of space, freedom and adventure gripped me. The excitement of going to sea, of the unknown, of what lay ahead, all still to be discovered. Had even the slightest hint of how this elegant little ship would come to rule my life, and for so long, been whispered in my ear before I ever boarded, I might have jumped over the deck rails, swum ashore and voted for peace and predictability. But now, as I leant on the varnished rail, I was happy simply to be at sea. A sea eagle, an otter, a killer whale, an ocean liner or a message in a bobbing bottle, there was always potential for adventure at sea, and the Baltic was a new sea for me.

People were unpacking, finding their way around, leaving me time for myself. Time to dream. Would my acquaintance with HH turn into something more? Did I want it to? I barely knew him. I succumbed to the temptation and dialled.

'Hello! It's me, Amelia.' I was wary of ringing him. Who knew where he was or with whom?

'What a wonderful surprise. How, and where, are you? Timbuktu?'

'No, Timbuktu is rather too far inland! And there'd be no decent accommodation for this lot, I expect.' I needed to be entertaining, a worthwhile interruption.

'Who are "this lot"?'

'I'm taking a bunch of Americans around the Baltic on a rather smart little ship.'

'Too many people for me, but where are you headed?'

I chattered on, delighted with his interest and ending by describing the four days in St Petersburg. 'Have you been there? Any tips?'

'No, I've not been there, so take lots of photos. You can show them to me when you're back.' I debated taking a photo of the voluminous bed in my luxurious cabin to send him. Behave, Amelia! That was just a cheerful conversation.

The cruise was designed to tick off the top spots of the Baltic, starting with Visby, the capital of the Viking island of Gotland, a city I longed to see, thanks to my mother, a keen historian. She had regularly mentioned this little port: once more important to the world than London, it was known as 'the City of Ruins and Roses' and been a vital cog in the trade of the Hanseatic League. The town lived up to its billing, with a maze of streets. The honey-coloured buildings had once been the homes of sea captains and merchants; now roses rambled and arched, smothering windows and doorways. The smaller weatherboard houses were painted black and many had model ships or a knot of bleached rope in the tiny windows.

Our next port was Helsinki. Naturally, G&S had put on a Sibelius concert in the rock-hewn church for us before 'free time' in the bustle of the famous harbourside market. Stall after stall displayed rows and rows of slippery fish. Silvery salmon, slim herrings with bright fresh eyes looked more enticing than their cousins imprisoned in thick pickling jars. I was unable to resist buying a hat. With suede outside, warm fur inside and ear flaps, it gave me a little Dr Zhivago glamour, even if it did smell of fish.

Leaving the Baltic astern we sailed into the Neva River to sweep past huge rusting letters – 'Leningrad'. This would be my second visit to Russia – the first had followed the Prague tour, so when G&S asked me to do another tour, I had again insisted on a recce before setting off for Norway.

Arriving at Heathrow to set off for that scoping visit, I had scanned the departure board, worried to find no mention of my flight to Moscow. The BA clerk looked at me, wearily, 'We do not fly to Moscow from Heathrow. All flights for Russia are from Gatwick.' She sounded almost triumphant.

In 1999, a Russian visa was linked with precise flights and no deviations or changes were permitted. Missing my flight would be disastrous and G&S would be unlikely to forgive such an unprofessional error in a new recruit. It cost me two hundred pounds, but the taxi made it and I caught the flight.

Watery May sunshine picked up the grit and dirt of Moscow. Barely a hint of a leaf showed on the sparse trees, but the streets were seething with people bent on holiday drinking and city entertainment. I had chosen the first weekend of May foolishly forgetting that fourteen thousand goose-stepping, uniformed troops and over two hundred vehicles and tanks would process through the city. The country people were out for fun. Vodka, singing, food-stomping dances, sex and jollity were on their itinerary. People had rampaged along the corridor outside my hotel room as I cowered inside, telling myself that a drunk was a drunk, even if he was Russian. I had dealt with many a drunk before in Oban, so I could handle this, even without a lock on my bedroom door.

I was therefore yet to be charmed by Russia but cruising serenely up the Neva in an immaculate white cruise ship gave a very different perspective. To port was a circular fortress: ranks of dark windows stared blankly towards us across the chilly gun-metal grey waters. The ship swept on, unperturbed, leaving the unwelcoming fort of Kronstadt astern. Next, the pale sun caught a huge golden cupola – the dome of St Isaac's Cathedral I thought, knowing it would be the tallest building on the starboard side. There was no mistaking the long ornate façade of the Winter Palace when it came into view. Turquoise and white, the pillars of the river frontage were partially obscured by a haze of exhaust fumes. We had arrived.

Clad in white 'pants', bomber jackets and baseball caps, the passengers sauntered down the gangway to the beat of the band. Resplendent in brass-buttoned greatcoats and huge peaked hats they blasted out 'The Star-Spangled Banner' in welcome.

Despite the warm July sunshine, our guide was swathed in a huge red coat, belted tightly round her dumpy figure. She waited on the embankment, unsmiling, as traffic roared past, engulfing her in fumes.

'Good morning, are you Irinia?' I proffered a hand.

'Dobray Ootra, Emila.' Her hand was warm and firm. 'Da, Da. My itinerary say Peterhof, yes?'

Keen to get out of the fumes, I gathered my little party together, searching for Rad amongst the throng. But, Maisie, her maternal instincts undimmed by the early start, had pre-empted his attempt to sneak away. She pounced, bringing him back into her fold.

I bellowed over the traffic, corralling them together. 'As you can see the traffic is bad, but it won't affect us, we're going by river. It's just a short bus ride to the hydrofoil taking us to the Palace of Peterhof.'

Irinia tugged my sleeve, 'We have no hydrofoil. Cancelled. Instead, we take bus.' She pointed at the source of the fumes. 'Please to climb in.'

'Why not the hydrofoil?' A chain of ear-splitting farts burst from a passing Lada drowning my query. 'Why can't we go by hydrofoil?' I repeated, annoyed at the prospect of the battered bus.

'Bomb. We have bomb. Please to get in bus,' she insisted.

'Bomb! What do you mean you have a bomb?'

'Bomb in river. Old Bomb. Bomb from war. River is closed. We cannot go. They will make . . .' She hunted for the word. 'They make explosion. Tomorrow. So now, please, go by bus.'

Irinia settled herself in the front seat, indicating I should join her. A thick dusting of face powder covered her cheeks, her eyebrows were heavily drawn in black pencil and her lips were plastered with thick red lipstick. Were it not for the crease of worry across her forehead, she could have been a clown. But already I liked her, her decisive aura and jolly Russian red coat.

'Traffic is bad,' she whispered. 'You like poliss?'

'Police! What do you mean "do I like the police?"' I whispered back.

'Da, da. Poliss! Poliss – you like Poliss?' She giggled, conspiratorially. 'They make traffic go quickly. It will be best.' She added quietly. 'You pay? You pay eighty US, and I get Poliss. They clear road.' Without waiting for my reply, she burrowed deep into her coat pocket, pulling out a mobile phone. 'Poliss are waiting. I asked my friend, so they are ready. We go now.'

There was no microphone on the bus, so I shouted over the excited chatter. 'I'm afraid the hydrofoil is off, sorry, so we will go all the way—' The nee-naw of sirens drowned out the rest of my speech and flashing blue lights bounced around the bus. The cavalry had arrived. With a car at the front and one bringing up the rear, our bus set off surrounded by blaring sirens and flashing blue lights. As if we were the Children of Israel, the Poliss parted Russia's Red Sea.

Peterhof seemed curiously peaceful in the morning sunshine as we strolled past the Gallery Restaurant, its long façade of arched windows leading us towards the Palace entrance. To our left, the gardens dropped away in steep terraces to the river, a mass of gold statues, fountains, topiary and flowerbeds with the bulk of Kronstadt visible in the distance.

'Are you Ok, there, honey?' Deborah asked as I pushed her wheelchair over the broken surface. 'I reckon I've put a few pounds on. Great view down there. Is that the fortress we passed as we came in on the ship?'

'Yes, that's right, out there in the riv—'

A deep thudding boom reverberated around us. It thundered over the buildings and seemed to hammer in our chests. Suddenly, unexpectedly the windows of the façade exploded showering us in glass. Glass arrows rained down, cascading everywhere. Shards stuck out of everyone's hair like Edwardian hat pins, slivers sparkled on shoulders and covered the ground like frost-crisp grass. A jagged, heap lay in Deborah's lap.

'Anyone hurt? Anyone cut?' I asked, surprising even myself with my calmness. Miraculously no one had a shard in their eye or slice across a cheek. There were a few nicks, but not even a bad cut. Like baboons we set about social grooming, carefully removing splinters of glass from each other's hair. Irinia took off her coat and gave it a good shake. Pieces of glass tinkled to the gravel. She shrugged her shoulders, 'Well, they say tomorrow, but here you never know.'

By the end of an eventful day, the ship felt especially welcome, a safe haven. Wearily, everyone silently tucked into tea. I went to the bar. I had two more days here in St Petersburg, and I fervently hoped they would be less dramatic. Officers leant on the polished bar top, a cluster of navy and gold braid, chatting and joking, not needed on the bridge.

'Hi Amelia, how was your day?' enquired the captain.

'Eventful . . . let's just say I could do with a drink.'

'That's Russia. We're going to our favourite nightclub later. Want to come?' It wasn't every day I had the chance to go to a nightclub in St Petersburg, so my reply was enthusiastic. 'Would you mind if I bring Rad along too?' I asked without thinking.

'Sure, ask anyone you like, but he's your responsibility. Ten o'clock at the gangway and don't bring much with you – passport, bit of money, but nothing else, no fancy jewellery.'

Rad was enthusiastic. 'What about my Mom? Will she let me?'

'Maybe you could say you're going with the captain? Ten o'clock at the gangway but take off that fancy watch, hide your passport in an inside pocket and bring a few dollars. Nothing else.'

We were so jammed into the shabby little taxi I almost fell out onto the pavement when we arrived at the back of St Isaac's Cathedral. Leading the way, the captain raced down the steps plunging into the basement. A blood-red glow and a blast of booze-laden, smoke fuelled air throbbing with noise burst out of the steel door. We trooped down after him – doctor, chief purser, a couple of his deck officers, the sturdy housekeeper and an eager Rad.

A mirror-topped bar stretched into deep shadows towards the back of the vault. Revolving spotlights twirled pools of light illuminating the three girls. Twisting and slithering, they danced slowly, provocatively to the throbbing music, hands sweeping suggestively up and down shapely legs. They bent double, bums pointed up at the arched roof, manes of long blonde hair tossed aside, eyes peeping tantalisingly. Their choreography was perfect. The whole deep red cavern could have been Blackpool but – all three were totally naked. Rad gasped.

A brunette in black rubber carrying a tray of drinks waved at the captain, pointing to an empty table. Shot glasses and bottles of vodka appeared swiftly, so the chief purser did the honours and included Rad. She emptied her glass in one, winked at the doctor, and the two women moved onto the dance floor, entwining arms around each other's waists. The captain whispered in the housekeeper's ear. She smiled coyly, and they too eased together onto the dance floor.

'Ok, Rad?' I bellowed over the music.

'Sure. I reckon the restrooms'll be at the back. Nature Calls.' He squeezed through the bodies on the dance floor. The naked girls continued twirling, blowing kisses between their legs, nipple tassels jiggling. Sitting on stools along the front of the bar, men sucked on cigarettes, staring. In a haze of smoke, booze, pulsing music and sweating bodies the night wore on.

'Ok everyone, time to go. Drink up!' shouted the captain. 'We've work tomorrow, time we all went home. Where's that boy, Amelia? What have you done with him?' Rad was nowhere to be seen. I'd been watching for him, hoping he would emerge.

'Not sure, but he must be here somewhere, I'll go and find him, hang on a moment.'

I pushed through the bodies on the dance floor, making my way towards the back where the walls were lined with cosy little booths, each with a red velvet curtain. One had the curtain looped aside by a gold rope while others were snugly closed. Gently I tweaked the edge of a curtain to peep inside. Empty. Relief made me bolder with the next, and there was Rad. Snaking across his bare torso was a pale arm. Her hand delved deep into his stripy boxers.

Another moment and I would have been too late.

In the heart of town was the Grand Hotel Europa on Nevsky Prospect and no one needed a guidebook to tell them it was *the* hotel in St Petersburg. G&S had a land-based group there being led by my boss, silky-suited Gregory who had insisted on a pre-breakfast meeting. His smooth confidence had been intimidating in the Cotswolds, but now things were different. I had acquired a little confidence too. My group was happy, I could tell, they liked me. I felt sure there would be no complaints over my handling of the lightning-struck train or even the bomb. Irinia and I were getting on well and together we waited in the hotel's opulent lobby. I studied the décor. Glass panels, elegantly etched with violins surrounded by swirling leaves and flowers, graced the doors. They were so very ornate and so Russian. Soft notes drifted from a harpist providing entertainment for breakfast. Irinia had a less glamorous view, as she faced the lifts.

'Ah, so we wait for Mr Cox. He is here again. I think he likes my city.' She paused. 'I know him, *very* well.' Unexpectedly her large red mouth split into a huge smile. 'Don't look about!' she hissed, covering her mouth to suppress a giggle. 'Don't look! Don't turn.' She looked over my shoulder at the bank of lift doors behind me. Reflected in the mirror panels I could see one of the lifts open to reveal Gregory Cox with a girl on either arm. Startled by the sight of us, he turned away, and the three of them swept past us.

'Good morning, Irinia,' he said smoothly a moment later, now alone and unflustered. 'It is good to see you again.' He turned to me, 'And how's the ship, Amelia? It's not one I know.'

Irinia butted in. 'Emilia. She has very tight group. All keep together, even with bomb.' He blanched, going white in spite of his tan. 'Bomb? What do you mean – bomb? I don't think our insurance covers bombs.'

'I haven't had a chance to file any reports yet, but everyone is fine.' I reassured him. Continuing as undramatically as possible I mentioned the expanding train tracks, the thunderstorm and yesterday's bomb. I omitted the nightclub.

We moved into the breakfast room to make our choices at the long buffet table stretching from end to end of the ornate room. Across a basket of mini jams, Irinia winked at me.

'Amelia,' Gregory said, the moment I was seated, 'I wonder if you could do a small something for me? I think you'll be leaving Russia before me and I need to get a parcel home. I'll have it delivered to the ship this afternoon. You wouldn't mind taking it back for me, would you?'

It was a foregone conclusion that one of his employees would do as he asked. There was simply no question. Irinia straightened up, clattering her knife to attract my attention.

'Well, there are ten more days of the tour, you know, Gregory,' I said.

He laughed rather too loudly. 'Well, it's not going to go rotten or anything! But the office needs it, sooner rather than later. I'd be most obliged if you could take it – so much easier than the airport.'

Breaking into the dining room hum, my handbag buzzed noisily so I delved inside for my phone. The blue screen was illuminated: HH. 'Please excuse me one moment.' Ignoring Gregory's look of surprise, I almost ran across the highly polished floor to the hush of the foyer.

'What a lovely surprise. This is just what I need to start my day.'

'What you need? I thought you were on a luxurious ship and wanted for nothing! Well, nothing apart from me, of course. Here I am, sun warm on my back, newspapers spread across the table, and you came to mind. But I can tell there's something wrong, what's the problem?' His perception was a surprise. I mentioned Gregory's request.

'My dear girl, there's no question, he should not be asking, and you certainly should not agree!'

'I thought you had never been to Russia?'

'Don't be so naïve! Everyone knows you don't take things out of Russia. Who knows what's inside this package, might be a lump of amber or an icon? I want you back, not locked away in a dodgy Russian gaol.' A thrill of excitement at his comment shot down my spine.

With perfect manners, Gregory stood as I returned to the breakfast table.

'I do apologise for that.' I tried not to grin, adding, 'About the parcel, you know the ship is very strict? Everything brought on board is checked. Bags, parcels, everything is inspected and opened up. Would that matter? I wouldn't want to jeopardise G&S in any way, so I think I'd better not take it. I hope you can find someone else.' I smiled at him. 'It looks as if Irinia has finished her breakfast, so we'd better get back to the ship.'

I had survived another tour and felt more confident, but I needed more work. Two luxurious tours a year were insufficient. Scotland, the *Monaco* years, experience gained wrestling with bureaucracy, bloody-minded fishermen and intransigent shareholders, must not be wasted. I determined to see whether I could be a guide amongst the islands of the West Coast, on *Hebridean Princess*. It was worth a try. It was all I knew.

Two days later the train took me north. Beyond the grubby window, the landscape lost its soft southern air and the Pennines began, soon I would be in Leeds. Should I have prepared something for the interview?

7

Yorkshire

Is the Future Tartan?

After Russia, an interview in Skipton seemed reassuringly familiar.

'Hi. Come on in.' The Chief Purser was surprisingly informal. The ship, I knew, was old school, possibly even old fashioned. The gladioli rigidly standing to attention in the reception area confirmed the air of formality.

'Let me tell you about *Hebridean Princess,*' he said, 'and then you can tell me about yourself.' He ran through the ship's virtues as my mind slid away to the only time I had been on board her. Not an event to remind him about.

In her latter days of operations, *Monaco* had many temporary skippers, and one had been particularly annoying. The moment we reached Oban, Griff, with no concerns over maintenance or anything else, would do a bunk, disappearing swiftly to the pub. Usually, he was easy to find, but on this particular occasion I had lost him. Had the sight of *Hebridean Princess* swooshing passed us in the Sound of Mull excited him? Could he have decided to get on board *Princess*? I had rushed up the gangway, pushing the glass door etched with a crown logo opening into Reception. How could I explain to the immaculate receptionist I was looking for a small, swarthy, incontinent Welshman? Thankfully there had been no one behind the desk, the passengers having not yet arrived. A faint whiff of fish tainted the air and there, polluting the royal blue carpet embellished with gold crowns, lay a small prawn head. Oban's bustling quay was always scattered with scraps of prawns and fish scales, but none of the crew would have been so careless. Griff must be here. I needed to find him and get him quickly off the ship. Following my nose, I went to the main lounge. There, happily ensconced in a tartan-covered wing-back chair, next to an occasional table, laid for tea, he sat surveying the Tiree Lounge. Little crested cups, a sugar bowl with tongs and neatly folded napkins graced the table, waiting for passengers. But only crumbs from the shortbread remained.

'Ah, Amelia.' He smiled at me swallowing his final mouthful, 'This is a great ship. Look you. There's even a fireplace yere, so smart.' To my horror, a dark stain was just visible at his crotch.

The purser's voice jerked me back to the present. 'So, how do you know the West Coast?'

'I ran a boat around the islands for ten years, maybe you saw her? The *Monaco,* a big green ex-trawler. We used to see you quite often, anchored off Iona or coming up the Sound of Mull.'

'No, 'fraid not. So which islands do you know?'

'I know all the ones you go to and about fifty more!' I told him. He picked up a blue biro, the gold crown logo catching the light as he twiddled it round. I waited, hoping I had not overstepped the mark.

'Well, how about you come and watch one of our regular guides? There's a four-day cruise coming up.' In spite of my rudeness, it seemed I had a toe in the door.

I strolled along the Fulham Road, passed the expensive antique shops, contemplating what I needed for a luxury cruise in Scotland. Even on a mini one there would be two black-tie evenings, but all my nice clothes were in storage, along with everything else I owned. I was discovering how much I loathed living in a flat on Fulham Road. It was an expensive flat, with big windows looking out over the communal gardens where the squirrel still ran head-first down the plane trees, but I felt like a rat in a trap. The prospect of a weekend in Scotland among the islands, cruising on *Hebridean Princess* with no responsibilities, thrilled me. A break from my lonely existence.

My mobile rang, making me jump.

'Hello.' The voice was deep, soft but with the underlying hint of an accent I still struggled to define.

'Hello? It's a bad line, who's calling, please?'

'Don't you recognise my voice?' he asked with a laugh.

Of course I did, but I needed a moment. Even via a bad mobile connection, Helly Handsome oozed confidence.

'Oh, it's you! Sorry, there's a lot of traffic noise... bit difficult to hear,' I lied.

'That engine of yours has been silent, no booming in the night. Are you back from Russia? Are you looking after your boat properly?'

'Are you at the marina? I thought you would be somewhere else, away on important business.' He did not need to know I had been on board *Monaco* the day before and naturally I had checked his yacht, hoping for signs of life.

He ignored the jibe. 'Yes, I've been away on and off. When are you coming down again?' He sounded casual but, I reminded myself, he was the one who had made the call. 'You never know your luck,' he went on. 'I might be around. We could have that dinner or something?'

'Oh, I'd love to, but I can't get down for a week or so.

I'm off to Scotland. Visiting a little cruise ship called *Hebridean Princess*. Do you know her?' I was hoping to sound important.

'No, No, I don't know her, but it doesn't sound my sort of thing. Too many people. Have fun.'
'But when I get back, I'd love to.' But he had gone. I stopped myself from ringing back.

Going to Scotland offered a chance to see my father in Yorkshire en route. Ever since my mother's death four years earlier, he had been rattling around the family house, unable to cope with a move and determined not to leave his much-loved walled gardens, the apple and pear orchards, glasshouses and vegetable patches. He was a regular bridge player and the 'Judge', had remained popular with a busy social life even without my mother to keep the dinner and lunch parties going. But I knew he was lonely. To my surprise, he had asked me to meet a couple who might be happy to help: they could live in the cottage next door and look after him, cook and clean.

'Here I am, Papa,' I shouted, pushing open the back door. 'Hello? Anyone at home?' He really should lock the back door; anyone could wander in. I walked down the stone-flagged passageway lined with watercolours and into the drawing room. He was sitting with his black and white spaniel curled on his lap, the fire crackling warmly as he worked contentedly at *The Times* crossword.

'Hello, how marvellous to see you.' Quickly he put aside the paper and stood up, the dog jumping to the floor. 'Come on, let's go for a walk, the garden's looking lovely at the moment.'

Delighted to have someone to share his passion, he led me

out of the French windows and up the steps on to the lawn. On either side were terracotta urns, frothing with trailing pink geraniums, dove grey nepeta and pale blue lobelia, while climbing roses tumbled down the warm brick walls. We strolled across the grass, arm in arm, on through the wrought iron gate with its design of linking horseshoes.

'There's a good cutting of asparagus and let's see how the tomatoes in the greenhouse are doing.' He was pleased to have something to give me. The kitchen garden was wholly enclosed by high walls and their warmth encouraged the tight green figs, furry apricots and peaches to ripen, even here in North Yorkshire. Sweetcorn, peas and beans grew in tidy rows with not a weed to be seen on the rich dark earth.

'The Browns will be here soon,' he said, and I detected an unexpected anxiety. 'I hope you will like them, as I've told them they can come, I've given them the Ok.'

'Papa, it doesn't really matter if I like them, the important thing is whether they will look after you, do what's needed and whether you like them.' I tried not to sound annoyed; it was too late now for any changes.

Awkwardly, we sat around the dining room table, Brenda and Mike tucking into the scones I had brought. Papa reminded Brenda her job was to clean and cook in lieu of rent. Mike could do much as he liked most of the time, but maybe, Papa suggested, he would be good enough to bring in the logs.

'I think you saw the cottage last time,' he said, standing up. 'Amelia has to get on up to Scotland, so we'll call it a day now.'

Outside by the wooden gates onto the village street, we paused to say our goodbyes. Mike, who had said nothing so far, looked at Papa.

'Aye, Judge, there's nobbut to complain about, and cottage is Ok, but d'ye mean to tell me, at my age, I'll be a kept man?'

'Yes,' my father replied, 'that's right, Mike, but most of we men are really.'

Standing in the late afternoon sunshine in his brown herringbone tweed suit, he looked the epitome of an English country gentleman. Unexpectedly, he began rummaging in his trouser pocket. Change jangled noisily.

'It will be good to have the cottage occupied, it's been empty for far too long,' he said, still fumbling about in his trouser pocket. With the air of a magician pulling a rabbit out of a hat, he produced a small silver penknife and carefully opened the slim blade. A paint blister, fat from the rain, had caught his eye. It bulged at head height. Taking a step towards the gate post, with surgical precision as if he were lancing a boil, he neatly pricked the swelling. A clear jet of water spurted out missing Mike by inches. Triumphantly my father turned to Brenda. 'I bet you've never seen a gatepost pee before!'

She burst into giggles.

As I wound my way laboriously up Wensleydale, I longed for my zippy red Ford Escort, the Flying Tomato. Soon I crossed the cattle grid and was out on the rolling open moorland, bleak hills heaved to the distant skyline. Patches of dark heather contrasted sharply with the green stubble of young bracken. I swept smoothly round the curve taking me through one of the arches under the long viaduct. It was a road I knew so well, and I loved the sense of space and timelessness. Through all the *Monaco* years of driving from Yorkshire to Oban, I had come to know every corner, but now, sitting high in the Discovery I had new views over the dry-stone walls. Dog roses arched in sprays of pink and white in the more sheltered dips as the road followed the beck. Peaty and brown it ran down the valley pouring over rocky ledges to dark pools dotted with flecks of foam. Celine Dion blasted out, 'My Heart will go on' from the car stereo. Would HH call me soon? Should I ring him for a change? After the cruise would be best, I'd track him down then. A frisson of excitement fizzed through me at the thought of being back among the islands and at sea. The voyage went south of Mull, to the misty blue stepped shapes of the Treshnish isles and Staffa's basalt columns.

A slight shudder rippled through the ship as she came to life. Oban, the town that had once been such a big part of my life, with its grey-faced houses ringing the harbour, began to retreat as *Princess* edged off the pier. As she nosed sedately out of the harbour, fishing boats, spiky with clam dredges like rusty chainmail lining their gunwales, slid away to stern. The Colosseum silhouette of McCaig's Folly broke the skyline above the town and the ship turned towards the stark obelisk on the bracken-covered slopes ahead. Hutcheson's Monument I knew, but did I know enough to be a guide? I would observe, take note, but meanwhile I should introduce myself to the couple leaning on the varnished rail.

'Hello, good afternoon, I'm Amelia, I'm going to be the on-board guide in due course.' I held out a hand.

'Hello, I'm Ruth and this is Duncan. Where do you come from?' Ruth was elegantly dressed in a pale blue puffa jacket, edged with beige suede, a heavy silk scarf tucked into the neck. She was a perfect match for her equally smartly dressed husband in his checked shirt, yellow jersey and dark suede jacket.

'Yorkshire, but I ran a boat up here for a while.' I was keen to establish my credentials.

'Ah, Yorkshire, it's the only place to come from,' Duncan said. 'This is our fourth cruise and it'll be good to have a new guide. Hear some new things.'

'Thank you. Well, I hope so. That's Hutcheson's Monument.' I pointed at the obelisk steadily getting clearer on the port shoulder, 'Hutcheson started Cal Mac, the ferry company, and this is an ex-ferry of course.' I thought I was getting off to a good start.

'I thought you said you would tell us something different.' As a true Yorkshireman, Duncan did not mince his words.

Joan, the official guide, was earnest and, in spite of the drama and bloody history available to illustrate Scotland's warring clans, her lectures were accompanied by a soundtrack of snores. As the misty blues and basalt columns of the Treshnish Isles slipped past, she was tucked away in the library, buried in a book. A dumpy woman, drowned by her clothes, she seemed entirely beige. Sensible skirts flapped around her shins and drooping cardigans in shades of brown, their pockets stuffed with tissues, were pinned by a large cameo brooch. But she knew her stuff in a way that I did not.

'Amelia, you will have time, I think,' the captain said, as the waiter poured cream onto my porridge. 'Could you do a job for me, on Iona?'

Iona was an easy place, everyone would be absorbed by the Abbey. I had hoped to slip away, cross the narrow island to the western side, to the romantically named 'Bay at the Back of the Ocean' where the beach was made of jewel-like pebbles and the view west to Coll and Tiree was stupendous.

'Come up to the bridge after breakfast, and I'll show you

on the chart. I'd like you to check out a beach for me. It might be useful to land the Zodiac there sometimes. With your knowledge, you could eye it up for me, see if it's workable.'

'Ok, yes. I can certainly do that.' I was delighted my experience would at last be of use.

The crisp April air was still, and the sun now had some warmth as I sauntered back from the Abbey, accompanied by three of the many elderly ladies among the passengers. They were typical *Hebridean* passengers, elderly but sprightly, well-educated and knowledgeable. Despite having had only a couple of days on board, I realised I would need to be switched on, ready for their astute questions.

'Amelia, it looks as if there are scrapes on the rocks over there, do you know what they are?'

I breathed out, thanking my personal interest. 'They mark the remains of the "Grantio Rosso" quarries of Mull. In the nineteenth century, the stone was used by Telford, Charles Barry and of course the Stevensons for their lighthouses. There are monuments made from it all over the world, from Aberdeen, across the Atlantic and even the Albert Memorial has columns made from it.' I hoped I sounded like a proper, knowledgeable guide.

Having answered their query, I excused myself to go over to the beach the captain had indicated on the chart.

'We'll wait here for you in the sun, it's lovely and warm. Don't rush, dear.'

To reach the beach I had to climb a wall, take a track across the short turf leading to the seashore. I clambered up the well-used stile with stones projecting either side to make steps. Carefully I stepped over the rusting strand of barbed wire that ran along the top. On the far side I put my foot onto the topmost stone. As it took my weight the stone twisted, turning my ankle. I flung out an arm to keep my balance catching it on the barbed wire. A deep gash ripped through the soft skin of my forearm. I could see muscle, flesh and ruptured veins. Blood pumped freely. With my right hand, I squeezed the gash together hoping to stem the blood that flowed between my fingers. It dripped freely onto the earth.

'Amelia! What have you done? Are you all right, dear?' I must not let them see: someone might faint.

'I'm fine,' I said shakily. 'I'll just walk down to the jetty and get back on board.' I tried to conceal the blood dripping between my fingers. 'You carry on, enjoy the rest of the afternoon and I'll see you this evening.'

The blood made big splashes on the road, like juice stains left by the chewers of betel nut in Asia. On the slipway, Donald was in charge of the coming and going for the tenders. The blood still running freely looked bad.

'Oh my goodness! What's that?'

'Bit of a mess.' I sank onto the quay wall.

'Let me see. That's terrible, so it is.' He picked up his VHF handset, '*Hebridean Princess, Hebridean Princess* this is Donald.' Clearly and graphically, he spelt out every gory detail, broadcasting throughout the west coast just how fast the blood was pumping, how big the rip was and ending with, 'It's an emergency. She needs help, and quickly.'

'Donald, please tone it down a bit. The whole west coast doesn't need to know!'

'Well, we need help, now. I'll get Dougie.' The grey smudge of the Zodiac, quicker than one of the navy-blue tenders, appeared speeding towards us across the Sound. Dougie arrived, a solid giant in his late sixties, eyes a little watery from a life at sea.

'Now then, let me take a wee look.' Tentatively I opened my reddened fingers and blood spurted. He studied the gash.

'Aye, well, it's a fair big tear you've got there. But I'm licensed to sew na' problem. Let's get ye back on board.' 'Licensed to sew' would probably mean sew a sail with a big fat needle and twine, I thought.

'Thanks, Dougie, but maybe there's a doctor on Mull?' The little ferry that crisscrossed the sound came alongside the pier and above the noise of its engine came a shout.

'Hey There! We've a couple here, wi a car. They say they'll gie ye a lift tae the doc.' Donald's broadcast on the VHF was paying off.

'Take this handset,' Dougie said, cramming his VHF into my pocket, 'and keep in touch. I'll tell the captain you're away to the doc.'

I walked shakily up the car ramp, 'It's yourself! And what you been doing, then, hen?' asked the decky. I almost burst into tears. To be remembered from the *Monaco* days was a surprise.

'You should know better than tae be taking wee holes oot of yourself.' He grinned. 'But it's gud to see ye, and the doc's waiting. These folk will take ye on, gie ye a lift. It's nae bother as they're going back to Tobermory.'

'Could you give the ship a shout for me, please? Tell them where I've gone, and I'll be back as soon as I can.'

'*Hebridean Princess, Hebridean Princes.*' Twirling the knob, he held the mouthpiece close to me so that I could speak to the captain myself.

'Hello, Captain. I've got a lift to the doctor. Are you still planning to anchor in Bunessan? I'm sure I can get a lift out to the ship from there. Will that be Ok?' I knew I would be able to find a fishing boat, or someone in the pub with a boat who would give me a lift.

'I'm anchoring early tonight. It's my Welcome Dinner. Try to be in time for that.'

When we reached the little bungalow all white pebble dash and prim lawns, the doctor came out to meet me. Opening the car door, he led me into a smart little surgery. I was beginning to bless Donald as the doctor had laid out swabs, cotton wool and plasters: everything was ready. I peeled back my sticky, bloody fingers. Blood welled from the tear, but it had stopped spurting. It was a long, deep gash, and the skin torn by the barbed wire had ragged edges. The doctor went white and collapsed heavily onto a chair.

'I'm not used to this. I'm a locum, just here for ten days, I come from Leeds.' I had nothing to contribute. 'I don't usually have to do stitches,' he said, eying up my bloodied arm. 'I send injuries to A&E at the Infirmary.'

He stood up, stiff with uncertainty.

Two hours later, between the two of us, we had created a wandering herringbone design up my forearm. Giant stitches trailed over the white skin from wrist to elbow. He had tied the knots while I did the sewing. It throbbed.

Bunessan, a wide sea loch I knew well, ran north-south. It was sheltered by the bulk of the Ross of Mull, and I was relieved to see the ship peacefully at anchor in the entrance. The Zodiac was ready waiting beside the jetty outside the Argyll Arms Hotel.

'I thought I'd come. See how ye're doin,' said Dougie.

'Thanks, nice of you. I'm Ok,' I replied between gritted teeth, nursing my arm against the jolts as we sped across the still waters to the ship silhouetted by the evening sun.

Stretching out over the port shoulder, the davit was ready and waiting. Dougie clipped the Zodiac harness onto the hoist and the winch began to lift us out of the water. As we swung and turned water drained nosily out of the flap. Higher and higher the davit lifted us above the sea until the Zodiac was clear of the ship's railings. Carefully we were swung round moving inboard over the ship until we were suspended high above the open well-deck. The hydraulic winch whirred and slowly, smoothly we were lowered into the stowage area. We inched down, passing in front of the panoramic windows of the Tiree Lounge. Assembled in dinner jackets and evening dresses was the entire complement of passengers. The Captain's Welcome Cocktail Party was going with a swing, but as we slowly slid past the windows everyone saw. Some waved but the captain, his officers and the crew did not.

The final afternoon of the brief cruise was to be spent in Tobermory, pottering among the shops and brightly coloured buildings lining the harbour. *Princess* drew alongside the pier and I looked down from the bridge wing as the Bosun threw the heaving line across the gap. This bustling little community had been so much a part of my life for many years, it had become more like home than anywhere else. Colin, the harbour master, who had sunk many a dram on board *Monaco*, looked up to catch the line. Surprised, he missed it. The rope slithered and snaked over the edge of the quay splashing into the water.

'You Ok down there, Colin?' shouted the captain, surprised. He was the Harbour Master after all. 'Have you a problem?' Colin stared up. I waved.

'Well, it's yourself. I knew it'd no' be long. Gud to see you.' It was the best greeting I could have had, and I knew the captain had heard.

As *Hebridean Princess* steamed towards Oban at the end of the cruise, Duart Castle slipped past to starboard, and I wondered if I would be back. Cruises on *Monaco* had always ended like this. Irritatingly, the final morning was always brilliant sunshine and calm.

'Amelia,' Joan, sensible brogues planted firmly on the deck, was swathed in a duffle coat. 'Andrew would like to see you now, before he's caught up with departures. He's in his office.' Her antagonism was palpable.

'Can I come in?' The door was always open, but I knew better than just to walk in.

'Sure, take a seat. So, you've seen how Joan works now, what do you think?'

'Thank you, it's been a wonderful few days. *Princess* is a lovely ship and I've had a really enjoyable time, but actually...' I seemed to hear myself from a distance. 'If you want the guiding done like that, I don't think I want the job.'

What had I done?

Andrew leaned back, turning his chair to make space before crossing his long legs. 'Well,' he considered, 'how about you come and give it a try. Show me how you would like to do the job?'

My cabin was again virtually in the bilges, down below the waterline with forced air but no light. Tartan curtains hung either side of a 'pretend' porthole and on the matching tartan bedcover lay a little white tent of thick paper surmounted by a gold logo, 'Welcome on board *Hebridean Princess*. The captain wishes you an enjoyable cruise and looks forward to meeting you in the Tiree Lounge at seven thirty, to introduce you to his crew and the guide.' I climbed the five flights of stairs emerging into a reception room crammed with people.

Everyone had an air of purpose. Feeling lost I went up on deck to watch Oban slide astern once more. By evening I was really nervous. I waited at the back of the lounge, butterflies fluttered and danced in my stomach. I clutched a glass of champagne reminding myself I had done two tours for G&S, that I had negotiated broken trains, mountain hikes and bombs. The captain, kilted and confident, was revelling in admiring gazes from forty pairs of eyes.

'We have many familiar faces on board again. Lovely to see you all, and I look forward to chatting with each of you again. Welcome to the new faces and I hope you will soon feel at home. The forecast is good, so I anticipate at this stage we will keep to the itinerary. Are there any questions in the meantime?'

A hand shot up.

'If you are here and your crew, who's steering the ship?' There was always one clever clogs trying to sound smart in front of his fellow passengers.

'Harriet,' said the captain.

Andrew, in full Chief Purser mode and resplendent in a McQuarrie kilt, detached himself from the bar walking between the tables to join the captain, so tall his head almost touched the ceiling, he was better looking than I remembered. There was a round of applause.

'Good evening, everyone, and nice to see so many familiar faces. Welcome back.' He listed the 'dos and don'ts', talked about lifejackets, irons and fresh milk.

'And now I would like to introduce you to our new guide, Amelia Dalton.' Placing my champagne carefully on the top of the bar, I went up to join him, wondering why I'd not had the sense to prepare a speech.

'Amelia is new to us, and I'm sure we'll all enjoy hearing

what she has to say.' He handed the microphone to me and returned to the bar, bending to greet people as he went.

Even using a microphone was alien. I looked at the seated guests, at the captain, at the senior staff now ranged along the front of the bar. Standing shoulder to shoulder they made a solid intimidating line of uniform and gold stripes. I pushed up the button on the microphone.

'Good evening, ladies and gentlemen. I am delighted to be here and very excited about the itinerary for our cruise, but the first thing I must do, is to make you an apology.'

A sigh came from the uniformed line accompanied by a clearly audible whisper: 'Doesn't she know never to apologise, you *never* apologise.'

'Ladies and Gentlemen, I am apologising because I'm English and I know the majority of you are Scottish, but I am going to tell you all about Scotland.' People smiled, some actually laughed.

The days passed quickly, and I discovered I did know enough. I enjoyed the deck talks, as we turned north past Ardnamurchan out of the Sound of Mull, pointing out the Sgurr of Eigg, with the Cuillins of Skye in the distance. I knew the lochs where we anchored, and I knew the distant island silhouettes better than some of the bridge crew. I spoke about the fishing boats, their skippers, where they lived, the names of their dogs and children and what they were catching. I knew the cargo boats and the famous wrecks, why they had sunk and what cargoes they had carried.

It was over and I'd done it. I knew the passengers had enjoyed my stories, but I was aware I needed to learn more history. I stood in the hubbub of Reception as passengers milled around, saying farewell to me and to friends. To one side stood a tall man, watching.

'Amelia.'

'Yes, Lady Burnsall?' I could tell the tall man was listening.

'You never did tell us why that peninsula on Islay is called the "Mull of Oa". Do please tell me if you've a moment now, before we disembark.'

'Of course I have time.' As the guide, I ought to know, but I had no idea. Inspiration dawned. One of Cubby's stories would do.

'You know the Scots came from Ireland?'

'Yes, dear.'

'Well,' I said, raising my voice above the chatter, 'the Irish were rowing across the North Channel, the stretch of water that separates Ireland, rowing like fury and suddenly they became aware of land looming up out of the spray. The fellow in the first boat looked over his shoulder and seeing the cliffs of Islay, said "Oh!" So, it's been the "Mull of Oa" ever since.'

Lady Burnsall laughed. 'Very good, dear. I'll remember that!'

The tall man had heard too. 'An apocryphal story, I think.' But he grinned, nonetheless.

Andrew too was there to say goodbye. 'Come and see me in the office when you've finished.'

His voice was peremptory. I waited in his empty office, looking at spreadsheets stuck on the wall, lists of sailing times, menu plans, orders for beef and champagne, the daily needs of the ship.

'So you've met our new Managing Director, then?' Andrew said as he came in, making me jump. 'I saw him with you and Lady Burnsall. How's the week been? Do you think it went well?' he asked.

'Thank you. It was great for me, but I hope the passengers enjoyed my talks?'

'Yes. You did well, not what they usually hear, but everyone seemed happy. Good luck in whatever you do – maybe we'll see you again. The company is getting a new ship, so whoever takes over from me will decide who the guides here will be, not me any more.'

8

Norway

Abandoned

Waiting for life to come to me was not the answer, I should do something, or I would sink into a well of emptiness. The ramifications of being divorced were becoming increasingly clear, and I liked none of them. Life in a rented flat in London was lonely. My only two girlfriends, part of that family life full of purpose and energy, were in Norfolk and Yorkshire, inconvenient for a natter and coffee.

Monaco, I was told briefly, had been sold. I should have been pleased, but it created another void. I smiled at the memory of my final bilge-pumping visit. I had spent most of the night with Helly Handsome, tucked away on his boat, in what he referred to as the galley. *Monaco's* galley was a working area, efficient stainless steel worksurfaces and two ugly domestic gas cookers, but his was stylish, sleekly fitted, cosy and appealingly sexy. Porcelain mugs snuggled next to a plate rack stacked with pale blue china, glasses hung by their slim stems. Nothing here would rattle or break. It was easy to understand why he liked being on board. It was orderly, well designed and ready to go to sea. This sleek yacht had nothing in common with the stationary fibreglass gin palaces on the surrounding pontoons. In the course of the evening, I also discovered he was good company. Entertaining, attentive, as well as charming. The night had felt far too short, speeding away in talk of the sea, places he had sailed to and where he would go when he could escape the duties of running his company. My life on Scotland's rugged coast felt provincial by comparison, but I knew I had skills he had not.

G&S had asked me to do another tour, but not until the autumn. Three months with nothing to do meanwhile. It was disappointing to have heard nothing further from Andrew after my week as guide on *Hebridean Princess*. I remembered his casual comment about the new ship. Might this offer me something? I unscrewed the cap of my fountain pen and began to write.

Dear Mr Fenton ... Would he remember me? He had met me only briefly, that moment at the end of the cruise. But nothing ventured ... I wrote that I understood he was establishing a new ship and therefore he would need me. Brazenly, I told him I was two people rolled into one. I could combine my marine qualifications with G&S guiding experience. I had the skills both to design cruises for their new ship and also to programme the shore visits for the ship's passengers. I posted it quickly, knowing that if I waited, my courage would fail.

Days flicked by, empty.

'Good morning, Amelia speaking.' I answered the mobile brightly, well aware of how important the tone of a voice was in any call.

'Good morning, Amelia. Michael here.'

He began by talking about guides, saying they were already chosen for the coming season in Scotland. I held my breath— 'But maybe you could write a couple of sample cruises for me? Based on about eighty passengers, international waters, reflecting *Hebridean Princess's* passenger style – islands, remote beaches. For the new ship.'

'Yes, with pleasure. Anywhere in particular?' I asked, hoping he would not say Indonesia or the Pacific. Scotland's turbulent, tidal waters and the two G&S tours were all I knew.

'No, you choose. Your ideas. Fax them to me and then we'd better meet, how about the 18th, that'll give you a few days. Come to the office here in Skipton about 11.00.'

'Ok I'll get going. See you then.' I had five days. I would need charts, pilot books and guidebooks if I were to replicate Scotland's varied west coast elsewhere. Remote archipelagos, deep lochs and secluded anchorages must be the aim; communities, small local museums, all difficult to access other than by sea and rarely visited, plus of course no long sea passages. There must be other archipelagos: the Small Isles, Outer Hebrides and coastlines of Mull, Skye and the mainland were not unique. Local museums and history, wildlife and the scenery would be the focus and the two itineraries must appeal to the types of people I had met on board.

Again the train whisked me to Yorkshire. Michael had merely acknowledged my fax, but the moment I stepped out onto the windswept platform at Skipton, I felt I had come home. I inhaled deeply, enjoying the unmistakable whiff of sheep shit, bog and moorland air from the surrounding Pennines before jumping into a taxi.

Michael, legs propped on his desk and phone tucked under his chin, waved at me through the glass wall. Elsewhere in the office the walls were covered with certificates from the Scottish Tourist Board and photos of *Hebridean Princess*.

'Yes, I appreciate that.' He sounded exasperated and grimaced at the phone. 'But we must have a ship soon. We have a deadline. I expect you to have found one by the end of the month. That gives you two weeks.' He put the phone down with a clatter and ran a hand through his curly hair.

He stood up, revealing well-worn green cords, and held out a hand.

'Amelia, good to meet you again. Thanks for coming. I have your itineraries here somewhere.' Sheaves of papers were scattered haphazardly across his desk. Pulling a plastic folder out of my newly acquired briefcase, with a feigned air of confidence, I placed the pages in front of him, pleased I had brought spare copies.

Were they in the correct format for a ship's itinerary? Was there such a thing as a 'cruise format'? I had no idea so had simply given each element a different colour. Blue for the ship, with the lats and longs, anchorages included a little anchor symbol. It had been fun to do, rather like drawing maps in geography at school. Distances, in nautical miles, were also in blue, with speed based on eleven knots. Shore visits, with an enticing (I hoped) description, were green, and finally overnight passages in red. Cruise No. 1 worked through the Norwegian fjords and islands, sailing from Trondheim to Bergen. The second took my virtual ship into the Baltic, embarking in Stockholm to call at Visby, Helsinki and St Petersburg. Using charts and pilot books, I had adapted the two G&S tours and added unknown islands, found small local museums and a couple of curiosities that had caught my interest. The most appealing was a nineteenth-century 'Hummerpark' on a little island called Espaevar, once an important call on Norway's coast. The local fishermen had enlarged a cleft in the rocky shore enabling them to corral over twenty-four thousand lobsters, ready for sale.

Michael gave only a cursory glance at my carefully coloured sheets.

'Well, that looks fantastic,' he said, without bothering to study the detail. 'Great. Let me have another six cruises. Can you set them up? Let me know if you need shipping agents. Get it all costed and ready for operations.'

There was no mention of my terms, expenses, or formal employment.

'Thank you, I'd love to, but are you offering me a job or am I doing this on spec?'

'Of course I am.' He looked surprised. 'Work out what you need and talk to Tony next door. He's the accountant, tell him I said to sign you on.'

'Well…' I realised I was pushing it, but I had no choice. 'To ensure the cruises operate successfully, we will need to know the exact logistics for these remote islands. The conditions ashore must be known, whether the jetties are safe, if it is a long walk and so on. We must tell the passengers what kind of landing to expect – shoes or wellies, steps or a beach.' Research had told me Michael had a ferry background. The nuances of passenger requirements for a chic cruise ship might be new to him.

He put his fingertips together. 'Ah, good point. What do you propose?'

'The places must be checked if we're to operate at the top level like *Princess*. I know most of the stops for these two itineraries, except for the most outlying Norwegian islands, but future cruises will need proper recces, real inspections.' He considered while I wondered if I'd asked for too much.

'Start with Norway and the islands you don't know, then we'll take it from there.'

The return train journey south seemed to whizz by as I plotted my very first recce for Hebridean Island Cruises. I had a job and an enviable one.

Ten days later, trundling along the Thames embankment in a black cab, I considered the smart acquisition lying at my feet:

a mini stainless-steel trunk. It had the air of a professional photographer's case, but also it reminded me of a mini school trunk, giving me that same sinking feeling I remembered so well at the start of a new term at boarding school. I had cut the black foam rubber filling the interior into appropriately shaped holes and all my new equipment nestled inside. The paperback-sized computer was tucked beside an equally small printer. There were spare batteries for my Nokia mobile and digital camera with slots for extra SD cards. Coiled in the bottom section were leads and international adapters. The first contact provided by Michael was his IT friend Stuart who had sent me a list for the techno shops of Tottenham Court Road, and now I was self-sufficient with a complete travelling office.

'Good morning, madam. Welcome to City Airport.' The taxi door was swept open by a green-uniformed airport official, gold braid glinting in the early morning sun. 'And which flight will madam be taking this morning?' It could have been Harrods except for the strong smell of kerosene.

The bubble of excitement grew inside me as the plane descended and a maze of channels, islands and fjords spread out below. The Norwegian coast was reminiscent of Scotland, but bigger. That, I reckoned, must be the Sognefjord. Flåm was too far inland to see. I had included the scenic mountain railway. No need for a recce there, I thought remembering the over-heating track and thunderstorm. So I was starting with Norway's most westerly island – Utvaer. Geographically well placed, I had discovered it had been a final stop for the Vikings heading for Scotland. Threateningly they had called to sharpen their swords on the rocks and apparently the marks were still to be seen.

Reminding myself to keep to the 'wrong' side of the road,

I left Bergen in a hire car. There was a long way to go and on the seat beside me lay notes of my route, a carefully made list of road numbers, ferries and small towns taking me north and as far west as it was possible to drive. I reckoned I had about two hundred miles to go to Kolgrov, but ferry crossings and looping round fjords prevented my being able to judge how long it would take. Driving long distances was a pleasure for me, and I settled in happily to enjoy the striking fjord scenery. Tucked along the shores were settlements of neat wooden houses coloured in soft yellow ochres and deep red, each with its church.

The first fjord ferry was across the entrance to the Sognefjord, at Rutledal. Ferries are as integral to Norwegian life as trolls, geometric jerseys and replica Viking longboats. I had left London before daybreak and by now I was starving. A stream of truck drivers, each wearing a patterned black and white jersey, snaked like a caterpillar into the bowels of the ship. They were making for the canteen, and I joined the queue, reminiscent of the pie and peas queue at the Fishermen's Mission in Peterhead. Here too I was the only female.

'Hei, hvordan har du det?' asked a Viking, a caricature whose bushy red beard merged with his tousled hair to create a fuzzy ball.

'Hi, sorry, I don't speak Norwegian.'

'Ja, no problem. Where are you going?' He enunciated each word carefully.

'I'm going to Utvaer. Have you heard of it?'

'Utvaer! Utvaer!' he exclaimed as the queue shuffled forwards. 'Everyone in Norway knows of Utvaer. It is famous! Why do you want to go there?'

'I understand it was a stop for the Vikings, to sharpen

their swords before attacking Scotland.' I grinned at him. 'But I'm starving, I left London really early this morning, so what's best to eat here?' His well-filled jersey suggested he was more familiar with food than Scottish history.

'You don't know?' he asked incredulously. 'Here is the most famous food in Norway. Svele. You must try... this ferry has the *very* best. Svele is full of... energy. You have it with brunost.' He turned to the girl behind the counter and spoke to her in Norwegian. Two plates, each with a folded pancake, so big it flopped over the sides, appeared; steam rose invitingly. Beside the pancake lay an unidentifiable muddy brown slab.

'That,' he said proudly, pointing at the slab, 'is brunost.'

The pancake was hot, gooey, sweet and delicious but even a whiff of brunost was revolting.

By the time I reached Kolgrov, I had tested three other pancakes. Each ferry had its svele, and I was becoming an aficionado, but with jam not the khaki-coloured, stinking goat's cheese.

As I worked my way north each ferry grew smaller, the roads narrower and more tortuous. Views out to the North Sea grew wider, colder and the humps of distant islands, scattered among expanses of chill blue water, flatter. Tight groups of rowan trees now grew around the villages that sheltered at the head of the fjords, each with its complement of small inshore fishing boats, quietly resting at their moorings in the still water, well away from the swells.

At last, I reached a cluster of three buildings – Kolgrov. I only knew I had arrived because the road ended on the jetty. Beside the small wooden pier was a blood-red weather-boarded building sporting the promising sign 'Rom'. It had been a long day, and I was tired, hungry again and stiff from driving. Supper, a bath and comfy bed would be good. After tucking the car into a slot on the pier I grabbed my bag. Inside the guest house all was neat, with gingham curtains and a fleet of model fishing boats sailing along a window ledge. Well-scrubbed pine tables with chairs tucked tightly underneath waited for customers, but there was no sign of anyone.

'Hello! Anyone here? Hello, anyone around?'

'Ja, Ja.' The voice preceded a scuffling noise as an elderly woman appeared. I had clearly interrupted an early night.

'Hello. Good evening, my name's Amelia. I rang a couple of days ago.' She stared at me. I repeated, 'I spoke to someone on the phone. They said you would have a room for me. One night. Ok?'

'Room Ja. But we have no food. You bring own? I show you room.' I followed her up the well-worn bare wooden stairs. There was an iron bedstead just like school with a mattress and pillow but there was nothing else. No bedclothes, pillow, duvet or towel.

'Could I have a duvet or something please? And a towel?'

'We are not a city hotel. You bring own in Norway, like bring own food.' She smiled happily. 'Village shop open nine in morning.'

I settled down wearily, fully clothed on the spartan bed. I had eight hours, the timetable had told me, before the foot ferry started fjord-hopping among the nearby communities, but it left before the village shop opened. I must be ready, waiting on the jetty, as Utvaer was a request stop.

On a calm silvery morning, the little boat chugged up the fjord, the arrow of its wake spread out across the still waters. When it came alongside, I caught the rope, tied a bowline and dropped the loop over the bollard. I still enjoyed the look of surprise on a skipper's face, even in emancipated Norway.

'Hello, good morning. I'm hoping you could drop me off at Utvaer, please?'

'There is no one out there,' he said. 'it's not summer yet, no one is living yet in the *rorbuer* – fishermen's cabins.' He looked up at me standing on the jetty. 'The island is deserted. No lighthouse keepers there for many years. Are you sure you want to go to Utvaer? You're not a local.'

'I read a Viking fleet sailed from around here, from Solund to England, and stopped at the island on the way.'

'Ja, Harald Hardråde with two hundred boats.' He had no problem with a conversation in English.

'I'm working for a Scottish company so the Viking connection will be good. I read you can see where they sharpened their swords on the rocks – do you know where?'

'Ja, ja. You can see the marks. We won, so the Vikings must have had sharp swords!'

There were three other passengers, all for villages elsewhere and soon we were heading almost due west threading between low-lying bare rocky islets. None had trees or even bushes, just patches of winter-dead yellow grass bent from the prevailing wind. Apart from an occasional gull the sea was empty, still and quiet in the bright morning sunshine. Visible above the islands, far into the distance a blood-red column stuck out: the lighthouse. It was well placed on Utvaer, its height showing clear above the low-lying patchwork of islands. Carefully the little boat slid into the cleft running up from the south, that almost split the island in two. As I stepped onto the metal framework of a jetty, I made my first passenger note: it would be sturdy and provide an easy landing for the passengers.

'Enjoy the island. In the summer I usually have two or three trips out here, but it's empty now, so you have it all to yourself. See you later.'

'Thanks very much. See you this afternoon, what sort of time?' I wondered why I had asked. After all, there was nowhere to wander off to.

'About two, I expect. See ya.' With a surge of power, he reversed away from the landing place, the little white boat swiftly disappearing east into the morning sun. As the engine noise fell away, quiet descended like a blanket over the island. Only the occasional harsh squawk of a gull and soft cooing of eider ducks pottering through the bladderwrack along the shoreline, broke the peace.

Lighthouse first, I thought as I clambered up the bare grey rock, next I would look for the sword marks, as they would probably be easier to see when the sun was stronger. Walking over the island was easy as a succession of ridges and hollows had been smoothed by aeons of eroding waves and long-ago ice sheet. As I jumped from one to the next the Mars bar lurking in my jacket pocket thumped against my thigh. At the last minute, I had remembered it in the car and popped it in my jacket with a small bottle of water. The lighthouse itself was a steel column, topped by the glass lantern; painted a typical deep Norwegian red, it gazed unperturbed out to sea. Norway's most westerly point. I sat down on a warm dry ridge at the foot, my back against the riveted steel. The surrounding seas were deceptively calm and benign in the sparkling April sun, but hollows in the smoothed rocks were filled with caches of broken shells, bright yellow, rich brown and pearly white, evidence of the storms and waves that washed over the rocks.

Time to look for the Viking marks. Having taken photos

of the lighthouse from several angles, I started back over the ridges aware of how hungry I was. A fresh westerly breeze blew in my face. It had come from across the North Sea. I waved. Waved to Muckle Flugga a hundred and eighty miles away, the nearest bit of Scotland. Time for the Mars bar. When I sat on a rocky ridge, my boots were buried in surprisingly lush vegetation. Nestling in the folds of the smoothed rocky surface were vivid orange and red nasturtiums, bright green leaves I recognised as squat potato plants, and in one hollow the stiff grey spikes of onion sets. The lighthouse keepers had created these mini kitchen gardens bringing back a sack or two of proper soil to fill the cracks in the rocks. They reminded me of the lighthouse gardens of Scotland. It was a profession that allowed time for gardening and fresh veg must have been welcome.

Running over the grey gneiss were long, deep grooves, the Viking marks, and they fitted the story well. I took the required photos before returning to the jetty for more photos and made a note of the number of steps. Work was done, everything for the ship and passengers I had noted and maybe a photo worthy of the brochure too. Utvaer, I was now confident, would make a good stepping-stone after crossing the North Sea. There was sufficient interest with its Scottish Viking connections, enchanting mini veg gardens and striking red lighthouse. I had about an hour before the ferryman was due, so I lay down, soaking up the warmth from the hard rocks. The research and my first recce could be counted as a success.

Two o'clock. He should be here about now, but there was no putter of an engine.

Four o'clock. Six o'clock came and went and still there was no sign of the boat. The sun slipped to the west and dipped into the sea. The light began to fail and now I could see Venus shining brightly in the dove grey sky. I was alone. Alone on a remote, uninhabited island. The island was too far west for a mobile phone signal. I realised not a soul in the world knew where I was, apart from the ferryman. And there was no sign of him.

I returned to the bulk of the lighthouse. Its massive metal tower still retained some warmth, and I felt less forlorn with its strength at my back. Dark sea stretched all around, the swell sloshing regularly up and down on the rocks. Above the sky was a huge bowl of brilliant stars and I could see the Milky Way, a lighter belt stretching across the whole firmament. I had no food, and there were no trees or wood to make a fire. About two decent mouthfuls of water remained in the bottle.

Nothing moved on the sea. Just the surge and suck of the swell, not even the lonely cry of a gull in the dark. There were no passing cargo ships, no human movement anywhere. I was truly alone. I tried to control myself from looking at my watch. What did it matter what time it was?

Slowly the light grew, turning the rocks from black to pale grey. I wandered around, ate a few nasturtiums, enjoying the fiery honeyed sweetness of the trumpet-shaped flowers. I took off a boot and used it as a trowel, loosening the soil around a potato plant; but there were no tubers. I pulled at an onion; it came up easily, just an earthy shaving-brush of roots.

Eight o'clock, nine, ten: I became increasingly despondent as my watch crept on to midday. What could I do? My stomach ached with emptiness so I tried to cheer myself by thinking how much worse it would be in the rain. I had not intended my life would end on a flat, uninhabited Norwegian island, I thought angrily. The sun crept higher in the sky, warm and benign.

Fitfully, above the sound of the waves, I thought I heard something. I kept still holding my breath. Yes, there it was again, coming and going on the wind. It was an engine. Through my binoculars, far to the east, silhouetted by the morning light, was a speck. A boat.

I jumped up and down. Waving, shouting, bellowing. I knew it was pointless, it was much too far away to see or hear. But still I jumped. The speck grew, it began to take on shape as it came closer. It was, it really was coming to Utvaer. Now I could see the ferryman.

'Hei! Hei! Here you are!' he called out cheerfully as the boat drew into the inlet.

'Well, where do you think I would be?'

'Ja, well. I'm sorry. I forgot.' He grinned, 'But I'm here now. I was in Kolgrov, tied up, waiting for old Inga. She always goes to Litle Varønya on a Saturday, to see her daughter. With the eggs, the eggs from her hens. She asked me if I knew what the stranger was doing. Why was there was a stranger in the village? Was something happening in Kolgrov?'

Without waiting for him to be properly alongside, I jumped on board.

'She's such a . . .' He searched for the word. 'A busybody. She spotted the Bergen number plate on your car. Good thing you parked by the jetty!'

9

Norway

Fjords and Pancakes with White Van Man

Utvaer retreated astern, quickly turning from a prison into just a low innocent smudge on the horizon. Never again would I be so stupid I vowed, as a vision of bacon, eggs, black pudding, sausage and tomato floated through my mind. In future, someone would know where I was, or better still, I would not travel alone. Perhaps I could have a minder, someone to do the driving, handle the logistics, leaving me to focus on the job. If I were to check out distant coasts and remote islands, I would value another opinion. Helly Handsome? He would certainly add a spark, possibly a complete conflagration.

The little boat pottered on, pulling the high hills of the mainland nearer and the lonely ordeal slipped steadily astern. The Nokia lying on the thwart beside me burst into life as it locked onto the network and slithered, vibrating, onto the planks at my feet. I grabbed it quickly before it had a chance to slip between the cracks into the bilges. Eighteen emails, two phone messages and then it rang, giving me such a fright, I dropped it, just catching it between my knees.

'Hello Sexy Redhead, where are you? I see your boaty has gone.'

I took a long, calming breath. HH.

'How nice to hear you,' I breathed out, hoping to sound unflustered and relaxed. 'What a surprise.'

'Are you Ok? You don't sound like you?'

'Thanks, yes, yes I'm fine.' I fought back the tears, longing to tell him how frightened I had been.

'I can hear an engine – wind. So where are you?'

'Norway, coming back from an island called Utvaer. Way out west. It is good... good to be on the way back. Where are you?'

'Dubai. Hellish place, but needs must, there's a conference here. What are you doing for the next few days? Come and join me? You would cheer the place up?'

My heart leapt. 'What a lovely thought.' I pushed away the feeling of his arms around me, fighting not to cry. 'Bergen tonight, it's about a six hour drive, providing the ferries connect. Then I have a day of meetings tomorrow, shipping agents and so on, followed by a day covering two more islands just south of Bergen. Then I'm free as a bird.'

'Mmm, that's four days, plus flying. Pity. I'll be in Singapore by then submerged in board meetings.' He sounded genuinely disappointed. 'Well, we'll have to make it another time. Send me some photos, I've always wanted to sail around that coast, see the fjords.'

It always rained in Bergen I remember being told and it did. All through the drive south I felt dirty, miserable and tired. Big puddles shone in the headlights as wearily I drew up outside a faceless concrete block on the edge of town. The hotel lift whizzed efficiently to the second floor as a vision of a deep, hot bath and room service filled my head. Norway did not go in for baths, so there was no luxuriating in scented water. Room service produced a slab of fjord farmed salmon, slathered in dill sauce with boiled potatoes. Too-solid waffles came with a dollop of red jam, but every mouthful was a treat and preparations for tomorrow's meetings would have to wait. After a shower, I slipped gratefully under the duvet and instantly fell asleep.

FIRE! FIRE!

Evacuate. Fire. This is not a Test. I repeat, this is not an exercise. FIRE. Evacuate. Evacuate.

Still woozy from deep sleep, I scrambled out of bed, dragged on jeans and a jersey, grabbed my phone, thrust my passport and room key into a pocket and burst into the corridor. To my right, where the lift and stairs lay as I watched a heavy fire door closed off the passage with a solid clunk. The fire alarm filled the corridor. No one else came out of their bedroom, I was on my own in a bleak corridor on the second floor of a concrete block. To my left, the passageway ended in a pastel green door, labelled EXIT. I ran and pushed hard at the bar. Nothing. No movement. I pushed again, pressing down hard on the steel bar. On the other side, I could hear clattering footsteps as people ran down the stairs. I banged. Thumped. Shouted. Yelled.

'Help! Help! Please open the door. Help! Open the door. *Open the door!*' Without a pause, the feet clattered on.

I shouted louder. Pushed the bar and shook the door. Nothing changed, no one stopped.

Congratulating myself that I had picked up the room key, I ran back to my bedroom and over to the window. Smoke billowed in dark clouds up from the ground floor almost obscuring an extension projecting twenty feet below the window.

Twisting open the catches, I pushed. But this was Norway, and it was a sensible modern hotel. The window opened only a few inches. The fire siren still wailed, filling the bedroom, making my heart race. Picking up a chair, I braced myself to hurl it at the glass.

'Ladies and Gentlemen.' A soothing voice spread calm. 'The emergency is over. Fire is now under control.'

'Hello, good morning. Could I speak to Michael, please?'

'Putting you through.'

'Hello. Yes, back from Norway. Eventful but successful. I went to Utvaer and some other islands. Utvaer is fascinating, lots of connections. I'm sure the passengers will find it interesting.'

'You've got some good photos?' he asked.

'Yes, no problem. It's very small, but perfect for a half day. The sword marks are easy to see.'

I could hear him shuffling papers and sensed he had more urgent topics.

'I think you will like this,' he said. 'We've got a ship at last. She's in Chile but making her way here now. Should be in dry dock to start the refurbishment in a month or so.' He sounded as if he had pulled a perfectly wrapped present out of a bran tub. 'That makes all your deadlines shorter.'

'What fantastic news.' I replied. 'I have a couple of points from my end.'

'Ok, go ahead.'

'I'd like her dimensions as soon as possible and I think, now, in view of the urgency,' I went on boldly, 'I will need someone to travel with me. A driver, logistics person, to leave me free to focus on the itineraries.' I held my breath. My request would add considerably to the costs of my recces.

I could almost hear the wheels of thought churning. 'Yes, I suppose that does make sense. Ok. Take anyone you like, providing you're sure they will do the job. They must do what you want.' He paused, then added, 'Expenses and fifty pounds a day.'

And so began the travels which were to change my life, again.

A week later, the Discovery trundled steadily up the motorway, leaving me time for a good look at the looming Angel of the North. It was ages since I had driven up the A1 past my home patch. Mike and Brenda had settled into the cottage and my father seemed reasonably happy, apart from the dinners Brenda produced for him. 'It all looks like a cowpat,' he commented. Brenda put his supper in the Aga at teatime and there it languished, keeping warm, going brown and drying out until he had changed into his well-worn velvet jacket, had a martini, lit the candles and was ready. Even alone, he kept rigidly to old-fashioned standards.

A red sign, perfectly placed, caught my attention and there, behind the chain-link gates were rows of what I now knew were mobile homes, not caravans. I had to complete the Norwegian coastal recce, and I was determined there would be no more miserable nights with no sheets and no food. A campervan seemed the solution and the source of them closest to the North Sea ferry crossing was a firm based in Newcastle. The idea of exploring like a snail, from a moving home, had much in common with life on a boat, and this particular company had offered a driver service too. Parked beside a large van was a long wheelbase Land Rover, piled up with battered scuba tanks, the driver's door open. A small puff of smoke hung in the afternoon sunshine and a long leg in well-washed jeans stretched down to the grass.

This must be my van and my man. He was to be my driver and fixer for the next three weeks of recceing. His head and chin were covered in greying fuzz, and he screwed up his eyes against the drifting smoke from a slim brown cheroot.

'You must be Amelia.' He looked me up and down. 'I'm Bill.'

I held out my hand. 'Hello, Bill. That's a lot of tanks, you must be a diver?'

'Yes, just moving them for a mate.' He walked away, leaving a whiff of menthol smoke in the air behind him. 'That's the van we'll be using, just there.' I followed him to a clean white van. He flung open a side door and stepped back as if ushering me into a hotel suite. The van wobbled as I climbed in. A sixties world of Formica in pale blue and beige awaited. Opposite the door was a table with bench seats either side, upholstered in herringbone 'tweed'. To the right was the cooking area with two gas rings, a small sink and a rack of blue and white plates. Opening a slim door, I found a diminutive stainless-steel loo and a washbasin with a rack for tooth mugs and hook for the showerhead. Across the back of the van, stretching under the rear window, was a double bed with a sky-blue duvet where swallows flitted between fluffy clouds. It was the neatest, most compact and organised little home I had ever seen. After the confines of life on board *Monaco*, I knew I'd be fine. Depending on Bill. His fuzzy head appeared through the door, but he held the cheroot carefully outside.

'What do you think? Looks Ok?'

'Yup, looks great, but . . . but there's only one bed?'

He grinned, trying to suppress a laugh. 'Oh, don't worry there's another above the driver's cab.'

'Ah, Ok. Then it all looks good to me, but I've never seen inside one of these before. What do you think? You'll be doing the driving. I don't think I could drive this, it looks huge.'

'That's Ok, driven one for years. These vans all belong to my cousin, so there's nothing for you to sign. All taken care of.'

'Thanks, but I would still like to see the paperwork, please.'
The office would expect me to do things correctly.

Bill, a menthol cheroot dangling from his lips, leaned out of the window as he drove the van carefully down the ramp. We bumped over the ridges and into the stomach of the capacious ferry. Behind me, beers clinked and the little freezer hummed steadily. Every cupboard was packed tight, crammed with 'man food'. My experience of sea passages rolling round Cape Wrath and Rattray Head in *Monaco* had proved invaluable. Bill had watched surprised as I had stowed the cans of beans, tins of tomatoes and Fray Bentos Kate and Sydney pies now wedged tightly with packets of pasta.

The ferry slowly ground away from the dock and Newcastle, buzzing with headlights and life, slipped astern. It was a warm, mild night and knots of people stood about the deck taking advantage of the unusually soft breeze from the North Sea. All were male, not a female among them. On the deck below were more groups, chatting and enjoying each other's company; again, men. Outside the bar, where we had agreed to meet, were brightly lit rows of slot machines and the duty-free shop. It was a standard, smelly car ferry, until I realised the men had something in common. Each had a moustache or beard and most had both. The display and colour of facial hair varied, but every face sported a luxuriant growth. Some moustaches were precise, neatly trimmed with stiffly twirled points, others were long, droopy Fu Manchu-style, while others were bushy handlebars with horns like a Highland cow. Moustaches and beards spiralled, curled, dripped, drooped and bushed. All were carefully manicured and one, Poirot-like, was supported by a protective little mesh bag.

Bill leaned on the bar.

'Hi Bill, have you noticed anything?'

'Just seems the usual grotty ferry.' He reached for his beer.

'Look around,' I whispered.

He glanced around. 'What? Looks pretty standard to me.'

'Don't you see?'

'Nope.'

'Well, there's barely a woman on board and everyone, including you, has a moustache or beard!' His eyes widened as he studied the busy bar. 'But yours has a way to go!'

'Wow, you're right. This is weird,' he said. 'Look at all the different styles.'

A Sherlock Holmes look-alike crossed the floor to the slot machine, chawing on an unlit pipe. He pushed back his deerstalker to get a clear view of the spinning cherries and apples.

Bill winked at me. 'What do you think's going on?'

'No idea. I've never seen anything like it.'

A particularly fine specimen approached. The moustache, stiff and black, twirled precisely in two looping curls. Each whorl was neatly held in place by a miniature clothes peg.

'Do you mind if I join you?' he asked. The pegs wobbled.

'Of course not. Please do.'

Bill, bent over his pint, smothering a laugh. The man put his glass on the bar top, perched on a stool and gently pushed the clothes pegs apart, clearing the route to his mouth. I was unable to contain myself.

'Forgive me if this is rude, but you have a truly fine moustache. There are lots of others around, beards too, but yours is magnificent.' He puffed out his chest and the clothes pegs perked up.

'Thank you, I appreciate that, maybe I'll win.'

'Win! Win what?'

'I'm going to Ålesund,' he said, as if that explained it all. 'The European Moustache & Beard Championships will be held there tomorrow. I won last year, so I am hopeful.'

Ålesund, washed clean by sea air, had a pastel-coloured core of art-nouveau buildings, and the pavements, outdoor cafes and bars bustled with bristles, beards, moustaches and more Sherlock Holmes deerstalkers. Bill and I slipped away north, leaving them to their hairy jamboree.

We christened our campervan 'Charley'. I liked naming my vehicles, only the Discovery was characterless, but the van was a 'lad', and I quickly came to appreciate his qualities. Being able to spend all day checking sites, not wasting time finding where to stay among the remote fjords and islands was a relief, and exploring, able to follow my agenda freely, enabled me to cover three or four sites a day. Bill, whose life in Newcastle revolved around football and beer, had done little travelling, and we got on well, despite the cheroots. Charley swayed along the tortuous roads hugging the fjord shores. Bill threw him happily round the bends, whistling, smoking and singing while I sat at the table checking the map, writing up my notes and filing the hundreds of photos I took each day. I could complete each day's notes, deal with emails and keep in touch with the office. Along the whole convoluted coast Norway's mobile phone signal never failed me, even extending through one ten kilometre-long tunnel. At seven o'clock, I would call a halt, and Bill would find a lay-by and park the van so that a view spread out from our dining table window. Then came the 'frying-pan test'.

'How is it now?' he would shout, kneeling beside the van and twisting the levelling leg.

'Not quite. Down a bit. Yup. Stop! That's fine.'

Our make-shift spirit level, the frying pan filled with water, worked well, preventing us from spending the night rolling into the van side. Bill had been adamant sleeping at an angle was a mistake. Then, when necessary, he would deal with the loo and set out the deck chairs. I, meanwhile, would fry fillet steak, and we'd sit surveying the still waters of one fjord after another. It was an idyllic way to make inspections. Without my notes, the indented coastline, villages, bays, churches and museums would have merged into a fluid whole. Some islands were memorable, and I immediately included them in the programme: Kinn, where the church had ornate carvings and a votive ship in full sail; Selje, serene with monastic ruins so reminiscent of Iona; and Espaevaer, with its unique 'lobster park'. A deep cleft in the rocks where since medieval days the locals had corralled spiny blue lobsters to ensure they had a good supply instantly ready to sell to any passing ship.

Continuing north, eventually we came to the Lofoten chain, where the islands grew out of the sea like a surfacing stegosaurus. Blue, spiky and mountainous they still had pockets of snow.

'Are these all islands or are they linked?' Bill asked.

'Well, according to the map we can drive down them. Only a couple at the very southern end are not linked.'

Bill looked thoughtful.

'What's the matter? Are you fed up with driving?'

'No, no, I'm enjoying the driving, thanks.'

'Well, something's bothering you, so give me a clue,' I persisted.

He grinned as he spun the big steering wheel. 'It's the prospect of no svele that's bothering me! It's good, and I like the ferries. Most of the truck drivers speak English. I enjoy a blether.'

'I'm sure we can find a café or three to keep you topped up with svele and blether.'

The final island I had my sights on visiting before Tromsø, was Bjarkøya. I was planning a morning at sea for the ship in the waters north of Andenes. There were local whale watching tours that guaranteed a sighting, and one of these could precede an afternoon on Bjarkøya. Bizarrely the small, sheltered island had a museum boasting the 'world's largest collection of stuffed seabirds'. Charley cruised into the harbour where I hoped to find a boat. The settlement of Harstad appeared once to have been populated by Apaches. Between the weatherboarded warehouses, painted blood red with traditional fish blood preservative, were ranks of abandoned tepee frames. The skeleton A frames over ten-foot-high were covered with spiky rows of menacing steel hooks.

'What goes on here?' Bill blew a minty cloud between words. 'Why all the wooden frames?'

'They're waiting for the fish,' I replied. 'Cod has been the big thing here, traded since the thirteenth century, the days of the Hanseatic League.' He looked at me quizzically. 'It's not far from the Arctic, the rich fishing grounds. So the fish are brought back here, hung out to dry on these racks. You can imagine the stink, the air must be filled with the pong of drying fish. You know, Bacalao for Spain and Portugal. It's known around here as "the smell of money".'

'Ah, well, I'm learning something new each day on this trip,' Bill said, providing reassurance for me that others too would find my itineraries interesting.

In the harbour, fishing boats bobbed gently, their reflections clear on the water, along with those of the distant blue peaks of Grytøya hiding my objective, Bjarkøya, according to my chart. There were no Google Maps or Google Earth then.

'Hei Hei! Anyone on board?' Bill, fulfilling his role as Logistics, shouted over to the boats tied along the jetty.

'Hei, du må bare si ifra hvis du trenger hjelp?' came an answering shout. Till now, everyone had spoken English.

'Bjarkøya?' I asked, pointing towards the hills. 'I want to go to Bjarkøya.'

'Ja. Oh, Ok.' A bobble hat, followed by body covered in a traditional Norwegian jersey with the inescapable geometric patterns, appeared.

'Bjarkøya?' I asked again pointing north.

'Ja. Ja,' said bobble hat. I stretched my legs across the gap to launch myself onto the gunwale. Bill simply jumped, landing rather solidly. Just a flicker of a frown crossed our skipper's face. I realised I must remember to tell Bill that jumping onto a boat was bad form. Unaware, he sauntered to the wheelhouse, digging into a pocket to pull out the green packet of his beloved menthol cheroots and offering one to the skipper. This slim, chocolate coloured stick, delicate and rather elegant, looked effeminate, so it was eyed with suspicion and curiosity.

'Go on, try one.' Bill flipped his Zippo lighter into action. A haze of minty, misty smoke billowed between them.

'Ya,' said the Skipper, sucking at the tiny cheroot, 'gud, ya.' We left the small settlement behind and the fishing boat began to lift in the motion as we moved out of the shelter of the harbour.

'Bjarkøy?' I repeated and then less confidently. 'I want to go to the Stuffed Bird Museum.'

'Bjarkøy, ya, Bjarkøy,' he replied, encouragingly.

'Dead Bird Museum. I want to go to the Dead Bird Museum.' I tried again. He shrugged, grinned happily and we all laughed. Bending down, he dragged open the small door of a hatch leading to the forepeak. Thrusting an arm inside, he pulled out a tattered chart, spreading it over the compass and fish finder. Bjarkøya was a good-sized island with several landing points, in turn he pointed to each, looking enquiringly at me as he indicated one after another. I had no idea where I wanted to go. The boat pottered on as I considered. Bill had found a perch among a pile of fishing net and puffed his cheroot contentedly. The sea cliffs of Grytøya scrolled past. Razorbills, guillemots and kittiwakes covered the crags, jostling each other on the ledges in shrieking colonies. Puffins, like self-important waiters, bobbed on the lifting swells and high above, the menacing shape of a sea eagle soared.

The skipper tried again, mentioning a string of what I assumed were the villages of Bjarkøy. He needed to know where to head for.

'Sundsvoll? Vedvika?' he asked, but I only knew the name of the island. Take me to the dead sea bird museum was clearly inadequate. Inspiration dawned.

I raised both arms and flapped like a bird. Then I mimed holding a shotgun. I took aim at a sweeping fulmar, shouting 'Bang', then crumpled to become a dying bird. I felt rather proud of my charade. He simply looked blank. I 'shot' another gull. Suddenly, grinning, he slapped me on the back, picked up the VHF and pressed the button. A sing-song stream of chatter followed, he altered course and now we headed in a different direction.

A couple of hours later, the little boat entered a bay, we passed the cages of a fish farm, where salmon jumped and splashed under the netting, before coming up to a jetty made of floating plastic boxes. I took a rope, tied a bowline and threw it across the gap, the man waiting on the quay dropped it on a bollard, pointed at me and shouted to our Skipper. My tying a bowline as usual produced a look of surprise.

'Hello. Welcome to Bjarkøy.' He stretched out a hand to help me up. 'So, you can throw a rope, tie the knot. The museum will be what you want, Ja. I will take you. I have my jeep here.'

Driving along the shore, we passed pockets of beaches, bright with white sand. The sea was still, a deep, clear blue. Eider ducks in family groups of six or seven cooed softly as they paddled around the broken shoreline. The colours here in the high Arctic were as strong as the tropics, and it seemed a charming, unspoilt island. To the west, the stegosaurus mountain spine of the Andøya peninsula would provide the ship with shelter while to the south the defensive peaks of Grytøya would create a wind barrier. Only from the north was the island exposed, but a strong northerly, I felt, would be unlikely in June.

He turned the jeep away from the shore heading straight uphill to cross a field. The track climbed steeply until he stopped at a metal door, propped open by a lump of rock. Hobbit like, it opened straight into the hillside. What would our classy passengers think about this? It would need something good to warrant a specific stop all for this scruffy doorway.

'Here we are, I'll come back to pick you up in about an hour. Enjoy the collection.' The jeep disappeared down the hill leaving a cloud of diesel. The silence of an empty hillside settled round us.

Bill stuck his head through the doorway and decided the warm sun outside suited him better. I ducked under the wooden lintel to enter the dark, fusty smelling cavern, triggering the lights. Straight ahead, fixing me with an unwavering stare, standing on his hind legs was a massive grizzly bear. Beyond him stretched a rabbit warren of cabinets, burrowing deep into the hillside. From all sides glass eyes glinted in the light, staring unwinkingly as I wandered slowly through the maze of showcases. Fibreglass rocks, mirrored pools and chicken wire branches were covered by cormorants, shags, razorbills, puffins, Arctic skua, storm petrels, shearwater and gannets; even a sea eagle 'flew' on massive wings, overshadowing a nesting eider duck.

Would people find this quirky collection of interest? I felt far from certain. The showcases were dusty, the lighting poor and it seemed barely worth the trouble. A movement caught my attention, a figure blocked the light, silhouetted in the doorway, completely filling the entrance. He moved a little, triggering more spotlights. From head to toe he was dressed in white leather. Running down his sleeves and trousers were fringes of golden tassels, while embroidered across his chest was a golden eagle. Wings outstretched, beak and talons ready, with sequins flashing in red, green and gold.

'You like my collection, ja?' he asked. 'Vill you take svele or waffles?'

'I think it is amazing. What a super display!'

A Norwegian Elvis who could provide seabirds, svele and waffles – it would be an unforgettable afternoon.

10

Greece
A Yellow-peril Tour

In front of me were two swarthy Greeks. Cigarette smoke and waves of chauvinism blew towards me as I sat in the back of an Athens taxi. The yellow Mercedes swooped along the looping coastal road, flashes of sun reflected on the calm blue sea dotted with freighters at anchor, waiting for their next cargo. Soon we would be at Corinth. I was anxious to get a clear view of the canal and surroundings, but already, only forty-five minutes into the beginning of this research tour, I felt uneasy. Nikos the agent and his chum Yannis, the driver, had not drawn breath since we left the centre of Athens. As they argued and gesticulated, smoking continuously, my presence seemed irrelevant and already forgotten. Ahead lay five days of inspections covering the canal, the Gulf of Corinth and around the peninsulas of the Peloponnese, and I did not want a sexist battle. This time I was alone, anticipating Greece would be less challenging. Without a moment's hesitation, Nikos had planted his bulk in the front seat. His appearance was discouraging: he looked lazy, his flabby stomach rolling over his belt like a fat sausage. Someone in the office had chosen him, but had anyone met him? Could he really be the flexible, interested, engaged agent I needed?

'Nikos,' I leant forward, 'we will be stopping at the Canal, won't we?'

'No,' he said. 'It's not relevant. Yannis wants to drive now. We go straight to Delphi.'

'So, we will have time on the way back for me to see the Canal?'

'Yes, at the end. It is the only way back to Athens.'

That would do. At the beginning or the end, made no difference for me, and I did not want a battle to start so soon. Yannis swung the big car, swaggering and swaying along the shores of the Gulf of Elefsina. He drove north west through mountainous country, eventually drawing to a halt in the dappled shade of a dusty car park. This must be Delphi I assumed.

'You go.' Nikos said, unbuckling his seatbelt and easing his bulk out into the sunshine. 'We wait here. Yannis needs a break now. We will take a beer. You go.' Pulling a crumpled yellow packet from the back pocket of his jeans, he offered another cigarette to Yannis and lit his own.

Ahead, the craggy limestone slope of Mount Giona rose steeply, creating a backdrop; across the hillside were deep patches of shade interspersed by white columns and grey olive trees. It was a Tuesday in April, mid-morning, and I was happy to be alone, relieved Nikos had remained smoking in the car park.

Slowly, absorbing the quiet and stillness, I walked up the steep path of smooth, polished limestone slabs, enjoying the warm air, the spring twitter of birds and the sweet tang of rosemary.

As a child, I had been dragged round every one of Yorkshire's many historic sites by my mother. A keen and knowledgeable historian, she had insisted I translate Latin inscriptions and marvel at piles of stones. Yorkshire has much ancient history. As a result, an almost instant sense of boredom at the very idea of an archaeological site would overwhelm me. I preferred life, people, flowers, animals, birds, anything but lifeless stones. But these ruins, in this dramatic mountain setting, were different. Delphi seemed almost alive, strength emanated from the bleached columns. The power of the pagan rituals or echoes of questions asked of the Oracle, her famous prophecies of doom, still hung in the air. Maybe I'd fall in love with Greece despite the ruins.

By the afternoon, we had driven round most of the Gulf's northern shore and were nearing the next place on my list, Nafpaktos, a tiny circular port guarded by high walls. Two castles almost closed the narrow entrance into the sheltered harbour. On the map, it had reminded me of a jigsaw. The 'hole' shape of the harbour seemed to be waiting for the appropriate piece to slot perfectly into place. Nafpaktos, I had read, had once been a vital link for the Venetians, an outpost surrounded by the Ottoman empire. As such there should be plenty of historical interest, as well as restaurants and shops to provide an entertaining evening visit. The ship's tenders could come and go through the harbour entrance passing the castles. The jetties had steps, shelter and there was easy anchoring for the ship outside the walls. The little town was exactly what I wanted and with Delphi in the bag too, the day had turned out better than expected.

I had high hopes of the hotel chosen by Nikos. It was part of the Melia group and only lacked the letter 'A'. However, it was simply a concrete block conveniently placed. Next morning, we went to nearby Olympia. Again, Yannis squeezed out from behind the wheel and propped his bum against the long bonnet of the Mercedes. Nikos dug out a crushed packet of Karelia cigarettes. Again, happy to leave them in the car park, I went to explore.

Olympia was very different from Delphi, it was flat and lush. The fresh spring grass was dotted with daisies. Judas trees, at the height of blossom, branches thick with rose pink flowers, grew among the ruins, brilliant against the grey stones. Petals drifted, settling like confetti among the stone curls on a lion's head. Butterflies alighted to sun themselves in the April warmth. A wren trilled and twittered, bobbing on top of a broken column. Olympia seemed more an English garden than a pile of stones. Greece was beginning to appeal and my dislike of ruins fading.

'Amelia, how's it going?' Michael, I knew by now, wanted good news, something encouraging, when he made his intermittent phone calls.

'Fine thanks, all good here,' I said. Moaning about Nikos's habits and shortcomings from the warmth and sun of Greece in spring to someone wrestling with figures and deadlines in an office in Yorkshire would not be fair.

'Delphi will be good. The tenders can come into Itea, it's only a short transfer.' I explained, wanting to include and reassure him. 'I'm at Olympia now, glorious, so warm and sunny. The ship would come into Katakolo, that's about twenty miles.' I went through the logistics with him.

By the time Yannis had swept his taxi, me and the indolent Nikos round the three fingers of the Peloponnese, I had the measure of the pair of them and had managed to find some positives. Nikos was a foodie. We had dined at tiny restaurants, at tables beside the water, from dishes of squiggly octopus, fat olives and roast lamb. Yannis, in spite of his casual driving style with one hand on the wheel, had negotiated the tortuous route through the Mani, prickly pear country, and we had stayed on the road. I had 'done' all of the places on my recce list, and the Venetian strongholds

NORWAY

1. Chatting with Helly Handsome from a fjord ferry

2. Passing a fjord village en route to the Seabird Museum

3. 'The smell of money' amongst the Lofoten peaks

4. Blue waters flecked by the occasional sailing dhow

5. The Indian Ocean programme to come – Zanzibar to Madagascar

6. 'Marie Antoinette's farm' amongst the paddy fields

7. My challenge: the muddy, shallow and uncharted waters of Baly Bay spread uninvitingly below

8. Coconut palms curved over the water

9. Dugouts for fishing were drawn up on the beach

10. Hugo, all six foot four of him, overwhelmed the flimsy plane

11. I took an exotic beastie with me, perched happily on my hat

12. Another exotic beastie, the Angonoka, with its horny prong

13. Overhead was an arboreal teddy bears' picnic: Sifka lemur

14. Regular traffic on the road across the island

15. Our beach was pristine and perfect, giving no hint of dangers to come

16. Exploring the Mitsio Archipelago with a much-used chart

17. Striking islands and beaches amongst the archipelago

18. 'You stay here, I know what to do.' Hugo takes over my job

19. My chosen 'dog-bone' island, beaches, coral, and snorkelling

20. Every girl needs a good sun hat

21. Shopping for lunch at the Islands of the Moon

22. Spices, lentils and beans, the exotic-scented, orderly markets
of Asmara

23. Dahlak Kebir, the guide shows me evidence of the ancient
civilization at The Gate of Tears

24. The Ship's Naming Ceremony; no hat but finery for HRH,
   the Princess Royal

of Nafpaktos, Methoni and Monemvasia particularly, were as attractive as I had hoped. Arrangements for visiting the Mani's harsh stone villages would be manageable and, assuming the guides could bring to life the colourful antics of the warring families who catapulted rocks at each other during the day but shared an evening meal, I felt confident. I was also pleased to have overcome my antipathy towards ruins. Finally, ancient Corinth, perched high above the Canal, came into view.

Leaning over the railings on the bridge, far below in deep shadow, lay the Canal. Slicing straight as a die through creamy-white limestone, it looked unnervingly narrow. I fought the temptation to spit and count the seconds until it hit the water. By now, Michael had sent me the exact dimensions for the ship and, assuming they were correct, there would be just enough space: she would have ten feet of clearance either side, not much for a ship almost a hundred metres long.

I asked Nikos to book the canal transits for early morning and evening rather than in the middle of the day. The light must be right, shining down the Canal and not into the passengers' eyes.

'No, that's not possible.' His response was as predictably unhelpful as ever. During the long drives over the past five days, there had been several occasions when I had almost ditched him. He was on thin ice and it was getting thinner.

'Why not? She can anchor by the Alkionidies islands, perfect for an overnight. Whether she's going north or south, the islands are less than twenty miles away.'

He pulled on his smelly cigarette, 'That is not the problem.' Ash blew in my face.

'Are the operating hours the difficulty?'

He took another long drag on the cigarette, the end glowing brightly then he puffed the smoke straight at me.

'No, the problem is earthquakes.'

'Earthquakes! What do you mean – earthquakes?'

'There is history—' He failed to suppress a grin, ending smugly '—of earthquakes here.'

'Ok.' The recce was almost done, and it was not worth a fight. Not now. I could check it out later.

'Come,' he shouted over the roar of a passing lorry, waving. 'I need a coffee, Yannis! Yannis!' Yannis stopped the yellow Mercedes in the middle of the bridge, blocking the cars, lorries and busy traffic crossing.

'It's Ok, Nikos,' I said, sliding into the back as quickly as possible. 'Thanks, but I don't need a coffee, I've only just had breakfast.'

'No, I show you something.'

We turned off the main road following a narrow track that dropped to curl round under the big road bridge.

'This is it!' He sounded enthusiastic for the first time in the whole tour. He almost jumped out.

'See it is wet, look, it has just come up'. He pointed at the flat strip of shiny metal stretching over the Canal. Water drained away, disappearing from under my feet leaving the metal surface wet and shiny.

'This lowers. It goes up and down. When a vessel wants to go through the canal it drops down to the bottom, out of the way, below the water, the yachts and ships go over the top. Then it comes up again to be a bridge, just for the local traffic. Clever, eh?'

'Nikos, that is really smart, amazing, thank you for showing me. I'll take a few photos so the passengers can see what they're sailing over.'

The weight of Nikos himself seemed to slide from my shoulders as the plane lifted off the Athens runway. The shiftiness, sexism and arrogance remained below among the cigarette fumes and dust. I had completed another section of the ship's voyages. I had managed without any overt battles, just a war of attrition, but I had succeeded in getting most of what I wanted. Delphi, Olympia, Monemvasia and Epidaurus were unforgettable and, usefully, each in a different way. With embarkation in Dubrovnik, a cruise round the three peninsulas of the Peloponnese ending in Athens would be good and varied. Next I would have to 'do' the islands, but those would be with a different agent and with the wealth of shipping businesses in Greece there was plenty of choice. I need never be involved with Nikos again. It was done, and I knew relating the days of ruins, smoke and chauvinism to HH would be fun. It would be good to be home in London.

'Hello, Sandra. Can I speak to Michael, please? Yes, I'm back. Tiresome agent, we won't use him.'

'Hi, Amelia, what was wrong?' her Yorkshire accent sounded encouraging and safe.

'Well, it would take too long, but let's just say arrogant, chauvinistic, slippery and shifty. I felt he would rather tell me a lie than the truth, just to score a point.'

'Fun then! Hang on, I'll put you through.'

'Michael? Yes, hello, Amelia. All OK, in fact, better than OK, really good.'

In the beginning of my recces, I had reported regularly, but I knew he was submerged in countless complications, so I was determined he should be confident of my side. I had been exploring, planning and travelling to isolated islands by now for so long I wondered if the whole venture would ever start. Would we have passengers to visit Bjarkøya's

Stuffed Bird Museum? Would we land on the same beach as had been used during the war for the Sicily Landings as the ruins of Selinunte's Greek temple kept guard? Would passengers get to hear Heilan Laddie skirl up the tiered stone seats at Epidaurus? I was fortunate, I had an enviable job. It was extraordinary to be paid to explore and encouraging to know Michael trusted me. I was simply pushing on, working to ensure I found the island chains, castles and inaccessible villages needed, determined the new ship would replicate the company's proven successful model in Scotland.

The sounds of office life, a ringing phone, low voices of a distant conversation, came clearly as he shuffled papers across his desk. Everyone else worked under these constraints, and I was continually concerned my privileged existence would end.

'Hello there. Great, good to know you're on track. Let me have your thoughts for a winter schedule. We'll have to get away from Europe, into the sun. Think about it tonight, give me a ring in the morning.'

It was typical Michael. He did not waste time. Six months of cruises from late October to early March was a big programme, but for some time I had been wondering what winter might hold. Passengers should be offered warmth, an escape from European chills, sun, sea, excitement and the already proven recipe of unexpected islands and ports. The season would be a minimum of a hundred and twenty days, every one of which called for the ship to be somewhere different. It was surprising he had not brought the winter programme up earlier and my concern had been that someone else was already working on it, not me. I was filled with relief and excitement at Michael's brief direction and would need to find shipping agents, guides, transport and local managers. However, this felt different. This programme would be truly 'foreign'. I had only once been east of Athens to visit my brother in Kenya. I had no experience to draw on. After a night of studying what charts and books I had, I gave him a call.

'Let's hear your thoughts.'

I took a deep breath, knowing my ideas were ambitious, exciting and also costly. It was 2000 and they would also be truly expeditionary, breaking new ground for chic, small ship cruising.

'The programme I have in mind is to work south among the Greek islands in late October and go through Suez, using Alexandria as change-around port. Then down the Red Sea into the Indian Ocean. We will have Oman, Zanzibar, Madagascar, Comoros, Seychelles... India, Sri Lanka to choose from, an unbelievable wealth of islands.' I wondered if I had overdone it. Silence accompanied by the creak of Michael's chair as he leaned back, thinking.

'Ok,' he said at last, 'but more in Egypt. Where do Cairo and Luxor fit in?'

'Yes, of course, no problem.' I hesitated. 'Do you think people will already have been to those more mainstream places? The sites are all very much inland.'

'Maybe, but we can't simply ignore them and sail past. We can do the visits in our style, not in a big ship way.'

'It will probably mean people staying off the ship, will that be Ok? We can't get to Luxor, visit the tombs and return to Hurghada in one day.'

'Check out the best hotels and let me know what you think.'

'Right ... it'll be expensive, reserving forty or more good rooms.'

'Get the costs, but you had better get on with the main programme too. We can add those in later.'

'Fantastic. "In the Wake of Vasco Da Gama" it is, then! Well, maybe not round the Cape, too lumpy and there's no shelter.' I was unable to keep the excitement out of my voice.

'Watch the costs, let me know when you're going where, and of course take a minder. I don't want you wandering about on your own, not that you wander around, I know that! You're good value, Amelia.'

What better compliment and encouragement could I ask for?

11

Madagascar
A Land of Exotic Beasties

Europe was Europe but now truly exotic lands lay ahead. Colour, warmth and excitements to banish February blues. Like Vasco da Gama our ship would sail the Indian Ocean and I could think of nowhere more mysterious than Madagascar. Not only might passengers see lemurs, a curious beast called a fossa and colourful chameleons, but also a very special tortoise. We would be the only small ship operating there.

Madagascar with its unique wildlife attracted many organisations, and I had dismissed the most obvious, settling for the Durrell Wildlife Conservation Trust. I knew our passengers would have been brought up on *My Family and Other Animals,* and Durrell had a team based there running various specialised projects, including one on the angonoka. I had a quick chat to keep Michael up to date.

'A what, Amelia? . . . What did you call it?'

'Angonoka. It's a tortoise, a very special one, the world's most endangered.' I too had only just heard of it through a conversation with an enthusiastic eco warrior in Jersey. The angonoka or ploughshare tortoise needed support. I had few real details of what the beastie was like and wondered what support for an animal encased in a solid shell entailed? Now only to be found in one place in the world, a remote area of coastal Madagascar, this stripy tortoise would provide further excitement in addition to the lemurs, birdlife and chameleons.

'Fine.' Michael's voice sounded distant. 'Just get on with it, we're running short of time. Keep in touch and good luck.' His attention had gone, moving back to the demanding figures and facts associated with establishing the new ship.

Cut off from the world on the shores of the Mozambique Channel, Baly Bay was genuinely remote, with no roads, no electricity, little drinking water and not even a good-sized village. The angonoka tortoise was specially adapted to the terrain. With a horny prong sweeping up in a curve between its front legs, it could tootle about on the rough ground without getting stuck. The high, domed carapace had radiating bands of brown and gold, creating a striking hexagonal pattern. It was a glamorous beast. Too glamorous. Finding one in the harsh, dry scrub was tricky, but worth the effort. A poacher, with one in the bag, would have funds for a year or so, though the dealers further down the line would make much, much more.

Chart number 3877 covered Madagascar's western shores labelled 'Baly Bay'. Anchoring in the bay seemed to me the only way to access the tortoises' home patch. But there were no useful soundings, no helpful depth contours. The whole of the bay was blank, a white area with the ominous word 'uncharted'. The isolation was a bonus for poachers, but for me it would be a major challenge. A ship wanting to access this unknown and probably shallow bay, judging by the surrounding land, would find it perilous. In addition, I would need to be sure we could land our passengers safely, comfortably and with no incidents. Then there was the actual tortoise.

Baly Bay had none of the romantic associations of the

African bush. It was not teeming with wildlife but dry, flat, scrubby country and, depending on the season, a vast lake lay between the shore and tortoise territory. Assuming I could make the ship's access and passenger landing possible, what about the tortoise? Would we be able to see one? Having eighty people wandering around the bush in the hopes of bumping into a tortoise would be a recipe for disaster.

Every element was high-risk, but I like a challenge. Feeling some reassurance I was on the right track would be encouraging. I gave HH a ring.

'Hello, it's me, Amelia, I've escaped from the Baltic and Greece. How are you?'

'Good, a little weary. Too much work. Where are you now, then?' His voice was flat, preoccupied. I wished I had not rung.

'London but going to Madagascar,' I ploughed on. 'I fly via Paris, I barely know my way round, but I know you do. What about meeting up there?' The moment I asked, I regretted it.

'Nope, sorry, I have to be in the US, but see you soon. Keep in touch and stay safe.' I made a mental note never to ring him: let him call me.

Simply getting to the world's fourth-largest island felt exotic, with an added element of not even being able to pronounce Madagascar's capital city. Antananarivo.

It was fun to be on an Air France flight. I could understand the majority of what was being said, thanks to my father's insistence I should learn French, and the in-flight lunch had included foie gras, unlike the utilitarian Scandinavian airline food that had been my diet recently. After two days of initial meetings, Hugo would be joining me, another reason to feel happy. Michael, anxious about the timetable, had insisted it would be both time efficient and cost effective for me to charter a plane if I felt it were necessary. With the refurbishment of the ship progressing fast, architects, shipwrights and interior designers were all hard at work. She would be ready in six months. At last, the project was a reality. I had been propelling a virtual ship from port to port, driving her round in my mind for months, but soon there would be passengers. The operations and the reality of my planning, recces, photos, notes and itineraries would soon become real. It was exciting and daunting. The European cruises had been approved, and now graced a glamorous brochure. My photos and descriptions of the alluring destinations I fervently hoped would prove irresistible.

When I had begun the job three years earlier a plane's every bump, bounce and change of engine note had made me freeze with terror, but by now I felt almost relaxed in the air. I had learned the value of a window seat: an aerial view provided the lie of the land, possible bays and anchorages as well as an idea of depths as deep blue sea changed to a muddy ochre.

Madagascar. A green fuzz of trees spread out beneath the wing. Woodland thinned, giving way to ridges of deep red earth, spattered with clumps of bush. Baobab, with their awkward, misshapen grey branches and bulbous trunks, were unmistakable. It did look quite African. Soon there were arid valleys, barren grey ridges and mountain peaks reared up closer as the plane began to lose height. A vivid network of green paddy fields whizzed close by underneath the fuselage. I held my breath, letting it out with a sigh of relief when the plane bumped over the uneven tarmac. Madagascar already seemed exotic.

'I am Aristide. Bonjour. Welcome.' Tall and slim, he held

out a cool hand to shake mine. 'I am your guide in Tana. Hello.' *Tana* – better than *Antananarivo* – at least now I could pronounce where I was. Aristide curled over the driving wheel as we drew out of the airport. It was years since I had been in a battered Deux Chevaux and there was no mistaking it, he resembled a chameleon.

'Aristide, is it far into town?'

'Today the traffic is not good, and here in Tana we have only one road.'

Barely wide enough for two cars to pass, the road wound like a grey snake along the top of an embankment. On either side bright green paddy fields, divided by low walls of vivid red earth, spread across the valley, sun glinting on the water among the precise rows of rice. Everywhere I looked was vivid with colour, bold and vibrant.

Tucked at my feet lay my new rucksack. Less bulky than the camera case, it was made of rubberised black cotton and had two small pockets on the front, each with a magnetic buckle and chic silver clasp. Hugo, to my surprise, was now working as a model, strutting his stuff along the red carpets of Paris, Tokyo and Italy. His first appearance had been in Milan, and he had returned with this swanky Prada rucksack. A present for my travels. Madagascar would be its first outing.

'Please could you stop a moment, Artistide? I'd like to take a photo – that's a really pretty group of buildings.'

He pulled as far as possible off the narrow road and the Deux Chevaux leant precariously towards the paddy field below. Lorries lumbered past, only inches away. A short distance across the rice, perched on a mound out of the water, was a picturesque settlement. It could have been Marie Antoinette's farm at Versailles with its steeply tiled roofs and green surroundings, except for the rice and the string of drying washing.

Aristide, unconcerned by the lumbering lorries, waited patiently in the battered little car. This, I was to learn, was a Malagasy trait. Life went on slowly with no great rush and Aristide had plenty of tolerance, plus a cheerful charm and informality. Providing I made my requirements clear and was not impatient, he would happily organise whatever I wanted, no matter how strange it seemed to him. But without direction he was equally happy to sit, red Coke can in hand, and snooze, leaning against anything convenient.

Tana was like a colourful patchwork tablecloth spread over steep valleys and hills. The town consisted of a tangle of ramshackle houses, chaotic street markets and steep stairways juxtaposed with elegant villas and once-grand buildings. It was a charming place, with the added attraction, I quickly discovered, of good food. Eclairs, dainty macaroons, exotic ice creams, golden baguettes, and even foie gras were all available. France had left its mark. Elegant ladies in patterned dresses, their heads topped by matching turbans, strolled the streets. Baskets balanced casually on their heads, a baby tucked into a fold of their dress or a toddler tugging at their hands, they were like a flock of jewelled birds. The men, by contrast, ambled unhurriedly, dressed in faded shorts, well-worn T-shirts and decrepit trainers. Many sported a jaunty hat. Hats of all different styles and colours were ubiquitous. Aristide told me that in Madagascar, as well as being decorative, they were a means of communication. Everyone had a hat and particularly the young men. If a young fellow wanted to advertise he was looking for a wife, he would tuck a flower in his hat band when going to market.

After a couple of days of meetings, it was time for Baly

Bay. Aristide led me across the lumpy runway, my suitcase effortlessly balanced on his shoulder. Little plumes of red soil puffed up at every step, settling in a fine russet dust on my new cream coloured canvas shoes. The front door of the plane opened and a tiny man in blue trousers and white shirt swung out like an ape, bounced on the wheel strut and landed on the ground. My pilot.

I was settled next to him in the cockpit and he began flicking switches. I waved to Aristide, now enveloped by a cloud of red dust and scrabbled under my seat, feeling for the buckles of my safety belt. Snapping it together, I pulled it tight as the plane began to shake, the whole flimsy machine wobbling violently as he revved the engine, going through the pre-takeoff checks. There was no chatting with traffic control or queuing on the runway, we simply taxied across to the tarmac and immediately gathered speed to bump along the strip. My diminutive pilot peered about, straining to see over the instrument dashboard that curved higher than his head. It completely obscured his view, but once we were airborne and the plane level, he could see. All became smooth, the clouds of dust fell away and below lay Tana.

Inside me grew a little bubble of excitement, I had never chartered a plane before, but even this frail, wobbling machine with its unconvincing pilot was unmistakably the start of an adventure. I recognised the road into town, and there was what I had thought of as Marie Antoinette's farm surrounded by watery paddy fields. Hills rolled past slowly and before long the landscape became greener and there were the pompoms of palm trees. After about thirty minutes the pilot turned left, and we followed a broken line of white waves where the waters of the Mozambique Channel met the russet shoreline of Madagascar. Below there was not the slightest indication of habitation let alone a landing strip. Anxious I might distract him, but unable to help myself, I shouted at his ear:

'Have you been to Baly Bay? To Soalala before?'

'Non, I have never been there.'

Crammed into my jacket pocket was the chart, so I pulled it out and spread it on my knees, hoping to work out where we were. I knew the settlement of Soalala was on the southeast shore of the bay, but where was it? Baly Bay, that wide expanse of shallow uncharted water should be easy to recognise. We flew on along the coast. Below, the landscape became arid and beige, just a few skeletons of dead trees breaking the monotony. By my reckoning, we should have been there by now. Still there were no signs of habitation, no villages or huts, just an occasional spindly track squiggling like a string of spaghetti across the dry earth. The plane banked, turned to the left again and a big bay opened up ahead. This must be it. Baly Bay. This was what I had come so far to see. I knew it would be shallow, but from the air, the colour of the water to my right, the open sea, changed rapidly from deep turquoise to pale green and then a dirty reddish brown. It looked horribly shallow. Desiccated trees, leafless arms stretching up to catch us, swept under the wings. The only indication we had reached the landing strip was a sudden absence of bushes in the scrubby brown landscape. We thumped down and the plane jumped, bumping up into the air again, finally slowing to a wobbling stop.

As I flung open the door, the heat, laden with salty humidity, slapped me in the face like a damp flannel. But after years of chill Scottish winters and dark February days, it felt glorious.

'Are you going straight back?' I shouted to the pilot through the open door.

'Oui, I return Tana,' he said cheerfully.

'Right. Merci. Un moment, I have given your office number to my son. He'll be at the airport tomorrow. OK?'

'But maybe not me...'

I grasped my bag to run quickly away, wanting to escape the swirling dust as the plane taxied towards a line of thicker scrub, turned and bounced back along the open track gathering speed. Like an angry white hornet, it lifted off the ground, quickly becoming a distant dot.

With the noise of the hornet fading away, the only sound was a soft shushing of waves. The coastal humidity of Soalala fell over me and my glamorous Prada rucksack began to stick to my back. The tortoise man, head of the angonoka project, had been detailed to meet me but there was no one. Standing in the sweltering sunshine, I wondered in which direction I should walk.

'Oh, sorry, sorry, I am here. I am here.' A slight figure ran out of the scrub, shouting and waving. 'Sorry, sorry.'

'It's Ok, don't worry. You must be Angelo. I've only just landed, no problem.'

'Good afternoon. I am so very pleased to meet you,' he panted. We shook hands formally. Angelo, I knew had spent time in the UK, working on a course in conservation, hence his excellent English.

'Shall we go? The boat is over here.' He led the way along a tiny track twisting and turning through the spiny bushes, a desiccated grey. As I followed, spiky seed heads snapped off from the grasses trailing over the path. They stuck to my shoes. As more and more became lodged over my toes, their sharp prickles pierced the canvas. I began to hop from one patch of bare red earth to the next. Angelo, whose wide brown feet were clad in make-shift sandals, sewn from strips of tyre and inner tube, strode on ahead, untroubled by the spiky balls. Before long, the scrub thinned and we arrived onto coarse sand at the bay's edge. Stretching in front of me was a huge expanse of unruffled water, glassy and still, barely a ripple moving on the muddy surface. I had been expecting a traditional wooden dugout, maybe with an outrigger on one side for balance and a couple of paddles, but there on the beach lay a modern fibreglass boat about eight-foot-long. It was white, with neatly painted blue bulwarks and thwarts and a ten horsepower Yamaha fitted at the stern. Together we pushed the boat into the water, Angelo lithely jumped over the transom and I scrambled over a gunwale. Water streamed from his sandals, while my hedgehog-like shoes were now a sodden, muddy red and still covered with spiny balls.

'Do you mind if we go to the village first, Emilia?' he asked, screwing up his eyes against the sun, 'I would like you to meet the chief. I have talked with him already, but he wants another consultation.'

'Yes, of course. Whatever you like will be fine for me.'

'The people in the village must be happy for the boat to come, with all the visitors. It is their village, and they are really important for us. They watch and tell us if there are poachers. It's their land.'

Chugging across the bay in the boat created a breeze and the sticky humidity eased. It was a picture-postcard scene, this unexplored tropical bay. White sandy beaches and swaying coconut palms lined the shores. It was tempting to drift off, let the afternoon slide away, have a swim, maybe a snooze to dream of HH, naturally with a pina colada. But this was work, even if it had the appearance of a holiday. I had my most demanding, potentially disastrous programme to set up. Would the ship's long overnight passages to reach this bay be sensible? Would the ship then be able to access the bay? Where could we get the passengers safely ashore? What about the tortoise? I was responsible for every element, from the ship's safety to the passenger's enjoyment. And then there would be expectations from the village and of course the Durrell organisation too.

Using the vital chart, I began looking around, trying to work out the logistics. I must fill in some of the blanks for the captain. He would need all the information I could acquire if he were to bring the ship into this unknown bay. As we chugged crossed the open water heading for the opposite side, the water began to change colour, becoming a deep blue and I could no longer see the bottom. This western side of Madagascar has a significant tidal range, and I would be relying on Angelo's help with the village fishermen to get information about the tides and currents.

On the south shore, smooth grey trunks of coconut palms curved out over the water; underneath them in the shade was a jumble of bright colours. As the boat grew near I realised these were the villagers. The boat scrunched onto the sand, children peeped from behind the long cotton skirts of their mothers, who smiled and waved. Men in shorts and T-shirts watched silently, less certain of my arrival. I jumped out, smiling and hitching the Prada rucksack onto my shoulder. An old man, with creased, mahogany skin, stooped and bony with age, separated himself from the gaggle and came slowly across the sand towards me. He was dressed for an occasion. Long shorts, tattered and now faded by the sun, might once have graced a Caribbean beach with their bold green and yellow patterns of palm trees. On top, he wore a worn tropical white dinner jacket several sizes too large, the sleeves hung over his hands. This was the head of the village, the all-important chief.

'Bonjour.' Bony, ebony black and smooth, his strong hand gripped mine. His deeply wrinkled face was topped with tight wiry curls, flecked with grey. Still holding my hand, he led me up the beach to the shade. Four palm trunks had been arranged in a square; he pointed to one and I sat down. The other men of the village followed, settling on the other logs like fledglings waiting to be fed. Angelo and the chief waited for the rows of men to be still before stepping into the middle of the expectant gathering. A hush descended, broken only by the rustling of coconut palms and the distant chattering and laughter of women and children in clusters further along the beach.

Angelo talked, steadily and without a break for over an hour. The warm breeze blew in from the bay, and I did my best to look attentive, but my bum grew numb. I tried not to wriggle on the hard log, but I wiggled my toes in the cool sand listening to the palms whispering overhead. What could he be saying? After Angelo, it was the turn of others. Three men gave speeches and then at last the chief stood up. He spoke for another hour. Not a head nodded, and by now I was too uncomfortable even to doze. Madagascar, I was learning, was all about speeches as well as hats. Suddenly, without any sign of a conclusion, everyone stood up and walked away. The chief too stepped out of the square and ambled off, then flopped on the sand to prop himself against the trunk of a palm. He began to pick his teeth.

'You Ok, Emilia?'

'Yup, fine thanks, Angelo.' I stood up shakily, pins and needles fizzing in my legs. 'Did that go all right?'

'Yes, the men are happy, now for the women.' He grinned, with a flash of white teeth. 'They are much fussier.'

We walked along the beach to join the ladies. With their hair piled in curls and whorls on the top of their heads, they were an attractive sight. Children were shushed and told to stop rolling in the sand. This was a serious business.

Angelo launched into speech number two. This time there was general discussion. The ladies were full of questions and occasionally he pointed at me. By now, the chief lay prone on the sand, exhausted by his efforts, his loud snores floating across the sand. It was an idyllic place, even if my bum and legs were numb again.

'Emilia?' Angelo turned towards me. 'The ladies want to know which CDs you would like. They are very pleased with a new one they have just got, it's called "Swinging Safari". Would you like that?' I imagined Bert Kaempfert bellowing out of a ghetto blaster, Swinging Safari rippling out under the palms and across the still blue waters of Baly Bay.

'Angelo, I was thinking more of some village songs? Would it be possible to have their songs? Songs they sing about life here.'

With plans now outlined, we re-embarked, travelling across the darkening water. The late afternoon light was soft, and the air was cooler as I followed Angelo between the mud houses and huts, tightly clustered on a low-lying peninsula. This was Soalala. There were no looping electricity wires, no cars and not even a motorbike; no glass in the windows, no doors, only cloth curtains hung across doorways for a little privacy. Roofs were made from palm leaves with one or two pieces of corrugated iron. The houses were low, the walls made from clods of deep red soil pressed tightly together, with an occasional shell deeply embedded, pale and glossy in the falling light. The paths were beaten earth, packed smooth by bare feet. Chickens pecked about, dogs lounged and over everything hung a thin haze of fragrant wood smoke.

'Here we are. Welcome to my house.' Angelo pushed open a rickety gate in the bamboo fence, almost entirely covered by the vine of a rampant gourd. This was his private little patch separate from the street. 'It is an honour to have you as our guest.'

Inside the fence was a concrete bungalow with a proper wooden door and one glazed window to each side. Two papaya trees grew upright and slim, their heavy green fruit bunched high up under the glossy leaves. Chickens scratched at the concrete base of a well and two cats lay stretched on the top, soaking up warmth from the concrete. Neither the cats nor chickens stirred as I entered his little domain.

'Hello, are you there?' Hugo's voice was clear and excited.

'Yes! Lovely to hear you. Are you in Tana?'

'Yup, at the airport, I've met the pilot. What's Soalala like?'

'Well, let's just say it's a good thing the village is not part of the passenger plan. But the bay is pretty. A bit shallow, but probably Ok. Let's hope the tortoises are worth it.'

'The pilot's waving at me, I'd better go. He doesn't speak any English.'

'Must be a different one from mine. I'm here, at the strip, so see you soon. It only took me about forty minutes. Can't wait!'

To have Hugo with me would be helpful and his artist's eye would provide a different perspective. Plus, I would have the pleasure of watching him draw and of exploring together.

'I need to get some supplies, water and food,' Angelo told me. 'Things we'll need for the night at the project.'

'That's fine, I'm happy sitting here, waiting for Hugo, no problem.'

Watching his boat's wake spread in a widening V through the glassy blue waters of Baly Bay was one of those wonderful moments of anticipation. The morning sun grew stronger. Plover, dainty and smart with their black chest bands, pottered busily along the water's edge, their thin legs elongated by reflections in the still water. A heron stalked slowly along the opposite shore and far away, visible with my binoculars, high above the mangroves to the south, a fish eagle quartered the water. Time spun out at African speed. Where was the plane? I tried not to look at my watch, again, it was only a moment since I had last looked.

It was now two hours since we had spoken, since he had said they were leaving, and I knew it was a short, forty-minute flight. Angelo had returned and was waiting too, supplies carefully boxed, tied with orange plastic string and stowed between the thwarts. My thoughts spiralled but there was nothing I could do except wait. The plane had only one engine. Hugo was my only son. I had already lost one. A mosquito whined in my ear. After my sleepless night it was no surprise, but how had it managed to get into my ear? The buzzing grew louder. I shook my head. The buzz turned into a plane.

Jumping up, I ran to the edge of the strip, heedless of the spiky seeds. The plane banked, then turned back over the sea. It turned again, losing height, this time heading for the dirt track. A cloud of dust erupted as it hit the earth, it bounced up several feet and then came down again in a series of hops, jumping along to a halt by the bushes at the end of the clearing. Just in time. The wings waggled stiffly with the effort. A door was flung open and Hugo, all six foot four of him, uncoiled into the sun. He shook himself and waved.

I had always wanted to meet a loved one like this, to run, arms outstretched along a runway. Dropping my rucksack, I set off across the earth. Hugo spread his arms wide too and ran to meet me.

'That was quite a landing,' I panted, 'Are you Ok?'

'Yup. I'm fine. I'm here! I've christened the pilot "Penfold".'

'Penfold! Dangermouse's trusty assistant, the hamster who went to pieces under pressure?' When the boys were small, no post-school tea had been complete without watching one episode of Dangermouse before homework.

'Yup, his twitch is . . . interesting.'

'What do you mean, twitch?'

'He has a twitch, it pulls his head back, then his arms. It gets faster when he's taking off.' He grinned at my look of horror.

'Makes getting airborne a bit bouncy too, like the landing.'

'Mmm, that *was* a series of bounds.'

'Well, we've got him for the flight back to Tana. Apparently, the plane isn't wanted for a few days. I don't think he's keen to try to find Soalala again!'

We walked towards the boat.

'I'll ask Angelo to fix him somewhere to stay. We're going to walk inland and camp at the project for two nights.'

'Where did you stay? Couldn't the pilot stay there?'

It had been an unforgettable, long night at the bungalow. Angelo, nervously hospitable, had asked his wife, Mirana, to cook something special. An overflowing tin bowl of rice, accompanied by another slopping with a thin yellow liquid, bones breaking the surface. Mirana had sacrificed one of their precious scrawny chickens to make me a fiery curry. The little house was one room and Angelo had suggested I would be cooler if I slept outside on the veranda. Not a breath of wind had stirred the air through the long humid night. Hot, sticky and with the curry rebelling, the hours of darkness had felt interminable as I lay on the plastic-covered mattress. Cats prowled, squabbled and screeched. Mosquitoes whined. Being cautious I had brought my own mini mozzie net, cleverly designed with little poles to stretch a mesh hoop over my face, providing a few precious inches of mozzie-free space. They had bombarded the netting ceaselessly, whining and buzzing inches above my nose, convinced they would find a hole.

'I'll tell you about it later, Hugo. But let's get going now. I'll sort something out with Angelo as we cross the bay.'

For every two feet I climbed up, I slid back one as the soft sand slipped from under my still-spiky shoes. Would people who were probably in their sixties and maybe even seventies, manage this? Would they even *want* to? All to see a tortoise. Even if it were the world's most endangered. I was rapidly losing my nerve; the number of hurdles was becoming simply too many.

'You Ok, M? You look a bit pink.'

'I'm fine. Hot but fine.' I panted, catching my breath as we reached the top. 'Wow, what a view . . . it's like an English park. Look at those huge trees.'

Open grassland dotted with large, shapely trees stretched ahead. Their spreading branches made patches of deep shade and in the far distance, a lake shimmered. Had there been cattle flicking their ears against the flies and chewing the cud in the cool of the shade, it could have been Surrey. I slid down the slope to join Hugo and Angelo's team of lads waiting patiently in the shade. A bamboo pole stretched between the shoulders of two young lads bearing our supplies. This Livingstone-explorer scene was marred by the bulging plastic carrier bags. Traditional rustic, hand-woven, baskets would have been photogenic, I felt.

'Can I take an end?' Hugo asked.

'Eh?'

Hugo rustled up his French. 'Puis je vous aidez?'

'Non, merci. ees Ok.' The bearer's face creased into a broad smile and the pole-party set off, singing as they went; moving swiftly they disappeared among the trees. Angelo came next, then Hugo and I brought up the rear. Walking along the flat sandy path, knowing there were no African-type carnivores lurking to devour us, was easy, it was an idyllic stroll. The patches of deep shade provided welcome relief as the sun grew stronger, and occasionally we stopped to look at a plant or birds. In the next clearing Angelo stopped pointing into the canopy above. A pair of deep brown eyes locked with mine. The lads quietly tucked the pole ends into crooks of trees and our supplies hung safely off the ground above a trail of ants. We all stared up at the lemurs.

'Sifka,' said Angelo, quietly. In the foliage thirty feet above was an arboreal teddy bears' picnic. Lounging overhead were five creamy-white lemurs. Sitting casually amongst the branches, their relaxed limbs dangled down, long-fingered furry feet and hands embraced the boughs. Their faces, in contrast to the white fur, were a rich chocolate, and their ears were like tiny crescent moons nestling in a milky-white ruff of fur. Soft brown eyes surveyed us steadily, quizzical rather than fearful.

'They look as if they're studying us as much as we're studying them, Angelo. Aren't they frightened?' I asked quietly. 'Are they always so easy to see?' If I were able to promise a sighting of lemurs, then a hot two-hour walk to see a tortoise began to seem possible.

'Usually, there are some around here,' he replied. 'They know they're safe and the lads usually know where to find them. The poachers are only after the angonoka.'

As we walked on, the trees thinned, giving way to open grassland with occasional pools of water rapidly evaporating in the hot sun. As the wet season ended the lake began to dry, making the walk feasible. Fresh new grass was interspersed with stretches of drying mud densely patterned with a trailing network of bird tracks. Avocets, precisely marked in black and white, were busy in the remaining patches of water; sweeping up-turned beaks back and forth through the shallows they hunted for frogs and water bugs. Sacred ibis, glossy and black, stalked and prodded the muddy edges of the pools, seeking out snails. There were teal, ruddy-headed pochard and elegant grey herons too and no sound apart from birds and the breeze.

If I could guarantee the lake would have evaporated, the birdlife would be abundant and the teddy-bear lemurs assembled to order, it might work. The village dancing was predictable, but what about the tortoises? Would people be happy with this walk? Two hours each way to see a tortoise? It was a big ask.

12

Madagascar
A Land of Dangerous Beasties

At last it arrived, spreading its long, spindly legs all over the table.

'What! M, that is ridiculous.' Hugo exploded in horror.

'Well, after Soalala and my night among the chicken shit, spider crab with clove butter is too good to pass.' I grinned at him happily. 'Do you want some?'

'No way.' His choice of fish and chips did look appealingly uncomplicated. Covering the domed spiky carapace with a napkin, I took hold of the body pulling it away from the legs.

'Oh!' I peered inside. 'There's nothing there, no crabmeat, nothing. It's empty. I'm going to ask for another.'

'You can't ask for another,' Hugo rebuked me sternly. 'This is Diego Suarez not London, or even Tana.'

Maybe he was right, but Diego, named by the Portuguese in the sixteenth century, had a misleading air of sophistication. It was Madagascar's deep-water port, a huge natural harbour engulfing a lone craggy island, strategically on the western side of the Indian Ocean. This safe haven had been fought over by the Japanese, the French and the British. After an hour's flight from Tana, we had spent the afternoon wandering the centre, a small collection of elegant colonial buildings covering only two or three streets. The hotel had a huge, clean and warm pool, plus I had had a delightful massage. I had hoped this Malagasy chic extended to the restaurant. It had seemed so promising. Our table on the wooden veranda had a crisp white tablecloth, folded damask napkins, sparkling glasses and a view of the bay. The heady scent of frangipani almost succeeded in overcoming the pong emanating from the fish processing plant next door. At my elbow was a gin and tonic.

A slim waitress appeared carrying a replacement giant orange spider crab accompanied by a bowl of steaming melted butter. The heady scent of cloves wafted enticingly around our table.

'Wow! That's hot.' Hugo pushed his chair back, away from the clouds of steam and stretching legs. I dipped a finger in the butter and licked it.

'Scrummie, it's really lovely. Here, have a taste. Now for the crab.' Using my napkin again as protection from heat and spikes, I wrenched open body number two. A shining, writhing mass greeted me. Where there should have been a mound of delicious brown and white crab meat, minute jet black beetles seethed. Having survived the boiling, they were now released and made a dash for freedom. Black bodies poured in a stream out of the shell and over the white tablecloth in a glossy torrent.

We both jumped, scrambling away from the table.

Breakfast next morning was reassuringly predictable, with hot croissants, strong black coffee and mango juice. My mobile buzzed.

'Roger. Good morning, how's things in Tana? All good in the Durrell office?' Roger, my contact at the Durrell Centre, I knew by now was a glass half-empty person. It was likely to be a down-beat conversation, but I was determined to sweep him into my enthusiasm.

'Yes, thanks, we're in Diego now. Have you had a chance to look at the email I sent?' I was afraid he would only see difficulties. I felt confident, assuming I could make the logistics work, it would be a memorable day and would justify chartering a plane.

I listened while he listed the problems.

'Please don't worry.' I tried to prevent exasperation creeping into my voice. 'We can work round these things.' I waited until he came to an uncertain finish before outlining the potential for the charity if the visit were to come off. 'You say you can collect up a few tortoises and "position" them. Well! That will be great, so we can guarantee to see them, fantastic.' Bolder now, I went on, 'And loos? They are a vital element. Do you think it would be possible to dig a couple of long drops? I think we'll need two. Can that be done?'

I knew exactly what I was asking for. Digging deep holes vertically into soft sand to create a long drop would take time and effort. 'A bit of privacy too, please. Nothing fancy, just a bamboo fence with some sacking and a seat of some kind, with a pole each side. I'm afraid we will need seats, some people may not be comfortable with squatting. The poles? Oh, they are for people to pull themselves up by.' He found it incredible I was proposing to ask eighty people to land by rubber boat onto a beach where so many white faces had never been seen before and then walk to see a tortoise. Maybe he was right, but Baly was everything I wanted – birds, lemurs, striking scenery, kids, the village, and the most desirable tortoise in the world.

I had to make it work. Besides, I had promised the head man.

'Also,' I went on, 'the path will need staking every thirty or forty yards. People will then be able to walk at their own speed without getting lost. We'll bring water, lots of water, from the ship. But don't worry, we've got a few months to go through all this. I will have a few hours in Tana before I leave, so let's meet and go over it all then.'

I sensed he was beginning to understand and to join in.

'Really? The village ladies would like to make cakes... it's their idea? That would be wonderful. Yes, everyone would love that, but please make sure it's costed properly. Those costs, tea and dancing must go direct to them. We will give some books for the school, reference books in French, of course.'

The ancient Toyota Land Cruiser was doing well. It ground slowly through the mud of a deeply rutted track, leaving a plume of diesel fumes in its wake. It was now three hours since leaving the shores of Diego's huge bay and so far we had covered only forty miles. As we drove west through a lush forest, the terrain grew increasingly broken. At last we crested a ridge and began to drop downhill, through a forest of looping lianas and thick woodland. The huge leaves thinned until suddenly we burst into blinding sunshine. Ahead lay a white beach stretching to a turquoise sea.

'We ave arrived, Emily. Ere we are,' Mijoro, our guide from Diego, triumphantly flung open the car door. Heat rose from the sand burning through the soles of our shoes. A line of flotsam including battered coconuts, scraps of dried seaweed, piles of broken chunks of coral and silvery shells, marked the top of the tide. There were no footprints, no discarded flip flops or abandoned mineral water bottles. The beach was pristine, private and perfect. In the distance, hazy in the heat, I could just make out the islands I had come to check. They beckoned tantalisingly, more than eight nautical miles east into the Mozambique Channel. Studying them on the Admiralty chart in the grey light of the Fulham Road, they looked perfect. As Madagascar did not merit a helpful pilot book, I was relying on charts, my maritime experience and nous from my days in Scotland. Again I had to fulfil the tricky combination of every aspect being achievable for the ship, with an acceptable landing place and also unforgettable for the passengers. I was optimistic one of the islands would have the right combination. The surrounding waters were a suitable depth for anchoring and offered shelter, if necessary, among the mini archipelago. One island was craggy and the other shaped like a dog's bone. The craggy one, if I were lucky, might be composed of Madagascar's famous 'tsingy', the jagged karst limestone with its unique vegetation, and possibly even some lemurs. The chart showed the dog-bone one having beaches on either side of the middle section. If I were really lucky, there might be good coral in the shallows for snorkelling. The only way to know was to go and see. The urge to succumb to a dip, laze in the sand and fall into holiday mode in these completely idyllic surroundings was powerful. I pulled off my shoes, buried my toes in the sand, scooped up my hair and crammed it under my hat.

'Please come with me. I take you to meet Jean and Francoise, they cook for you.' Mijoro looked down the beach. 'They live down here. We walk, Ok?' He waved a hand towards the trees at the back of the beach, 'Ere is the hut for you.' Tucked under the shade of the coconut palms bordering the sand, was a simple wooden hut with a makuti palm roof: our 'beach-front villa'.

'I'll go and meet them,' I told Hugo, 'but you can stay and have a swim, make the most of it. It'll be a busy day tomorrow.'

Hugo had already taken off his T-shirt.

'Mijoro,' he asked pointing out to sea, 'is that where we're going? Is that Nosy Lakandava?'

A look of terror spread across Mijoro's smooth face.

'Non! Non! My friend. You must never do that. Bad, bad *fady,* very bad. You point like this.' He lifted his arm with his fingers tightly curled into a fist, only his partially uncurled index finger aiming forward, his knuckle pointed at the island.

'Ah, you mean like this?' Hugo carefully copied him. 'Ok? And what's fady?'

'Oui, that is right. We are ok now. No bad fady, no taboo. Spirits happy!' They high fived, grinning at each other.

Our hut was basic with no running water, no electricity or shower, but the view, with the shutters propped open, was holiday-poster stunning. Inside were a small table with two tumblers, a candle wedged into a glass full of sand, a box of matches and a china basin: these were our 'facilities'.

'See you later.' I called over my shoulder, 'Reserve a lounger for me, please. There might be a rush!'

Mijoro and I walked along the sparkling sand, carrying supplies for the French couple, owners of our 'villa'. Living in the bush, hours from a shop, fresh meat, veg and some passion fruit would be welcome. I returned to find Hugo lazing in the sea.

'It's not as remote as you thought. Look over there, looks like a tractor has been here.' He pointed his knuckle further along the beach where a giant caterpillar track appeared from the water crossing the beach to the palms at the top.

'That's caused by turtles, not a tractor. They make their nests in the softer sand at the top.' I answered joining him in the silky warm water.

I poured a bottle of water over my head to wash off the salt. Soon the light would be gone and we must get everything ready before we joined our neighbours for supper. It would be pitch black by the time we came back but, if we were lucky, we might even see a turtle haul itself out of the water, its flippers making those caterpillar tracks. Madagascar has a big tidal range and spring tides were as helpful to turtles as to me.

We made up the two narrow iron bedsteads with proper sheets and Hugo hung a mosquito net from a rafter above each bed. New and intact, the nets were the only things I had stipulated to Mijoro as being vital. After tucking the edges under our mattress, putting toothbrushes and paste ready beside the plastic washing up bowl, we sauntered along the beach. Shadows from the trunks and fringed leaves of the coconut palms made swaying patterns across the sand in the soft light of evening.

'Thanks so much for supper, delicious,' I said, standing up to take our leave.

It had been a long day and two plastic glasses of wine with chicken and fruit were making me sleepy.

Specks of mica in the sand made it silvery and luminous, lit only by the stars. A perfect night I thought for turtles, but we saw none, just millions of stars in the inky-black up-turned bowl of the heavens.

In the shadow of the palms, Hugo flashed his torch, illuminating the hut. Instantly moths, bugs and biting beasties joined us as we moved inside and got ready for the night. Hugo fidgeted with his bed.

'What are you doing?' I asked impatiently, torch clamped between my teeth. I parted the mozzie net, untucking it slightly from under the mattress to open the side.

'I'm checking my bed for scorpions,' he said still messing about with his sheets.

As I squeezed through the mozzie net gap, I put my left hand in the middle of the bed for balance. The candle by the window flickered creating a maze of dancing patterns, the perfect cover for a startled scorpion. He darted out from under my pillow. Curling his translucent tail, he stabbed his barb deep into the ring finger of my left hand. Instantly, a red-hot needle of pain shot up my arm and on up the side of my neck. The pain jabbed into my ear, spread into my armpit and then down to my waist. I could feel it reaching my thigh and then my knee. My hand, arm and neck throbbed, and my heart began to thump wildly. Everything went fuzzy.

'Hugo.' I tried to keep the panic out of my voice. 'Hugo, I've been stung by a scorpion.'

'What! No, are you sure? Keep calm… It's probably nothing.'

'I'm trying to, but…' Swaying with pain, I collapsed onto the bed. A truck seemed to be driving over my arm: it thundered up and down, back and forth, reversing and grinding over and over again.

'Lie down, here have some water. Try to stay calm. I'll go down the beach and see what the French people know. Won't be long.' He dragged on his Timberland boots and disappeared, the sound of his scrunching steps running across the sand fading fast. In that typical African way, Mijoro and our driver had melted into the forest long ago. Gone to find friends somewhere.

Silence fell over the hut. Blood pounded in my head. The truck thundered on, grinding up and down my arm. Will I die? How long does it take to die from a scorpion sting? The torch flickered, the beam died to a glow and then darkness enveloped me. The candle had blown out ages ago. Maybe I would die. The poison had seeped further and now my left foot felt numb too. Dying in a hut in Madagascar had not been the plan.

'Mummy!' Hugo's voice was sharp with fear. 'I'm back. Are you Ok?'

'Not great,' I croaked. 'Hurts like hell, but I'm not dead yet.'

'They're no good, they don't know anything about scorpions. But they say I might get a phone signal if I go up the hill at the back of the beach. Weird to live here and know so little about anything.'

'Take my Blackberry.' I squeezed the words out. 'Try Mark, he might know. Be careful.' Mark, one of my three brothers, lived in Kenya, and I knew had been to Madagascar.

'Have you drunk anything? Here, have a drink before I go. Water's always good.' Hugo pushed a bottle of water through the mozzie net; he studied me by the light of his torch.

'You Ok?'

'Yup.'

The sound of snapping twigs retreated followed by the crashing of undergrowth as he fought his way uphill, battling through tropical vegetation in the dark. My heart seemed to be flopping about. My arm throbbed deep inside and the skin was numb. I lay in the dark, waiting. Waiting to slip into a coma.

'Mummy?' His voice surprised me, I had not heard him return. 'Here! Come on! Wake up, drink some more water. Let me light this candle again.' I was barely conscious.

'Mark's not there,' he said. 'But apparently, he'll be home in an hour, I'll try again then. Let's see your finger.' He pushed aside the netting and sat on the edge of the narrow bed in flickering candlelight. My hand and fingers were black. Tentacles of deep red tracked in a network of spidery lines from my wrist and up my arm to the elbow. The whole arm was swollen, blue-black.

'Hugo, I need a pee.'

'Ok, can you stand?' Cautiously, I pulled myself to the edge of the bed while he held open the net for me.

'Hang on a moment. Let me give your shoes a shake. Make sure there's no more of the buggers hiding in there. Here, use this, take the washing up bowl.'

His second attempt to get help was a little better.

'I got Mark, here, have another drink. He says he doesn't know about scorpions, but he'll try a mate of his who's a vet in Tana. I've to ring again in another hour. How is it now?'

'Pretty hellish.' I tried to sound less frightened than I felt. 'Feels like a sledgehammer banging down on my hand... pain shoots up my arm.'

'Sounds horrid but keep going. You'll be Ok.'

'Do you think if I was going to die, I would have done it by now?'

'Well, you're not going to die. But you're probably right. I'll go up the hill again soon.'

This time Mark had an answer. His friend said there were no fatal scorpions in Madagascar. I immediately started to feel better.

The dawn light, pink, golden and turquoise, rose above

the trees behind the hut where Hugo had been scrambling about searching for a Vodafone signal. It was a relief to have the darkness fade. Through the open door of the hut I could see the idyllic view. Coconut palms, the empty beach and clear blue water, all growing brighter in the strengthening light, banishing the horrors of the dark. I had allocated two days for these inspections, thinking the small islands would not take any longer. Yesterday had been day one, today was the recce day, a full day to check them. Tomorrow we had a flight to Tana, a few hours to wait and then Air France home. Over my hand and arm, the imaginary truck ground on. Just the slightest movement made me faint. Spending a day bouncing eight miles out to sea in a dugout in strong sunshine was impossible.

'I'll go, Mother.' Hugo was firm. 'You stay here, it's not a problem. I know what to do and Mijoro will help, he'll be here in a moment. He said "early".' My heart was less jumpy now, although my brain, sluggish and befuddled, was still overwhelmed by pain.

'Tell Mijoro . . . tell Mijoro he must find another outboard motor. You are not going eight miles from shore with only one small engine.'

Hugo looked sceptical.

'Yes, Hugo.' I was determined. 'I mean it. If you go soon, I reckon you can be back by two. Have you got water?'

'Of course,' came the indignant reply.

'If you're not back by three, there'll still be enough daylight for the driver to get me back to Diego. I'll get a plane and find you.'

'Don't be ridiculous.'

'I'm not. Take the mirror from my rucksack,' I told him. 'If anything happens, if the engine stops, you're drifting, whatever, use it to flash to make a signal. They put mirrors into life rafts for exactly that reason.'

I knew I sounded melodramatic, but he would be in a small canoe on an empty sea with unknown currents.

He knew better than to argue with me. Reluctantly he delved into my rucksack. 'Sure you'll be Ok? Let me tie back the mozzie net so you get some air. Have you enough water?'

'Don't worry about me, I'll be fine.'

Draping a towel round his neck, he crammed on his baseball cap and pushed a bottle of water into his backpack.' He grinned, unable to suppress his excitement at the adventure. 'See you soon.'

Without his reassuring presence, the hut was lonely. I crammed his pillow under my throbbing arm and dozed. The truck was still at work, driving up and down, but my heart no longer jumped and beat irregularly. The sun was bright on the beach outside, the breeze shuffled the palm leaves making patterns of light and shadow dance on the sand; the heat grew. I waited. Occasionally I got up for a pee, noting each time the sea had retreated, the beach growing wider with the falling tide as the day dragged on. What if the engine broke down? What if the offshore daytime wind became too strong for the engine? How would I know where to find him? I had lost one son – would I lose another?

My arm was now mottled from the fingers to my armpit. Puffy and grey, it was an unattractive mix of bluish black with yellow patches and wandering trails of red. It throbbed relentlessly, even the faintest breath of breeze over the skin increased the pain. The shadows moved steadily across the beach. Hugo's time was almost up.

One o'clock, one thirty. I had said three. I told myself not to panic, wait, be calm. Don't start imagining things.

And then I heard a faint, distant buzz. It grew louder, until I knew it was the sound of an outboard motor. He was back and within ten minutes of our agreed time.

13

Tanzania

Burn-out in Dar es Salaam

To this day there is a mark on my finger from that scary scorpion. The almost equally scary doctor I visited in Deigo Suarez assured me there would be no after-effects, but I have a discoloured patch of skin and a ridge in the nail as unfading reminders.

Next in the Indian Ocean cruises came the 'Islands of the Moon' but the stream of emails all headed 'Urgent' had produced nothing. Did the Comoros islands really exist, I wondered? There had been no responses from any of the proposed agents, whether shipping or land. But the colourful text I had written for the brochure had worked. Bookings had flooded in, and the ship would be full. I had promised swimming from pure white soft sandy beaches, curious fish, entertainment by colourful dancers and a sumptuous seafood barbecue. All these attractions must become real.

The archipelago was without doubt exotic, unknown and the pilot book encouraged me to be confident. The depth at the harbour quay was more than adequate, but every other aspect was shrouded in mystery. Few people seemed to have heard of these remote specs of land, and I could find no one who had actually been to these far-flung tropical islands. For me, they represented stepping stones across the Indian Ocean, providing visits ashore between the African coast of

Tanzania and Madagascar before the cruise finished in the Seychelles. Exotic spices – nutmeg, pepper and vanilla – grew on the volcanic slopes. The islands had once been part of the Sultanate of Oman and surely this archipelago named 'The Islands of the Moon' must be romantic and interesting?

There was no choice, I had to go, and the best route was via Tanzania, but with only two flights a week, connections were critical. In view of the expense, I had relaxed my stipulation to Michael that I must have a 'minder' and set off alone from London to the tiny capital of Moroni.

'I hope I've made it,' I gasped at the BA check-in girl. Sorry I'm so late, the M4 was down to one lane because of the snow. Have you closed the gate? I've a really tight connection in Dar so I must get on this flight,' I added, hoping this might help my cause. There was something forbidding about her immaculate appearance, her scarf was pinned with a shiny brooch, its blue and red stripes spread across on her bolster-like bosom.

She studied the computer screen. 'It's Ok, the flights are running late because of the weather. At the moment, they're still able to take off but they're about an hour late.'

So I'd made it, and eventually I arrived in the bright sun of Dar, to find Tehsin waiting for me.

'This is a change from our usual meeting at the Travel Market in Docklands,' I said, shaking his hand. 'Sorry I'm late. I hope you haven't been waiting here all this time?'

'No, I knew the flights were delayed from the UK, but you've missed the Comoros connection. The next one is not until Thursday; they don't fly on a Friday or Saturday of course, but I've booked you into Seafarers – big gardens, beach and a couple of nice pools.'

'Sounds like heaven!' Two days relaxing would suit me fine.

The hotel golf buggy bumped along a concrete track winding behind the row of beach-front villas. Coconut palms rustled high above, iridescent superb starlings hopped on the short grass. Frangipani trees, their white flowers, waxy and fragrant on silvery branches, grew among widely spaced wooden chalets. Bougainvillea, a striking magenta, romped over the grey coconut palm roofs. All the buildings dotted through the gardens had these makuti roofs blending harmoniously with the surroundings. Tehsin had chosen well, I had a haven of tropical delights for my enforced wait.

After a stroll along the beach and a warm swim, I washed away the salt. Hot water gushed from a shell fixed to the curved wall, splashing over me as soap suds and bubbles frothed in the drain at the corner. The beach and outdoor shower were a world away from cold, grey February in London. Feeling entirely refreshed, I put on the one pretty dress I had brought and strolled along the path, romantically lit with candles in lanterns. I felt good, though I was on my own, the dress was perfect and fitted me well. You never knew, I might meet someone nice.

'Hello, good evening, could I have a table for dinner, please?'

'Good evening, Memsahib. Will that be for the special Chinese New Year celebration buffet or the inside dining room?'

'Oh, the Chinese buffet, please.' I had totally forgotten it was Chinese New Year.

'Yes, Mam, I have a nice table for two.'

'For one, thank you.'

'Oh, for one. Just a moment while I see if we have a table available.' Behind him were several empty tables. Dining alone was grim and equally miserable whether it was

Doncaster or Dar es Salaam. I waited, watching the red paper lanterns swinging in the breeze, their long gold tassels almost touching the buffet. I waited until he found an outside table; I was not prepared to be relegated to the stuffy dining room.

The long buffet table groaned with New Year delights: dumplings in bamboo boxes, spring rolls arranged in crispy log-cabins, prawn toasts interleaved like waterlilies, were arranged beside a phalanx of stainless-steel tureens: 'Lemon chicken', 'Beef in black bean sauce', 'Chilli crispy beef and carrots', 'Egg-fried rice', 'Jasmine rice' – and at the end came the shredded Peking Duck. It was a westerner's cornucopia of Chinese dishes.

By now, I knew how to manage dinner alone. With a book to provide cover, I could people-watch with impunity. The breeze brought smells of the sea, salty but not overly humid, wafting from the ocean it created a pleasant draught under the soaring coconut palm roof. Contentedly, I prepared a duck pancake, spreading plum sauce, adding cucumber strips and spring onion before the duck meat and crisp skin. I gazed around, surveying the tables. Holiday couples chatted cosily or gazed at each other over glasses of rosé or bright green cocktails complete with obligatory mini umbrella. In the romantic shadows by the lawn, two men were dining, deep in conversation. What were they doing here, in a holiday hotel? They must be gay, enjoying time together, I concluded. Another spring roll and maybe some lemon chicken would be nice. I sauntered over to the row of chafing dishes so I could see them more clearly. They were engrossed in their food, heads bent, chopsticks neatly ferrying mouthfuls from the array of plates and bowls covering their table. It must be ages since they have seen each other, I thought, they are so absorbed.

Ping. The spring roll popped out of the tongs. It scuttled across the tablecloth, whizzed under a burner to clatter onto the floor. I bent to retrieve it.

Did I recognise the back of that head? Did that figure seem familiar?

No, surely not? It couldn't be. Not here in Dar es Salaam?

In a daze, I put a delicate portion of jasmine rice on my plate and then crossed the polished floor. I needed to get closer, have a proper look.

'Hello,' I said quietly, rather hoping to make him jump. Slowly he turned and looked round, a smile spreading into his eyes.

'You! How delightful! What a surprise. What are you doing here?' Helly Handsome rose from the table. Cool, appraising brown eyes shone into mine and he kissed me, a proper kiss, rather more than a friendly greeting.

'You look beautiful. Ravishing.'

He was composed, unruffled by my sudden appearance. He looked good in pale chinos, brown crocodile belt and a blue striped shirt, his only concession to the heat partially turned-up sleeves. I was the one who had spotted him. I had had time to adjust but he was the one who was calm and totally collected.

'And I could say the same to you! Well, not beautiful,' I replied, flustered. Why did he always make me feel slightly out of control? It was annoying. 'I'm stuck, missed my flight connection,' I went on. 'The snow in London delayed the plane. And you? What are *you* doing here?' I was aware I was gushing.

His companion was agog, obviously wondering who I was.

'We came in from San Jose this afternoon.' He turned. 'This is Greg.'

Greg got to his feet, stretching a hand across the table.

'Amelia works in tourism she'll know what we should do. What are the best things to see in Dar?' Did I detect a hint of condescension or was I being oversensitive?

'Actually, there's not a lot to do in Dar. Get out to the bush, go on safari like everyone else.'

'What about the coast?' he asked.

'The coast? That's why I'm here, well, for the islands, the Comoros.' I hoped this sounded important. After all, I was working, not just swanning about.

'The Comoros. They are beyond our patch, we're sticking to the mainland, the Tanzania coast.' He moved things on the table. 'Come and join us. Can you squeeze that plate on the table?' The invitation sounded a little like an afterthought. Perhaps it was awkward for him, with Greg picking up vibes, observing. But HH smiled, his eyes inviting, encouraging.

It was completely unexpected to find him here, at a holiday hotel, beside the sea. His last email, over three weeks ago, had made no mention of Tanzania. I would have remembered. I had assumed he was in Gloucestershire and had been wishing he would make contact. The occasions we met had been beguiling. He had seemed to be entirely in the moment, leaving his phone unchecked, not referring to others in his life, and I had no real idea what his business was. Our lunches had been washed down by glamorous bottles of white Burgundy and were as spoiling as entertaining. He appeared absorbed wholly in me, in what I was doing, where I had been and how my work was progressing. Frequently I felt lonely in the remote places I went to, whiling away time in airports or long drives. His erratic emails, proving he remembered my existence, made my heart flutter disconcertingly. His company was heady stuff.

'Why do you want to see the coast?' I asked again, thinking it might be better not to join whatever the discussions had been before my interruption.

'I may need to get some surveys done,' he said, sitting down again. 'Of the coastal zones. There's possibly a bit of expansion for us here.' He seemed a different person, a man occupied with business. 'We've a chopper at first light. Can I get you a glass of wine? We're on beer, more hydrating. It's a hell-of-a schlep from Costa Rica.' He suppressed a yawn. Two empty bottles of Serengeti stood on the table.

'No, thanks. I'll leave you to it.' It was not difficult to sense he was simply being polite. 'I envy you. I could do with a chopper. Be a great way for me to check out the shores and islands.'

I returned to my table, relieved I had my book, but I had lost interest in jasmine rice.

I walked back to my villa alone. A bright moon sailed through the tops of the palms in a dark sky, creating the familiar pattern of fringed shadows shifting on the mown grass. There, silhouetted against the sea was my wooden chalet, with hammock, day bed and loungers on the veranda. It was a glorious, tropical night. A night for enjoying the stars and moon with company. I gave myself a mental shake. Time for bed, Amelia. Banishing thoughts of HH, I flung open the windows and turned off the air conditioning, grumpily wondering why the evening turn-down staff had put the air con on full blast making the room so horribly cold.

Something had woken me. I lay motionless, listening, holding my breath. Life on a ship had left me hypersensitive to smells and noises. The breeze shifted the gauze curtains and with it came an unmistakable waft of woodsmoke. Grabbing a sarong, I went out into the moonlight. On the far side of the gardens, beyond silhouetted tree trunks, was a flickering orange glow. Flames crackled, rising high in the air, driven by the ocean wind. As I watched, showers of sparks and glowing embers blew across the grass, over the beach and out over the sea. The huge makuti roof of the dining room, with its soaring peaks, was an inferno. In front of the flames figures moved almost picturesquely, like a magic lantern, dashing back and forth.

A golf buggy buzzed along the path.

'Hi!' I shouted at the uniformed driver, and he came to a halt. 'Is a fire engine coming? I think these villas will be Ok, providing the wind stays like this, but we should wake people up – just in case.' He stared, frightened into immobility.

'Come on, come on!' I shook the steering wheel. 'You take the villas on that side, and I'll go this way. Bang on the doors, wake people up!'

Working my way along the row, I banged on doors, shouting 'Fire, fire!' People grunted, cried out, surprised. At the next, there was no reply. I stamped on the wooden veranda and banged harder on the door.

'Fire! *Wake up*. Fire!' The door burst open, and there was HH. Wrap casually tucked round his waist. This was no chilly marina in Southampton, this time not just his legs were visible, his top was naked, muscular and attractively tanned.

'Ah, at last! Hooray, you're here.' A strong arm curved round my back, pulling me towards him. 'You shot off from dinner and I didn't know where to find you.' He kissed me as a puff of smoke wafted past and orange shadows danced on the villa walls. 'Thank you for preventing me from being burnt alive. My saving angel. Hang on a second.' He disappeared inside. 'I'll put on some trousers. We'd better go and help.'

'I think it's really got hold now. The whole roof is ablaze.' Even at this distance, the noise of crackling rose above the regular swoosh of the waves.

'Looks like it. Do you know what time it is? I've a car at five and the chopper at six.'

'Well, you'd better get going, that's in thirty minutes! Good thing I woke you up.' I commented surprised. He disappeared inside to dress while I returned to do the same before joining the crowd outside the still blazing dining room. Sparks, smuts and smoke spiralled up into the dawn sky as the soft early morning light grew stronger.

I too had an early flight but not in a private chopper.

14

The Comoros
Islands of the Moon

As I waited in the half-empty elderly Dakota, the smell of the fire and smoke seemed to be stuck in my nostrils. A cabin steward walked up the steeply raked aisle, flipping the backs of seats flat as he went, including the one beside me. Next came a large woman, she flowed and wobbled, hampered by the folds of her dress, a fireball of swirling orange and yellow. Pushing and squeezing she negotiated the narrow aisle. It was particularly challenging for her hips and the cumbersome basket she carried was an added difficulty. Occasionally the basket gave a leap. It bounced and jerked, clucks and squawks bursting through the latticework frame. She battled on, eventually reaching the emergency row where she collapsed so heavily the whole row of seats shook. Feathers flew from the basket, wafting upwards to the lockers, then drifting down to settle among the plaits of her black hair. She pushed the basket along the floor wedging it across the emergency exit, and a cockerel cleared its throat, ready for takeoff. No one, not even the flight attendant, looked surprised. More passengers piled in through the rear door and took their seats until the plane was almost full. We waited.

A plaintive keening drifted into the cabin. A stretcher appeared. Carefully, keeping it as level as possible, the two men carrying it lowered their burden until it lay along on the flipped down seat backs. The keening grew louder as six elderly men, chanting and sobbing, filed up the aisle, each touching the shroud as they passed. They took their seats by the chickens.

I hugged the window, imprisoned in my seat and cut off from the aisle; inches from my elbow lay the body. The shroud had a wide green stripe running through the folds like a giant squirt of fluoride toothpaste, which did nothing to disguise the lumps and bumps of the corpse.

What, I wondered, had been the cause of death. Was it infectious? The back door slammed shut and the plane jolted as we taxied over the pock-marked concrete runway. Would the body slip? Or the stretcher unbalance and slide onto me?

This stretcher, mourners and chickens were my introduction to the 'Islands of the Moon'.

Before takeoff, I had again checked my emails, hoping there might be at least one reply. Nothing. Did anyone know I was coming? Would someone meet me? I wished I had insisted on bringing a minder. Turning firmly away from the stretcher, I focused on the view, four hundred miles of sea, and then suddenly, the cone of a volcanic island appeared. We circled, losing height, providing me with a view of the harbour and capital, Moroni.

It was clearly a bad decision to have come alone. I must look confident. Collecting my rucksack from the heap dumped on the runway under the wing, I walked into the grandly named 'Arrivals Hall', a recycled steel container. The opposite side had been removed allowing a free-for-all scrum of waving, shouting and jostling. Hands tugged at my sleeve, and I was pushed and pulled on all sides as I hesitated, unsure what to do.

'You are with me!' shouted a fellow in a brightly striped tea-cosy hat.

'Come, I show you,' said another from betelnut-stained red lips.

'You. You. You come with me.' Each tried to outdo the other, shouting and increasingly insistent. The stained teeth, stinking breath and hustling persistence were intimidating.

'Good morning.' A curiously quiet voice cut through the hubbub. 'You must be Amelia?' A dark, almost Indian looking man smiled uncertainly, head and shoulders above the others. 'I am Josian of Tourism Services, Comoros. Welcome to Grande Comoro.'

'Josian? Oh, hello.' I tried to extricate myself from the pulling hands.

'Yes, I am Josian, hello. These guys are Ok, don't worry, just a bit too keen.' He shouted this time. 'The memsahib is with me.' It worked like hot water on jelly and they melted away.

'Amelia, I have your emails. Come, my car is outside.' Relieved by his air of authority and charming smile I walked unhindered from the hot container.

'Shall we go to the hotel? First a coffee and a chat?' he asked.

'Wonderful, yes thanks. You can tell me all about Grande Comoro, it looks beautiful from the air.' I hoped I sounded more confident than I felt, as I heaved myself into the shiny 4x4. 'Are we going to Moroni? How far is it, please?'

'About fifteen kilometres, and we cross the lava flow on the way.' His accent sounded French.

Undulating across a coastal plain, the road weaved through a moonscape of black lava. The sea was a brilliant blue on my right and all around the colours were strong, powerful in the bright sunlight. He turned off the unexpectedly good road to the hotel, a low-slung bungalow redolent of the sixties, with a huge tarmac car park edged by broken chunks of concrete. In better days, these kerbs must have been painted white, bordering what had once been flower beds. Grey streaks of mould ran down the bungalow's façade and the glass was broken in many of the windows.

'I'll get coffee organised.'

'Ok, fine. I'm going to use that call box. Check in with my office now, it'll save time.'

The low-ceilinged reception area was empty. Green glazed tiles, some with chipped corners, reflected light between concrete pillars and dirty gauze curtains fluttered in the breeze where the glass was missing.

'Hello, Michael?' I bellowed down the line. 'Yes, yes, made it at last. In Grande Comoro. Quite an adventure so far. The hotel in Dar burnt down last night, the plane was full of chickens and I had a dead body on the seat next to me on a stretcher. But the good news is I think I've found an agent.'

The Yorkshire Pennines seemed very distant on this forgotten tropical isle. Mosquitoes buzzed inside the little wooden cubicle, the air was torpid and I could feel them attacking my bare legs. Quickly, anxious to finish the call, I told him my plan to set off early tomorrow to go round the island and to inspect the port. Michael, though, was in a talkative mood. Life in the office must be slow and a call from the Islands of the Moon provided a welcome break. I eventually managed to tell him I had a meeting next day with the Minister of Tourism, after I'd checked out the harbour.

'I'll know more tomorrow, I want to be sure of the harbour first. Give you a ring then,' I said, swishing my legs about in an attempt to ward off the voracious mozzies. Michael, however, relishing the 'news from the front' went on talking.

'Sorry, it's really difficult to hear you, bad line. Don't worry. I'll try to call tomorrow. Bye.'

Josian, having received my emails had waited to see me in person rather than reply. He told me a little about the island and that my ideas might be possible. Weary from the drama of the last twenty-four hours and the uncertainty of what I might find tomorrow, I went to my room. It was fully in keeping with the rest of the establishment. A single iron bed with thin, slightly grubby sheets, a lumpy pillow and tattered mozzie net with a worrying number of holes. Dusty wires sagged across the bathroom ceiling, looping to a broken strip light above a cracked pink washbasin. The wires skimmed over a steadily dripping shower rose. But the dribble was just enough to splash my face. Both hot and cold taps on the basin swivelled round and round, emitting weary croaks but no water.

Next morning, sticky after a humid, sleepless night, I was ready rather than refreshed with camera, tape recorder and notebook lurking in the Prada rucksack when the big white Toyota appeared. Palms and banana trees made dark silhouettes in the dawn light, and Josian was on time, a good start.

'Good morning, Amelia. How did you sleep?' he asked, jumping down from the driver's door to open mine.

'Hi Josian, good morning, I'm fine, thanks. Have you stayed in this hotel?'

His long face looked worried. 'This is the only hotel in Moroni, and there is glass in some of the windows.' It seemed churlish to point out that glass was only in the metal frames of the bar windows.

'Ok, let's go. Show me your island!' My rosy-tinted idea of a long empty beach with soft white sand, with an occasional washed-up tropical shell or piece of coral, backed by sighing coconut palms, now seemed optimistic, a foolish dream invented in London, and the promises I had made in the brochure completely ridiculous.

'Sure, I will show you the island. First, we start where I suggest we have the barbecue and the place for the swim.'

'Great, but please remember we need to be at the port by midday.'

'Yes. Now we go to the beach. It was owned by one of the Presidents and was reserved for government employees, but this president has run out of money, so he closed it down.'

We drove north along the coast, passing a string of small coves, each with an attendant line of jagged volcanic rocks sluiced by the Indian Ocean. The road weaved between old flows of craggy mounds of black lava. In every direction stretched a moonscape, barren and unforgiving. As Josian drove, I asked about his background. He had come from Mauritius seven years ago having fallen in love with a Comorian girl who had been working there in the Oberoi hotel. In those days French money had paid for roads here, the museum and development throughout the islands. They had married, returned to Grande Comore and hoped to make it in tourism.

'Here we are. Mitsamiouli,' he said, turning down a track towards the sea, crunching coconuts under the wheels as he drove on to the short grass edging the sand. I jumped out. Curling right and left was a long bay, an expanse of golden beach. There were no footprints padding along the edge, no washed-up bottles, no pink plastic doll bodies or faded flip flops, just smooth unsullied sand. Turnstones scuttled along the water's edge poking long beaks into the wet in search of worms and crustaceans. Shells in mottled heaps made colourful mounds along the high tide mark, ghost crabs scuttled to hide under scraps of dried seaweed. It was a perfect, empty beach, and I was rapidly falling in love with the Indian Ocean.

Josian pointed into the shade. 'At the back, there among the coconut trees, is the resort. I can get some of the chalets opened for changing. They are not very smart, but I hope will be Ok? Maybe we can set up the barbecue over there? What do you think?' he asked anxiously.

'This is a beautiful beach, it's absolutely perfect, thank you. It will be lovely, it's an idyllic place.' I strolled out of the shade and into the hot sun. 'We can bring towels from the ship and there is lots of shade. What about undercurrents, is it safe for swimming?' I wiggled my toes in the warm sand, longing to strip off and slip into the turquoise water.

'Yes, naturally it's safe.' He sounded offended. 'That's why it belonged to the president.'

'Of course. Tell me about the barbecue, the food and how you would like to organise it. What do you think about some music? Dancing or singing?' I felt encouraged by the stunning surroundings to push him further.

'The food will come from the hotel. Their chefs will do the cooking.'

Dinner had been utterly disgusting. Dried up chunks of chicken, blocks of wood masquerading as chicken breasts. Breakfast had been no better: hardboiled eggs, cold, with slices of spam and flabby, industrially produced white bread with a melting packet of margarine. No jam or even the ubiquitous rolling hotel toaster were on offer.

'Josian, do you think tonight the chef could cook some of the dishes he suggests for me? Like a mini barbecue? I'd love to try some, whatever he chooses will be fine.'

I was always walking a tightrope, balancing between wanting to ask for what I would like, what I could create, what our passengers would expect and what was possible. I needed Josian excited not over-awed. No cruise passengers had ever visited this remote, lost little archipelago, and a luxury expedition ship would bring money to the island as well as his business but, as ever, the visit must work. Cockroaches, food poisoning, sea urchin stings and scorpion bites were not an option. I did not want super-slick or sophisticated. The exotic mix of peoples, rich history left by the Portuguese and Omanis, the marine life, tropical birds and plants, the spices and the colours of the Indian Ocean would be sufficient, as long as people were safe and each place left a bank of happy personal memories.

We continued our drive round the island. The higher volcanic slopes of Mount Karthala swept up to our right while on the left a calm azure sea stretched to the horizon, the blue only broken by the occasional triangular sail of a dhow fishing in the productive waters. As he drove, Josian told me the names of the villages, mere clusters of thatched huts – Chezani, Bambadjani and Heroumbili, simple settlements along the way. But during the whole drive there were no other bays or beaches, the shoreline was harsh and spiky with black volcanic lava. After six or seven miles the road started to climb towards the lush green centre of the island. Nutmeg trees, cloves, mangoes, pawpaw and banana with their flapping, elephantine leaves, edged the road, all grown in carefully tended plots, boundaries marked by stakes thick with rampant vines of vanilla and pepper. The hillsides were bursting with abundance from the red volcanic soil. As we turned a corner an elegant pair of white stone pillars with ornate wrought iron gates appeared, incongruous among the rampant tropical foliage. We seemed to have arrived at a French chateau.

'What happens here, Josian? It looks smart.'

'Come, I'll show you.' He stopped at the gates, jumped out and pushed them open. There was not even a latch. 'They're just for show.' He grinned at my surprise. 'There are no wild animals to bother about here.'

Grotesque gnarled trees, barely six-foot-high, grew in neatly tended rows. The knotted branches were thickly covered by greenish-yellow clusters hanging like fantastical bunches of ash keys jammed tightly along the entwined branches. It was the weirdest group of other-worldly trees I had ever seen. I took a deep breath: the air was thick with a heady, almost overpowering sweet scent.

'Ylang ylang,' said Josian, walking towards a tree. 'This is the best plantation in the islands. It is owned by a French company. They distil the oil from these flowers and send it to Versailles, to their perfume factory.' He plucked a bunch of the chartreuse-coloured dangling petals, handing the fragrant cluster to me.

'Why are the trees such weird shapes? They look spooky, like a witch's orchard, almost haunted?'

'They are pruned to stay low, or they will grow too high for the ladies to reach the flowers easily. The petals have to be picked quickly and distilled straight after picking or the scent is lost.'

Colourful, exotic and unexpected, the Comoros – 'The Perfumed Isles' – might yet be a success; at least we didn't need to use the hotel. Leaving the scented orchard, we descended through thick tropical woodland again, back to Moroni and the chaos of people and street life impeding our route to the port.

The machine gun pointed through the jeep window inches from my head: I had not realised I looked so threatening. Through the mesh of ten-foot-high metal gates, another soldier pointed his gun directly at me. He stood, casually, relaxed behind the gates that barred our way. A third soldier appeared from a sentry hut beside the gate; he sauntered across the pitted concrete, pushing aside his beret, tight black curls sprang out. He tucked his machine gun under his arm. We now had three machine guns pointing directly at Josian's car. Without a word from Josian, he pulled a key from a pocket in his camouflage trousers. After much fiddling, the links slackened, the padlock fell to the ground with a thud and he pushed the gates open a little. One stuck on a bump in the uneven concrete. With minimum effort, he gave each a push in turn until a gap appeared, inches wider than the car. Josian saluted and drove through smartly. The scraping noise of metal on concrete confirmed we were locked in.

The port bustled with life. Half-naked figures, loincloths loosely tucked, sweat glistening on their long muscular limbs, stood in a line along the top of the quay; in turn they began to descend a flight of stone steps leading down to the water. At the bottom, not pulled in tight but leaving a gap of some ten feet, was a wooden lighter, a *jehazi*. Low in the water, it was weighted down, piled high with filled paper sacks, each stamped with the blue triangle logo of a cement company. One by one, the sacks were dragged from the pile to the bulwark and lobbed across the gap to the next pair of hands waiting on the steps. The sack was passed on up to the next in line who, staggering with the weight, climbed the steps to the quay top. He passed the sack to another man's shoulders and he in turn stumbled over to a waiting lorry. While I watched, two sacks missed the catch from the boat and fell with an exhausted flop into the water, slipping through the gap between the lighter and the steps. Instantly sea water penetrated the paper and the concrete inside began to set. With every dropped sack the mound of solid concrete bags grew, and the *jehazi* was pushed a little further out from the steps. Each dropped bag increased the gap and thus the likelihood of bags sliding into the water. It was impossible for any boat to come properly alongside the steps and that would include our tenders.

'Josian?' I searched for words that would not offend him. 'This is bizarre.'

'Why, Amelia, what is the problem? The steps are good, I think.'

'The steps, as you say, are fine. And I appreciate that without a crane it is difficult to get concrete ashore, but that growing pile of solid bags will prevent us from bringing in the tenders. We won't be able to get people safely ashore.' I tried not to sound exasperated. I congratulated myself for insisting we were here at low water; at high tide it would have looked fine. Josian shifted his weight from one foot to the other.

'This must affect everything coming to the island,' I went on. 'It needs to be sorted out or soon you won't be able to land anything.' No wonder the island was crumbling and fading into obscurity.

'What about the Minister of Transport, when's my meeting with him?' I asked as I looked round the picturesque harbour. White buildings that had once been elegant palaces lined the black lava walls, crumbling now but evocative of former days. Rows of elegant arched windows stared blankly across the shallow water, relics of the island's rich trade with Persia and Oman. Wooden dhows, bleached by the sun and salt, lay on their sides, masts angled rakishly skywards, waiting for the sea to come lapping and creeping back. It was a beautiful Indian Ocean scene, redolent of history and romance, but it was also a useless harbour. So far, I had only sorted out the beach. Transport, the sumptuous buffet and guides all were yet to be organised, but now it looked as if getting people ashore would not be possible anyway.

'Amelia, come. I will show you the town and the museum, you will like those, I hope.' Josian almost pleaded, desperation creeping into his voice.

Backing the harbour was a tangled maze of streets and alleys. Ladies, their faces daubed with pale-yellow sandalwood paste, laughed and chattered, colourful as butterflies in their flowing dresses. Children peeped round corners, bursting into giggles at the sight of me. Richly carved frames surrounded elaborate doors, some fitted with round brass bosses, others sharp bronze spikes. Most were unpainted but occasionally one was a vivid Islamic green. Men in crisp white robes and embroidered pillbox hats lolled on steps in companionable groups, engrossed in what looked like games of dominoes.

'These doors are beautiful, Josian, such intricate patterns. Is the wood mangrove? And why the spikes?'

'No, mangrove is only used to support ceilings, the doors are Burmese teak. It's easy to carve, resistant to weather and rot, too. The richer the carving, the richer the merchant, and the spikes are traditional too. Supposedly they were to prevent elephants battering the door down. There is no need for the paint, but they like the bright green.'

To my amazement and relief, the museum had working air conditioning and clear labels, in French of course, but a faded air of sophistication remained, a hangover from former days.

All my life I had dreamed of seeing the strange creature that is a coelacanth. I had read there was one to be seen here. Thought to have become extinct over sixty million years ago, one of these grotesque fossil fish had been found in the market of the next-door island, Anjouan. And now, there one lay, languishing in a glass box, cloudy with dust, and with little of the preservative formaldehyde remaining. A predecessor to Damien Hirst's shark, it was bizarre and fascinating. A huge mouth gaped open displaying fearsome rows of teeth; muddy brown scales covered the three-foot-long body. Limb-like fins, fat and muscular, were evidence of the link between water and land. When alive it had patrolled the deep trenches of the nearby Mozambique Channel and, despite being a sad remnant of a true monster, it was still a wondrous creature.

If only there was a solution to the harbour: Grande Comoro was easy to like.

While the resident mozzies in the shower attacked me, the trickle of tepid water slowly washed away the day's grime but not my concern with the harbour. I knew I should bring Michael up to date, but first, even on this Muslim island, I needed a beer. I worked my way through empty rooms following signs to 'The Ocean Bar', to find three men, dressed in long European shorts and polo shirts, studying papers, deep in conversation. Through the open window an area of coarse grass, the hotel's obligatory 'lawn' was bathed in the last of the day's sunshine. A row of oil drums was lined up, each cut in half and balanced precariously on a metal frame. A haze of heat shimmered above them. My barbecue.

'Bon Soir gentlemen,' I ventured. They looked up but said nothing. 'My name is Amelia, and a barbecue has been organised for me out there under the palms – you can see the chefs. I wondered if you would care to join me? I must assess the food and I'd love to have your opinions.' Silence. I carried on, hopefully. 'Be nice also not to eat on my own.' They simply looked at me. No polite words or even a Gallic shrug.

I stepped out onto the thin grass to dine alone, clutching my bottle of Three Horses beer. A small table draped in a white cloth was laid for one and it had a glorious view. At the side of the lawn, blurred by the heat haze, were the chefs, four in all, each with his barrel of white-hot charcoal. Immaculately dressed, whites glowing in the twilight, tall hats carefully in place, they straightened up; white teeth and tongs flashed. Suddenly I felt rather relieved I had been spared stilted conversation in my halting French. The barman appeared, shook out the folded napkin and spread it over my lap.

'Bonsoir, Madame. You wish maybe a wine?'

'Thank you, yes please, a glass of white wine with some ice if possible and water.'

'Oui... Oh sorry, I forget, we ave no wine. Maybe another beer? Please you go help yourself.'

There was an unexpectedly varied selection. The first barrel had little woven packets made from strips of banana leaves, which had probably been fresh and green once but were now dark brown. Lobsters, giant prawns, tightly curled octopus tentacles, all lay desiccated but still sizzling. Above the final barrel a large bowl was balanced almost touching the fiery coals; inside was what appeared to be a dried-up river bed. Once it must have been a pool of sauce but that had evaporated leaving lumps tightly glued together surrounded by a network of fissures.

'Hello, what is this, please?'

'These —' Tongs pointed proudly at the brown lumps. 'These are meaty balls. You like?'

Chef number four was in charge of the side table. Neat in his white robe and toque, the little fellow stood on tiptoe to reach over the bowls. With a whisk of palm leaves, he waved at the flies enjoying the heaped tinned vegetables. Soggy mounds of grated carrot, coleslaw, red beans, butter beans and peas – nothing was fresh or local, everything had been liberated from a tin. There were no exotic salads of palm hearts, green beans or avocado. I reminded myself this was the point. This was why I was here, and I must taste every dish, do every chef justice. I started my rounds. First came half a lobster, next a huge spiky prawn, then the desiccated tentacles and suckers of octopus clattered onto my plate and the final chef popped one of the banana leaf packages beside the seafood. The river-bed chef, not to be outdone, had succeeded in prising a wizened 'meaty ball' from its socket.

I sat at the table, gazing out to sea. There was nothing to be seen out there, no lights, no twinkling boats fishing through the night as in the busy Mediterranean, no red or green port or starboard lights of distant ships. It was an inky-black sea, disappearing into the night. Waves crept gently back and forth on the sand beyond the grass. Above me, a velvet sky was awash with stars. My thoughts drifted to HH. Was he still in Tanzania? Doing what? The next time we spoke I really must find out.

I set about the mound of spikes, shards, suckers and legs, but at each movement the table wobbled. Carapaces and claws skittered and clattered, crab legs shot onto the grass. Everything was completely dry, cremated. It was more like chewing driftwood than food and in the darkness difficult to know what was what. I crunched through the burnt leaf package to find a bullet-like nugget inside, a bullet with a hint of fish. Not one element was edible. Disheartened, I thanked the chefs in my bad French, the end of a long day in a place so full of promise. It was up to me to tailor this forgotten island into the promised tropical paradise.

'Morning, Josian.'

'Amelia, good morning. You have had breakfast, yes?' His long face looked worried. I was trying, and clearly failing, to look happier than I felt. I had three more hours before I needed to be at the airport, three hours to turn disaster into perfection.

'Yes, thanks, Josian. Do we have the meeting fixed?'

'Yes, it is at eight thirty, in half an hour. I hope that is Ok for you?'

'Good. Which Minister? Tourism or Transport? I think I should try to see both, although probably the Minister of Transport is the more important, because of the port.'

'Yes, I understand, but that is easy. Here they are the same person. How was the barbecue last night?'

'Well...' Much of the night, when not swatting mozzies, had been spent wondering how I could give the chefs a cookery lesson, but as dawn flooded the sky a dusky pink, inspiration struck.

'I've been thinking about the barbecue. The hotel chefs did a great job, beautifully presented and lots of variety. But, I think the guests would really enjoy choosing their own food.'

'But it will be a buffet, yes?' He looked concerned.

'Yes, but can we arrange for all the seafood to be spread out? On a table, laid over seaweed to keep it cool?' I explained.

'Each person will come up, point to what they would like, a lobster, octopus, fish or whatever, and then the chef can cook it, while they watch.' I waited, allowing him time to consider this novel idea. 'It would be nice for the chef too. Many people will speak French, and they can have a chat while their food is cooking.'

Josian still looked sceptical. Then, having considered it carefully, he said, 'Amelia, I like this. It sounds good. We can make the table look nice too, with flowers. Ice and seaweed are not difficult, we bring those along with the food. I think the chefs will like to do this, and it will make more of a party.' He smiled, confidence returning.

With any luck, I thought, the seafood will not have time to turn into dried-up, chunks.

The Minister's office was cavernous. A ceiling fan twirled slowly but did nothing to stir the heavy air. The dark, sunless room was crowded with oppressive furniture, appropriate to the elevated position of someone responsible for two ministries. The mahogany was unmistakably of Indian origin, ornately carved with curls, bosses, leaves and flowers as well as being richly inlaid with ivory and mother-of-pearl. It would have delighted Old Jolyon Forsyte. The desk, enormous and entirely devoid of papers or phone, filled one end of the room. There were six matching high-backed chairs, three of which sat in a line under the metal-framed window, broken strips of cane hanging from their sagging seats.

The minutes ticked by bringing my flight time remorselessly closer. After ten minutes I stood up, my attention caught by a movement outside the window. On the far side of the compound came a diminutive man on a battered bicycle. He tootled up to the building, propped his bike against the wall and trotted in. I gave a little bow, thinking he might not like to shake a female hand.

'Bonjour. I am Mohamed Massounde.' He settled himself behind the desk. I could only see the top half of his head, from his nose up. He opened and shut a couple of drawers importantly.

'Good morning, Minister, thank you for finding time to meet me.' As forcefully as I dared, I outlined the problem with the concrete, explaining how it would prevent my bringing tourists to his beautiful island. His air of surprise was almost convincing.

'Zees ees news to me. You are sure? I zink they manage veery well down there.'

'Oh, you didn't know? Goodness! Well, the tide is falling now so the *blockage*' (pronounced this in my best Franglais) 'will be visible. We have a car outside, so come with us and I can show you.'

'Minister.' Josian joined the cause. 'It would be helpful for you to see how the Port is working.'

In the hot sunshine, the three of us stood on the quay, looking down at the clear turquoise water lapping below. Curiously the harbour now was completely devoid of life and quiet.

'Minister, here we are. You can see the problem?' I pointed at the bags of concrete visible below in the clear water. A crab scuttled over one, and seaweed waved, fish lazily circled the concrete pillows. Nothing else moved in the harbour.

'They are heavy so *naturellement* from time to time one is dropped.' My French was embarrassing even to me, but I pressed on. 'Et *puis*, the concrete sets in the water, it goes hard. *Vous comprenez* – you understand?' He looked down into the translucent water.

'*Oui,* I see a *petit problème.*'

'*C'est facile.*' I tried not to sound too bossy, remembering that as a female I was not supposed to understand these things. '*Vous* can *fixé.* A few men, here at low water, they could *travailler* on the sacks,' I suggested. 'Get them up, jackhammers would move the *sacs*, and your *port* will be working again *tout de suite.*' A muscle twitched in his cheek. Had I gone too far? I smiled sweetly at him. 'We can bring our tenders, bring the tourists to this wonderful island. And for you, your *port* will work, will *marche bien,* you can land all the things you need.'

'Ah, *oui. Oui!*' light began to dawn. 'I fix. All will be *préparé.*'

'What do you think, Josian?' I asked during the drive to the airport. 'Do you think he will actually get anything done?'

'It'll be Ok, don't worry. He can see it will be a coup for him, and I will make sure the work is done.' He sounded relaxed as he swung the big white Toyota around a pile of rubble that had once been a statue on a plinth, gracing the airport entrance.

'Everything hangs on the harbour being functional.' I wanted to drive the message home. He looked at me and grinned.

'Now for check in.'

I wondered why he was grinning.

In the shade of the tin roof, I stepped onto the red platform of the scales, my suitcase and rucksack tucked between my feet. From there, I was told to move to the door where a measuring stick was glued beside the frame. Josian noted down my height and weight before laying my papers and passport in front of three men, who sat at a trestle table. The first studied my flight ticket which I had printed before leaving London. Number two nudged number three, who was asleep, his head pillowed on his arms. He sat up and opened a green exercise book. Laboriously, in big curly writing he noted the ticket number, takeoff time, flight number and finally my height and weight before sliding the book, ticket and my passport to his left to number three. Number three flicked through the pages. He flipped them back and forth several times.

'You cannot travel to Dar. You 'ave no visa.'

'It's Ok, I do have a visa,' I said as patiently as I could.

'I cannot see visa. There is no visa. I tell you, you cannot fly.'

Josian stepped forward and, bending over the table, he said something quietly. The man again flicked through my passport, studied the Tanzania visa then viciously stamped four times, each time on a different page, and snapped it shut. I had obviously spoilt his fun for the day.

'Ok, you go,' he muttered.

Josian grinned. 'The plane is usually twenty-five minutes late, but don't worry. I will know if it does not arrive, it comes in over my office.'

'Josian, thank you. Thank you so much, it has been very good to meet you. I love your island; it is a truly fascinating and unusual place. You must let me have the costs and soon. Please don't hesitate to email me. We *must* keep in touch,' I said pointedly.

'Yes, yes, I will do that, don't you worry, everything will be fine. Goodbye now and have a good flight.'

He seemed completely relaxed, unruffled by any of the problems.

This time there were no bodies, no baskets of squawking chickens. I had four hours to while away in Dar before the onward flight to London. I found the only lounge and plugged in my laptop. Emails flooded in. Shipping reps, guides, agents, drivers and managers from Norway to India, every one of them with queries.

My mobile vibrated in my pocket. Flipping it open, the little screen glowed green 'HH'.

'Hello! This is a nice surprise.' I hoped I sounded crisper than I felt.

'And how are you, Amelia, the travel guru? Where are you now?'

'I'm sitting in the glamorously named Tanzanite Lounge in Dar.' Nowhere could have held less charm. The décor was a particularly depressing shit-brown rather than brilliant Tanzanite blue. 'I've three hours before the flight home. What about you? Where are you now?'

'I'm finishing up here, back in Dar this evening. I was hoping you might still be there.'

'Oh.'

'What about staying on?' His voice was smooth and persuasive. 'We could do a safari, a night or two in a tent, beasties roaring around outside. Just your sort of thing? Can you get your agent to fix something up?' This seductive idea spun round my mind. Could I? Should I? I was flying Business, so a date change was perfectly possible.

'What a lovely idea, sounds wonderful. I'll have to let the office know. Can I call you back?'

'Ok, but make it quick, I've a meeting in twenty minutes, and I need to fix other plans.' Click and the phone was silent.

'Michael, it's Amelia, can you hear me?' Cracking interference made conversation almost impossible. 'I'm back in Dar.' I listened to his distant voice, hoping to get a feel for how things were in the office and for his mood before continuing.

'Yes, I've finished in Grande Comoro, I'll send a report shortly. It's a really exciting island, just our sort of place. Colourful history, remote, lush and a beautiful beach. It will be great, a few challenges of course, but I think it will be good. Michael, I'd like a few days off, please, while I'm here in Africa. A brief safari, it's so easy from Dar.'

In spite of the interference, I could hear all too well.

'A meeting covering the Indian Ocean cruises. The day after tomorrow?' Excitement drained from me. 'The officers too. Right,' I said wearily, 'I'll be there.'

15

The Maldives
Cyclones & Seaplanes

The train drew into Leeds station and I crossed to the outer platform, the one for Skipton. I took a deep breath of February Yorkshire air, so different from hot, scented ylang ylang. Bracing, I told myself, though in truth it was cold and smutty, with the industrial smell of stale eggs. Even so, it was always good to be back, back in gritty Leeds. I settled into the carriage. Through the filthy windows the views of Wharfedale would feel like home. The suburbs slipped past in a grey blur. Millstone grit villages and Victorian textile mills and chimneys lined the river as it flowed down the valley, winding between the Pennine hills. After so much time among vibrant tropical vegetation, it seemed very English. My thoughts were filled with safaris and *Monaco*. I had no regrets at not having to creep about in the dark to pump out dirty bilge water, but I did for the safari.

Monaco, Digby's death and divorce as well as so much travelling had changed me. Cubby's obsession with safety and the dangers of the sea had taught me much that I needed and had used. Without all of that, I would not be on a train to Skipton equipped with the skills for establishing an international cruise ship. Sheep, oak trees, wind-sculpted hawthorns and dry-stone walls rolled past. My disappoint-ment at having to forego the safari with HH, the starlit evenings round a campfire drinking sundowners while watching hippo, receded. Emotionally I was home. Had I missed out completely? Would he make contact again?

I could feel my eyelids drooping in the stuffy boardroom. It had been a long flight and two train journeys, plus I was four hours ahead. Sleep crept over me. Voices droned on. I pinched my thigh under the table to wake myself up.

'Yes, you are right, but finding a proper storage place for the ice axe is very important,' said Andrew, the future purser. 'It's a significant piece of equipment, and it must have a proper place; the authorities will insist and there'll be inspections.'

Dopily, I wondered what this was about. We had been in the board room over three hours and so far, had only covered two topics.

'Does this ship really need an ice axe?' Michael asked, exasperated.

'Of course. She can't possibly reach the required standards without one,' was the affronted reply.

'None of the itineraries I'm establishing is in the Arctic,' I said. 'There's no need for an ice axe, and she's certainly not going anywhere remotely near the Antarctic.'

'Amelia.' Andrew looked at me over his glasses, 'the ice axe is a small chain saw, so the correct storage is vital.'

'Sorry, but I still don't understand why the ship needs to have a small power tool designed for ice on board when she won't be anywhere near ice.' Six pairs of eyes looked at me. I had not succeeded in hiding my irritation. 'If she gets into ice a small chain saw won't be what's needed!'

Jeremy, from the hotels department, stared at me.

'Amelia, the ship won't meet the required standards without one and it's traditional. There must be a stylish ice sculpture at the entrance to the dining room, the passengers expect it.'

I had assumed chain saws, even miniature ones, were for lumberjacks not chefs. Deciding I had better listen, I kept quiet. Eventually, we reached item four on the agenda. 'Storage of Umbrellas'. Surely this must be simple. Storing umbrellas for passengers' use could not take almost two hours of discussion like the chain saw. Determined to keep my mouth closed, I drifted into a daydream.

A tent, with views of thick mopane woodland visible through the mozzie-netted panels let into each of its canvas sides. The decked terrace, complete with binoculars, was a delightful place to while away the time. Two gins and tonics waited on the small table by my elbow. In front, the ground fell away to muddy water, the river flowed lazily past, parting round grassy islands. From the surrounding bush noises drifted gently to me on the warm air, the melodic descending coos of an emerald spotted wood dove, the teasing chuckle of a hyena and deep grunting from the hippos wallowing in the water below. I wished HH would hurry up, whatever could he be doing? The ice in his gin and tonic was melting quickly. A frisson of excitement ran down my spine.

'Amelia, what do you think? You have been to the places, what's your view?'

I jerked myself back to reality. 'Sorry, please could you repeat that?' I had no idea what the topic was.

'What do you think? The brollies for the Indian Ocean?'

We were still on brollies. 'Well, if it looks like there'll be a tropical shower, they will definitely be needed. But can't they simply be stored by the main door? Everyone will have to be clocked out by the security staff anyway, so can't they just pick a brolly as they go ashore?'

'I know you've been travelling,' Michael said with some impatience, 'but we are discussing the big umbrellas needed for shade on the aft deck. They will need to be large, so they will be really heavy. They can't simply be left up or they'll be torn to pieces, and dangerous if one takes off.' I realised there were many things I had yet to learn, and which life on board *Monaco* had not prepared me for.

Finally, we got to the item on tenders. This was a safer subject, one I felt more confident to deal with. I studied the architectural drawings. They were to be jet-driven, allowing them to turn on a sixpence and operate in shallow water, even onto a beach. They were proper little boats with seating inside and out and not the horrible, shoe-like, multi-purpose lifeboats which so many ships used. The transfer from ship to shore would be an enjoyable experience, taking in views of the surroundings. It would be a mini cruise, not purely functional.

'Michael, they look perfect and delightful for the passengers. Jet drives are fabulous for the shallow waters, tricky to drive, but fine once you have the hang of them. How long will they take to build?'

'Well,' he went on, pleased with my approval, 'the shipyard is adapting one of their regular styles, so not long. We'll have them in time for the round-Britain show-off, the shake-down voyage.'

'Great. That'll give us time. We can practise in British winds and tides. If the crew can manage those, they'll be Ok for Norway, and the fjords are less challenging, apart from downdraughts. The Baltic and Med are easy too, and by the time we're in the Indian Ocean they'll have had lots of use.'

'How about a little drink before we go to the Bull? You look as if you could do with a sharpener.' Papa had collected me from the office, and I had one night to catch up on his news. It was months since I had seen him. He looked well and was, as always, cheerful, but I knew he was achingly lonely since my mother's death, and I admired his determination. His only complaint was – as before – the dinners Brenda cooked for him.

'She puts them in the Aga in the early afternoon, so by the time I want dinner it all looks like a cowpat.'

'Papa, I'll cook dinner, no need to go to the Bull. What's in the fridge?'

'Yes, I know you can, but you look all in.'

I looked in the fridge. Two cream buns and a packet of soup.

'There's a new chef at the pub,' he said, 'and it'll be good to have a change of scene. You enjoy that martini while I go and have a quick change.' Even at home on his own, he still changed each evening and put candles on the table. His old-school standards remained intact, and it was heartening to see the welcome he received in the pub.

'Evening, Judge,' said a fellow leaning on the bar. 'I see you've been at it again.'

'I hope you feel it's an improvement. Sadly, the Council won't do it, but someone should.'

'Aye, that's true. The last lot are looking good now. What are these new ones?'

'Flowering cherries. White ones. I'm less keen on pink, too suburban for here, I feel. What do you think?'

My father had a lifelong love of trees and had become a rogue planter of roadside verges. The village street was now graced with whitebeams along the road past the church, so it seemed he had been at it again.

'Judge, if you want to do it, you carry on. No one's objecting, that I know of.'

Next morning, I awoke to a glowing bedroom, red and orange patterns danced across the walls as the sunlight played on the curtains. Downstairs, there was no sign of my father, just breakfast ready laid for me in the dining room. I had woken late. Quickly grabbing a piece of toast, I went in search of him.

When my parents had bought the former vicarage, everything had been overgrown. From the orchard and woodland to the grass tennis court, all had been abandoned in favour of concrete dog runs. The vast walled kitchen garden with its two Victorian greenhouses and the other formal areas of flower beds by the house, had been given over to breeding greyhounds. Starting with jackhammering the dog runs, my father had transformed it all and now there was a croquet lawn, roses cascading over walls, fig and apricot trees and a spreading cherry, just showing its flower buds. Running alongside the croquet lawn was a dense holly hedge, perfectly clipped apart from a small elderflower tree which grew up through the middle of the dark, spiky leaves. Standing under the arching branches, in deep discussion, were my father and Les, the part-time gardener. The body language was not good, even though they were great mates. Many hours together in the potting shed, planting bulbs, pricking out seeds, waging war on bugs and weeds had created a mutual recognition of knowledge and friendship.

'That'll have to go, Judge.' Les tapped his stick on the slim trunk growing up through the perfectly pruned hedge. The elder quivered and my father looked down at his feet, saying nothing. Eventually, he raised his head.

'No, Les. It's necessary,' he said firmly.

'Begging your pardon, sir. It's a weed, it's time it went. I'll take it out this afternoon.'

'I know you want to get rid of it, but I would like it to stay. It keeps the witches away,' Les spluttered, unconvinced.

'Well, Les, you haven't seen any, have you?'

Les knew when he was beaten, and I was still smiling when I kissed Papa goodbye on York station. I had kissed his soft cheek there a hundred times during my life when going south to yet another term of boarding school but this time I was heading much, much further south to another distant archipelago looping across the sea. To the Maldives.

'My dear girl, I can think of nothing nicer than to loll around with you on a deserted island. When are we going?' I could barely believe it. Would it really happen, this time? Together, à deux with Helly Handsome.

'I know February is not the best time of year for the islands, but it's mad for me to go in high season, just too expensive.'

'That's fine for me and I'm ready for some fun, business is tiresome at the moment.'

Fighting not to allow myself to be over-excited, I watched the atolls, like strings of pearly bubbles spun across a translucent turquoise sea, looping across more than three hundred miles of ocean, there were over a thousand to choose from. The Minister of Tourism had told me the ship would be welcome anywhere, I merely had to say where I wanted to go. I hoped I had painted my vision clearly enough. The island must be uninhabited and unsullied, a place where people would be unable to resist wiggling their toes in the sand, strolling under palm trees and swimming in the warm sea. The shipping agent had told me we must use his preferred operator, who would be available to show me the 'best' island. This was not encouraging, but by now I had learned some patience. The Imray Guide 'Cruising the Indian Ocean' had an inadequate couple of pages detailing the whole of this vast archipelago of more than a thousand coral atolls, but I was determined to find that secluded island with soft white sand, waving palm trees and warm, clear water, with or without the minister's involvement. Visions of lolling around with HH in these idyllic surroundings filled my head, exactly as they would for our passengers. Of course, the agent for Customs clearance, the passenger bureaucracy and local guides had to be dealt with, but at least our tenders would provide the required transport.

With an hour to wait before the boat transfer to my island hotel, I had time for a wander around the national capital of Malé. There was little to hold my interest, apart from the fish market, which even now, at midday, still bustled with wrangling fishermen. Mounds of slim fish, slippery and slender, lay graded according to size, on the cold concrete. Next door, in a more prestigious site, were their colourful cousins, a riot of frills, stripes and rainbow colours, the fashionistas of the reef. Keeping watch from the wings was the heavy mob, muscular tuna, like bouncers protecting their fancy clients. With sharp fins and angular tails designed for speed, even in death they looked predatory.

Tepid water splashed over the gunwale as the fibreglass boat with its stretched green awning sped towards a green fuzz of coconut palms blowing away the grey of Heathrow and fustiness of the flight. I must find time to get a tan before HH arrives, I thought.

'Good afternoon. Welcome, Mrs Dalton, please follow me. I will take you to your villa.'

'Hello. Good to have arrived.' I burrowed in Prada feeling for my passport.

'No need for the passport here, we have all your details.'

Suspiciously, I wondered whether I was being watched, or maybe it was simply a nice touch, but I decided I didn't really care. HH would arrive tomorrow. A knot of excitement tightened in my stomach. I had promised him a warm turquoise sea, waving palms and a secluded hut, so the hotel would need to be good if my reputation was to remain intact.

The villa was designed to replicate the whorl of a seashell and was constructed entirely of bamboo and teak to blend with the palms and island vibe. Slatted shutters folded back opening onto an uninterrupted view across the private beach. In the middle of the 'shell' was a circular space, filled with a huge four-poster bed. Gauzy net curtains, tied to the uprights by scarlet ribbons, moved gently in the soft breeze. From the bed, the view of the ocean would be unimpeded. On the inshore side, there was a dense screen of pandanus, their knobbly fruits hanging like unripe pineapples. It was a romantic hideaway.

Kicking off my shoes, I sauntered across the sand. It was almost too hot to walk on, so I speeded up and ran into the sea. Ahead of me, where the pale turquoise turned to aqua in deeper water, a school of fish swam slowly past, yellow dorsal fins frilled along their backs, a crisp contrast to their grey sides flashing silver as they turned in the sunlight. Time to join them.

Stepping from the sand into the shallow foot bath to rinse off my feet I heard a little electronic beep. A discordant note among the soft sounds of sea and rustling palms. The green screen of my mobile flashed with the sign of a missed call. HH. But he had left a message. He rarely left messages, but he must be feeling jolly and maybe had called as he boarded his flight. Twelve hours and he would be here, here to share the 'shell'. I pressed the little black phone close to my ear, not wanting to miss the slightest intonation of his voice.

'Hello, gorgeous. It seems I've missed you, pity. I'm boarding now but will try to ring again when I land, in about five hours. Catch you then. Ciao baby and keep smiling.'

How could he ring me in four hours? He was flying direct and that was at least ten hours.

I went for another swim, unable to concentrate on anything, but even the water had lost some of its sparkle. I lolled away the time, waiting. The breeze gained strength, by the time it was dark, I needed to close the shutters and pull on a jersey. Maybe the company of the dining room would help time to pass.

'Good evening, Madame. I am afraid the restaurant is closed, because of the weather, but we will send some food to you. Which number is your villa?'

I strolled back. Still another hour before I could expect his call. Finally, it came.

'Where are you?' I tried not to be exasperated.

'Well…'

'Are you still there? I can't hear you.' I could tell what was coming.

'Yes, I'm here. I'm afraid work has intervened. A deal I've been chasing for years. It's finally come to a head.'

'Oh. what do you mean "intervened"?'

'I have to be in Georgia, sorry.'

'Are you there now?'

'No, I'm in Budapest. Georgia tomorrow. If I'd known this would happen you could have come too. This is a lovely hotel, Four Seasons, Gresham's bank, Art Nouveau, all curls and swirls. The room has a great view across the river towards the museum. You should be here.'

'Yes, if I had known.' My voice trailed off, saying anything further would simply have sounded as bad tempered, angry and disappointed as I felt. Time together, whether on safari or sunning and swimming in tropical waters was again to remain a fantasy.

Nursing my disappointment, I slowly became aware of the buffeting and strengthening wind. Silhouetted against the outside light, branches writhed, palm fronds were swept aside like fringes of hair. With the shutters closed, my little teak villa felt snug but lonely. I have always enjoyed weather and there was no denying the cyclone was exhilarating. I had anticipated the Maldives would be calm and picture-postcard pretty but now, with no HH and bad weather, I simply wanted to get the job done. My interest in lazy sun-drenched days had been blown away. Before slipping between the cool sheets, I emailed the agents reducing the time of my inspection visit and bringing the date of my flight home nearer by three days.

Through the night, the crashing of waves kept me awake and the whole structure creaked and groaned. Dawn, grey and heavy with rain was more like February in London than the tropics. The downpour thundered on the makuti roof while the wind, unabated, squealed through the slats of the shutters. Outside, on my private terrace, the solid teak furniture had all disappeared. Table, chairs and lounger were nowhere to be seen. Today was obviously a washout. And having reduced my time and changed the flight, that would only leave one more day.

'Hello, good morning. Is the dining room open for breakfast?' I asked the waitress. Neatly dressed in pink with a matching scrap of fabric pinned to her wiry black hair, she was sweeping the polished black floor. Leaves and bits of broken palm roof lay scattered among the tables.

'Yes, Ma'am. Please take a seat, anywhere you like. All our other guests left yesterday.'

'Oh, I arrived yesterday. How long do these storms usually last?' She propped up the broom and looked worried. 'I don't know, lady. But I'll go and ask.' In a moment she was back.

'Ma'am, my boss he say if we are lucky today will be the end, but sometimes it go on for two or maybe three days.'

I filled my time, filing photos, emailing, reading and missing HH. The day was grey and chilly and soon everything I touched was sticky from the humid, salt-laden air. It was a relief when an email from the agents popped up. They would come in the morning with a boat and show me the 'best' island. Asking the name of the island and in which direction, resulted only in 'one hour boat ride or maybe two.' Again, I hoped they understood what I needed to find.

But by the morning the storm had blown itself out, and the sunshine was warm as I stepped into a nasty little fibreglass boat. It bobbed in the choppy waves, bumping and thumping against the wooden jetty. Six fat fenders lay unused inboard. Along the jetty came a swarthy man. Casually he sauntered along, flapping shorts, baseball cap, cigarette in hand, reflective sunglasses and a heavy gold bracelet. A caricature of a low-grade agent on any tourist island anywhere in the world. Two bulky Yamaha outboard motors were strapped to the transom, each boasting a hundred horses corralled within.

'You Mrs Amelia? I am Akhil.'

'Good to meet you, Akhil. What's the plan?' I asked, holding out my hand. He ignored it as the boat continued to rock and thump against the jetty.

'We're taking you to Kookamatti,' he said as the engines roared into life. 'It is top-end resort. You will like it.' Instantly I knew I would not, the very word resort filled me with dread.

It was far from what I had specified, and our passengers would not want to be dumped among the holidaymakers of a resort, even for a day.

'How long will it take to get there, please?' I was conscious of my time constraints and concerned this inspection would waste the one precious day.

'It is a long way. Another atoll. The driver, he say an hour, maybe two, but don't worry, I have arranged a lunch there.' He grinned; a gold tooth winked in the sunlight. 'They do really good curry.' By now I knew some agents used my recces as an opportunity to show off, enjoy a big lunch and a day out of the office. For me, sitting around through the middle of the day, eating an unnecessary, huge meal was a total waste of time. And I hated curry.

Above the roar of the outboards, it was impossible to speak, but there was no need. Akhil had disappeared into the little cabin, the soles of his brown feet filled the doorway and occasionally his toes twitched as he slept. Ninety minutes later we arrived at Kookamatti. A chain of concrete bungalows lined the beach, jolly with bright yellow umbrellas. Tanned bodies sprawled across plastic loungers or splashed around a floating bar. Akhil was determined I should see all the delights of the resort. Travelling by golf buggy he took me along the tarmac tracks as Celine Dion crooned from speakers tied to the trunks of coconut palms. Bronzed bikini wearers played on the swings, bashed balls on tennis courts and pedalled past in chattering groups.

'Akhil, thanks for showing me round, but I'm afraid I would like to go as soon as possible. I have a meeting with Mr Jensen, at the seaplane base. Please can you drop me off there instead of the hotel?' Looking from the air at the sea and islands below as I arrived, it had dawned on me that it would be almost impossible to appreciate these coral atolls unless seen from the air. The colours and chain of the islands strung like pearls across the ocean, the fringing coral reefs and lagoons, the vivid change of colour from palest turquoise to deep blue, would all be lost unless seen from above, and of course, our passengers would be arriving by sea. They must be offered views from the air.

'You don't want curry?' he asked incredulously, as the waitress appeared with dishes of curry, poppadum, rice and relishes.

'No thanks, but you enjoy yours. I'll be on the jetty.' He shrugged, took a pull from a half-empty bottle and set about his lunch.

The jetty led from the sandy beach out into the deeper water; halfway along, still in the shallows, baby reef sharks twisted and turned, curling round the wooden uprights, sinuous and stealthy, the black tips of dorsal fins and tails clearly showing. As I watched their antics, the sunshine began to fade and clouds spread steadily across the eastern sky. By the time Akhil and his mates appeared, there was no sunshine and the sky was heavy, dark and threatening. Fat warm raindrops splattered down, splashing into the sea, making the surface dance. Quickly we all got on board and the Yamahas thundered into life. Our driver, tall, in a flimsy T-shirt, pushed the white throttle knobs as far as they would go, until they touched the dashboard. Ahead lightning forked, illuminating the white foam caps of a dark sea. We hurtled across the waves, charging through the blinding rain into the storm. Sea and sky merged into a wall of grey water.

'You,' the diver shouted, pointing at me. 'You go into cabin.' He gestured at the small opening in the for'ard bulkhead, where Akhil's feet already twitched in a curry and beer induced stupor. I hunched over my rucksack, trying to shield the camera and phone, as rain stung my face and ran down my back, so that I was unable to open my eyes. The driver squinted at the compass and gave a slight twitch to the wheel, then having corrected the course, he grasped the wheel, tucked his elbows tightly into his sides and closed his eyes. Two hundred Yamaha horses blindly propelled us into the storm. Even if soaked, I reckoned I was safer beside the sightless driver than trapped by Akhil's bulk in the cabin. I hummed 'Men of Harlech' fervently hoping there were no floating coconuts or chunks of wood bobbing in our path, anything would hole the boat at this speed.

Miraculously we made it, and as the seaplane base appeared out of the gloom, the rain stopped. A watery sun shone on the red and white bodies of dripping seaplanes. Floating beside the pontoons, they were grounded, waiting for the end of the cyclone and the final squall to shriek through. I clambered off the boat and squelched along the pontoon towards the incongruously modern Seaplane HQ, pushing open the plate glass doors. Immediately my sopping wet shorts and T-shirt clung to me, the chill of the efficient air conditioning an icy blast.

'Good afternoon, can I help you?' asked a uniformed check-in girl, politely ignoring my dripping hair and soaking clothes.

'Thank you, I have an appointment with Mr Jensen. He's expecting me.' I added, conscious water was running off me, seeping into the carpet. She pressed a buzzer and sunlight flashed, catching the movement of a glass door. With a name like Jensen, obviously he was Danish but nonetheless, the tall, blonde figure walking towards me was unnervingly cool. He looked at me and smiled.

'Cappuccino?' he asked.

Next morning, the occupants of the now full hotel dining room looked up from their breakfast papaya and omelettes, their attention caught by rainbow fans of sparkling water. Even at a distance the seaplane was eye catching and I tried to hide a smug smile. It taxied towards the jetty. I stood, leaving my table, tucking my notebook into my Prada friend, and sauntered nonchalantly down the boardwalk.

'Good morning, Mrs Dalton.' A figure, immaculate in tropical whites, stood at the end of the jetty. 'I am Henry and the pilot is George. Welcome on board.' He held open the red and white door.

'Thank you, Henry. Good morning.' I ducked inside. 'Hi George.' I stretched a hand over the back of the seat.

'G'day,' came the Aussie reply as he pushed back his headphones.

'Thank you for being so punctual,' I shouted above the whirr of the engine. 'Mr Jensen gave me lot of suggestions yesterday, but I'm happy to start wherever you like.'

'Well, the final clouds of the cyclone have gone now, so I reckon we can go south, down to the south of Huvadhoo Atoll, you can see the local crafts down there. Strap yourself in and enjoy the flight, about a hundred and twenty miles.'

It was impossible not to. The only tiny cloud on my own horizon was that HH was not here to share the fun. Pushing thoughts of him aside, I surrendered to the beauty laid out below. A few remaining puffs of white cloud made patches of shadow on the water, stretching endlessly in all directions like ruffled silk. Definitely, I thought, an ocean, not a sea. As we flew along the colours of the water changed. The rich blue of deep water grew lighter when atoll after atoll, each with a wavy edge of reef coral or a motionless, pale lagoon, slid below like abandoned deck quoits. These shallower, enclosed waters were every shade of turquoise, from the palest azure over the white sand to stronger peacock blue, speckled with brown where the mounds of coral bommies almost broke the surface. The seaplane itself was exhilarating, and the idea of not needing a runway added an intoxicating sense of freedom.

We landed on the smooth waters in a spray of crystal droplets. The island was the predictable tangle of sandy paths running between thatched huts. There was a school and a tiny mosque with arched windows prettily edged in green. A gaggle of children clustered in a sandy playground and I realised they had a routine for visiting tourists. Lessons would stop and the children would assemble to dance and sing. I was shown into a house, drank cool milk from a fresh coconut, had an opportunity to buy a hat made from coconut leaves and that was it. It was fine. The island would tick the box of 'meet the locals' but it did not match up in any way to my fantasy of an uninhabited Robinson Crusoe island. I had only a few hours left. Tomorrow I was leaving.

'Hi, George. That was good, thanks. Where to now? Mr Jensen suggested some uninhabited islands. Please could I see them, three, I think?'

'Yeah, Ok, further north. Back the way we've come, about seventy miles. Bithdadoo first, You strapped in?'

I peered through the small window as we taxied over the crystal sea. It seemed curious to be slipping over water, it slapped against the floats as the plane picked up speed, spray fanning up in arcs of silver until we were airborne.

Of the three atoll bubbles, welling up out of the indigo water, each was almost right but not quite good enough. Each was uninhabited, but there were signs of beach parties, the remains of barbecues, volleyball nets or beer cans cashed under arching casuarina branches. I felt sure, if I was determined enough and could keep George motivated, that patch of tropical perfection would be somewhere.

'George, you're doing a great job, I'm loving the flying, too, fabulous. Do you know Madivaru? I read about it in a dive magazine. Could we take a look there, please?'

'Wait a mo, let me find it, and we'll give it a go.'

The cobalt blue of deep water stretched into the distance beyond the wing tips while below, the pale turquoise of shallowing water slipped past as we dropped down to Madivaru. George banked the plane, turning left to circle the lagoon, a brilliant white lifebelt of sand. Smoothly, he brought her down into the middle of the lagoon and taxied towards the beach. By now I felt at home in the seaplane and Henry didn't have to reach across to open the door for me. I flung it open myself and stretched a foot onto the float then jumped into the water. It was warm and only knee deep, the plane was in so close.

Madivaru was a tiny island. In forty minutes, I had walked all the way round. Forty perfect minutes of peaceful isolation. Stretching north from the central cluster of palms was a long white spit of sand. Broken shells lay along the waterline, crab plover skittered ahead poking their black beaks into the shallows searching for molluscs. Ghost crabs scuttled over the sand, disappearing into burrows as I drew near. Shells, moved by their hermit crab inhabitants, twirled away from my feet as I walked. The sand was so white the glare was almost harsh in the afternoon sun. Everything was perfect. There were bommies too, dotting the deeper waters of the lagoon, perfect for snorkelling, and protected from any motion. The break in the outer reef made a route for the tenders to ferry passengers back and forth to the ship standing off in water too deep to anchor. The palms gave shade and finally, the seaplane had the quiet waters of the lagoon for use. Every passenger could have a flight, no one would miss out on seeing these islands, like a necklace of pearls, strung across the ocean.

16

The Seychelles
Fruit Carving and Dumper Trucks

Beneath me again lay ruffled silk of the Indian Ocean. I pinched myself; it would never do if I were to become blasé about this extraordinary job. This time, I was flying for the first time on an Air Seychelles plane and Business class too, which was charmingly called 'Pearl Class'. I had both slept and eaten well. The island nation of the Seychelles, being French speaking, had chosen their airline should have alliance with Air France. While much of the world worried about the dangers of deep vein thrombosis on a long-haul flight and obsessed with easily digested meals, the French airlines took a better view. It had been champagne, red wine and foie gras all the way from Paris.

The Seychelles again offered something different. Now I knew there were two kinds of islands: the inner ones, composed of granite rocks, the hills covered by tropical vegetation, and the outer isles, low-lying and flat, with long beaches, coral atolls with barely a hillock among them. Having realised a recce would be costly, I had booked incognito onto an ancient local cruise ship. Using this vessel as a convenient platform, I could spy my way round the islands with no one aware my aim was to establish a rival programme for a much more glamorous vessel. After the luxurious *Renaissance V* of the Baltic, the elderly *Etoile Royale* was undoubtedly scruffy, with no highly polished rosewood or soft towels made into swans paddling across my bed. I reminded myself this was not a holiday. As work went, cruising across the Indian Ocean while I watched flying fish was not bad. Silvery and swift they skittered across the wave tops in front of the bow, skimming low. Having managed to escape the predatory beak of a brown booby they ran out of puff and collapsed into a wave top. The next morning was not so benign. A large swell unsettled many of the passengers, leaving only the more robust ones to lounge on deck, soaking up the sun and enjoying the motion. The elderly vessel rolled across the ocean, throwing up sheets of water that splashed on board. I loved every moment. In addition to the sense of freedom, the afternoon offered a new excitement:

Fruit Carving and Napkin Folding.
14.30 beside the Pool

Neither of these had seemed important to my life before, but now, as I positioned myself on the balcony above the pool, I realised they were vital. I had an excellent view. Below, on the starboard side of the pool was a long folding table, carefully set with a colourful selection of tropical fruit. Seated around the pool edges, chattering with excited anticipation, were the non-seasick passengers. The chef appeared in full whites and tall toque. He minced round the edge of the pool to the table waving a huge, Samurai-style knife. The applause was fulsome, followed by rapt attention, the only other sound the swish of the sea as our vessel swept over the ocean. Dexterously, using his huge knife, he transformed the fruit. The mango became the body of a cat, its head a tangerine with spaghetti whiskers. A pineapple became a koala, strawberries were turned into mice. Lined up on his table, the growing menagerie watched the passengers. Suddenly a swell came broadside at the ship. She rolled heavily, lifting first the starboard side high, swooping back, sinking the port side as the wave passed by. The ship's motion was reflected in the swimming pool. A tsunami sloshed out of the pool, out over the deck, washing the table and the fruit zoo into the pool. They bobbed about, an incongruous party enjoying an impromptu swim. Undaunted, people jumped to join them in the pool and swam around, gathering up the floating menagerie. It was another introduction to the world of cruise ships, but napkin folding would be taking it too far. Emails and photo filing called me.

After a week, we had visited the granitic isles and I knew what they offered: spice and botanic gardens, craft shops and little museums. But I knew Praslin, Silhouette and La Digue, while glorious with their photogenic beaches and tourist sites, merely skimmed the surface of the magic of the Seychelles. The coral atoll isles, scattered across the ocean to the south, were what I really wanted. Lonely, largely uninhabited and teeming with wildlife, they must become part of our cruise programme. Of these, Aldabra was my goal. This huge, raised coral atoll, the largest in the world, had a lagoon the size of Manhattan and was so remote and isolated there were many endemic species, including the famous giant tortoises. It was unfortunately over seven hundred miles away from Mahe, the main island. While on board the *Etoile Royale* I had asked, emailed, enquired repeatedly how I might get there. It was simple, charter a plane or boat. With the best offer starting at thirteen thousand dollars, I fixed a meeting with our proposed shipping agent. I needed to make him aware just how determined I was. I persisted, waiting for long periods in his office reception, until eventually he came up with a most perfect solution. I could take advantage of someone else's plane and boat.

I settled back into the soft cream leather aware the nineteen other seats in the cabin were empty. I was the only passenger in the charterers' plane and would then have the use of their boat as it returned through the island chain to the marina at Mahe.

'Good morning. Are you Ok back here?' asked the co-pilot. How could I not be, as puffy white clouds floated past the windows of my own private jet quietly eating up the miles?

'Another ten minutes and we'll be at Assomption. You'll get a great view of the strip. We usually give them a buzz to let them know we've arrived, give them time to move the tortoises.'

'Move the tortoises?'

'Sure, they like to live on the runway, and you can imagine what they do when they hear the plane – just hunker down. This is not like Africa, buzzing a strip with antelope works there, but here the tortoises simply retract into their shells.' He grinned. 'That leaves massive immobile obstacles all over the runway.'

'So, what do you do?' I asked torn between wondering if my leg was being pulled and how the plane could land.

'You'll see, don't worry.'

The plane curled down towards a flat expanse of limestone. The coral platform was long enough to provide the only airstrip for hundreds of miles in any direction. All around was only wide blue ocean and a few specs of smaller atolls, including Aldabra itself, about ninety miles away. My boat, like a bath toy, was the only object on the sea and I was happy to see it there, waiting just for me. We landed smoothly. What had the co-pilot meant, I wondered. Walking down the metal steps, immediately I was wrapped in a warm tropical breeze. There, across the concrete strip, I could see mound after mound, a solid line of brown humps edged the runway. One lump grew higher, legs appeared underneath, and the giant tortoise shambled slowly back onto the runway. Another still sat in the scoop of the yellow JCB. As a way of clearing a runway it seemed as novel as the obstacles were unusual.

'Hi! You must be Amelia.' A fellow was coming towards me from the beach. His muscular arms and thick neck were fuzzy with curly ginger hair. His short legs, also covered by a wiry ginger mat, were only visible from the shins to his toes, his shorts having been designed for someone taller.

'You must be Steve. I saw your boat from the air, *Ocean Endeavour*?'

'Hi. Any more luggage?' he asked, taking my holdall and turning to walk down the beach. 'This is Mike, my mate.' Mike was the complete opposite: lithe, tall and athletic, he pushed the rubber boat into deeper water. Dropping the outboard motor, Steve pulled the cord and we pottered across the calm sea. Assomption, inhabited by resilient tortoises and scrubby dry bush, had little to offer apart from a long white shelly beach.

Ocean Endeavour had been an inshore survey boat in her earlier life before being fitted out with six double en-suite cabins. She would be my floating home on the move for ten days, my *Monaco* in the tropics, but this time the crew of six was just for me and my only responsibility was to explore, extensively. I asked Steve where we'd be starting.

'Aldabra of course. We'll be there just before sunset. Beers ashore!'

From the anchorage outside the reef, Aldabra looked like any coral atoll with its white shoreline and line of wind-snapped trees. In high expectation, I slipped over the rubber tube of the Zodiac into ankle-deep water and followed Steve, cans in hand, onto the wiry grass. Dotted with the mini cones and long dry needles of the casuarinas, the grass barely covered the coral underfoot. The breeze was warm and salty, and the view across the still water to the unbroken line of surf edging the reef was unremarkable, indeed the whole place seemed unremarkable. I pulled the ring on a can of Seybrew, waiting. This coral world, which I knew was not merely remote, but unique and fascinating, had yet to reveal its wonders.

'Over there!' Mike shouted, jumping to his feet and running beer in hand towards a palm. Scrambling steadily up the trunk was a giant crab. Huge, mottled and blue, its legs were splayed out reaching right round the trunk. Steve simply picked it off the tree, presenting it to me.

'Hold it round the body so it can't get you.'

'Are you sure? It's bigger than my head and those claws look fearsome.'

'Don't worry, they can't reach you like that. It's a coconut crab, quite rare these days. Gone from most islands – good to eat but safe here. Aldabra's a great place for them. Sandy soil for burrows and plenty of coconuts. Those claws can get a coconut open in moments.' Warily I held the beast, inspecting its carapace before I navigated round a giant tortoise and returned it to the same palm tree.

'Look!' Steve pointed towards the shore. 'I was hoping we'd see one this evening.' Picking its way daintily among the broken chunks of coral came a leggy bird, its mottled back almost dull compared with the rich russet head, stabbing and poking along the shoreline; a white throat patch completed the bird's striking appearance.

'Aldabra rail, endemic, read about it later, there's a good bird book in the saloon. Its survival is quite a story,' he added. I was learning Steve was much more than a stocky fellow in shorts. 'Lagoon in the morning,' he went on. 'Early start. The tide's right so we can enter over to the north west and come out through West Channels.'

'Wow, are we going through Passe Houareau ?' Mike sounded incredulous. 'I've never been through there.' Adding 'Nor have I' seemed superfluous.

'It's a good opportunity, and for once we're not in a hurry.'

It was barely light at five thirty next morning, but I was ready. By now Aldabra had me gripped and I was very excited. Standing on deck, I ticked off the contents of my rucksack: water, hat, sunscreen, camera. In the brief time ashore last night I had experienced just a couple of the species here on this isolated atoll, a Pandora's box of natural treasures. Pottering slowly by Zodiac through the huge lagoon would be breathtaking and an experience of a lifetime. Crossing the vast expanse of water and exploring amongst the mangroves took us over five hours before we reached the west side. The roof of the Picard research station was just visitable through the scrubby trees.

The lagoon had been unforgettable. It had started with spotting a manatee. The water, just a few feet deep, was crystal clear, lit by sun bright on the silvery bottom, and we had watched her peacefully breakfasting on seagrass. Frigate birds had swooped overhead, wobbling red spotty inflated pouches as they flew, white-crested terns scanned the shallow waters, sacred ibis with their bushy black tail feathers perched precariously on branches over the water, and of course there were colonies of brown noddies, raucous and rowdy.

The abundance was exhausting. Everywhere, in every direction. The unique wildlife, rich, rare and specialised surrounded me. In places, the coral cliffs were four or five feet high and were studded with huge fossil fans and giant clam shells. Mangroves formed a ribbon of forest around the lagoon edge, their network of roots providing calm channels for mudskippers, molluscs and hermit crabs. It had been an extraordinary five hours, peering through binoculars, staring into the clear waters, searching mangroves and all the while trying not to get burnt to a frazzle.

'Ok, Parc Caret, here we are. We'll do a drift dive through the channels. Mike, can you pick us up outside, please?' Steve directed. 'You Ok with that, Amelia? Keep near me and avoid getting pinned by the current against the base of one of those limestone mushroom islets, the coral is razor sharp.'

Now I would become less an intruder and more part of the environment; for me, this was a major charm of diving.

Holding hands, we were swept along by the ebbing tide, the sea pouring out from the shallow lagoon into the surrounding deep waters of the Indian Ocean. Just as the current bore us through the channels, so too it carried a myriad of sea creatures. We all drifted along at the same speed borne on the outgoing tide.

Turtles were everywhere, effortlessly swooping and turning: a flipper tapped my shoulder and slowly I turned my head to receive a stare of curiosity rather than fear. Above, surgeonfish were silhouetted against the patterned shafts of sunlight. A party of reef sharks lazily flicked their black-tipped tail fins, seeming less of a threat when we were all part of the same tidal flow. Eagle rays, flat winged and elegantly spotted, slid smoothly beneath. Occasionally, the swirling tidal currents affected the visibility, making the ride even more mysterious, and Steve would give my hand a squeeze, pointing out something I had missed. All too quickly the water grew cooler, the blue around me deeper, and the bottom fell away as we left the shallows of the channel. Giant lacy fan corals appeared, bending in the current. Napoleon wrasse at home among the intricate branches of red tree coral finned stiffly past. Clams, tucked into the indented reef, had curly electric-blue lips, unmoving as they filtered the rich currents.

It had been an experience never to be forgotten. Again, I was in a magical place, again I vowed to make it work. Others must have an opportunity to witness this extraordinarily wonderful place.

The days that followed were equally memorable, and every one was different. Steve had been adding to his knowledge as a diver and marine biologist around the isles for years. Mike was an acrobat, taking a break from the trapeze he usually swung around with at Cirque du Soleil. They were an unlikely duo, and my recce became one of the most extraordinary and privileged times of my life. I dived, walked and explored one isolated coral atoll after another.

Cosmoledo, romantically named after Portuguese sailors, had a lagoon as tidal as Aldabra. In the rubber inflatable we whizzed across the shallow waters to see the red-footed booby colony on Ile du Nord. I strolled the white reflective sands of Wizard island and learned to avoid walking on the trailing, salt-resistant stems bright with citrus yellow flowers, but spiky for bare feet.

Sailing steadily north, we reached the Amirante archipelago and like Vasco da Gama, we paused to explore again. The atoll of Astove instantly felt different. There was an overwhelming air of sorrow and the wildlife was missing. This had been a coconut plantation and home to a pioneering couple, their Spanish-style hacienda now crumbling into decay. Deteriorating quickly in the tropical climate, the low buildings were empty, abandoned and silent. Carved teak doors, imported from Zanzibar, swung forlornly into echoing empty rooms. The struggle of life in such a lonely place had been too much, and the island was sliding back into deserted peace.

For ten days I saw no one other than my ship's crew, not another soul crossed my horizon, only abundant and varied wildlife. Atoll after atoll, empty beaches, dives, snorkels, strolls, Zodiac rides and swims. My days were spent watching turtles, rays, sharks, birds and butterflies. There was only a tiny cloud on the horizon: I had no Hugo or HH to share this utterly beautiful, extraordinary coral world with.

17

Eritrea
The Land of Punt

'Do you really feel that country is suitable?' Michael asked. Everyone round the table looked at me.

'Yes, I do. I realise the capital, Asmara is inland, up in the hills, but I think it's manageable, as manageable as Cairo.' I was determined to convince them. 'Massawa is the port and fascinating in itself. It's known as the "Pearl of the Red Sea".'

I went on to explain that Asmara had extraordinary architecture, Modernist, Art Deco and untouched since the forties. I admitted it would be a challenge, but I believed Massawa would make an ideal preliminary port for the Red Sea passages. 'Absolutely no one else goes there, definitely a coup,' I concluded. By now, I knew Michael better, and the idea of a 'first' would appeal to him.

'OK, but you must take someone with you. Someone tough. Stuart would be good,' Michael said. 'I'll give him a call. Great guy, you'll like him.'

Stuart's help assembling my travelling office had been invaluable, but as a Minder in Eritrea?

Weary, I dozed as the train bore me south. As so often HH crept unbidden into mind. It was frustrating not to know more about him and his personal life. Despite the hours I'd spent with him on his yacht, I still knew so little. Did he have a wife, children? But he had not asked about me, so I did not ask about him. Whenever we had met, the mood had been too enjoyable to risk our growing closeness. Our encounters had all been flirtatious and full of laughter. Had he gone on a safari alone? Where was he now? Never mind, Eritrea would be exciting and take my mind off him.

My phone vibrated and slid across the carriage table.

'Hello! You must be psychic!'

'Hello, Travel Diva. Where are you now? Sounds like you're on a train.'

'Yes, on my way back to London. And you? Are you back from Africa, did you go on safari?'

'Came straight home as you wouldn't join me. Where are you off to next? Timbuktu?'

I felt confident he would not know Eritrea. It was far more exotic than Timbuktu.

'I've been to the Seychelles since we last spoke,' I said, quickly adding, 'And now I'm off to Eritrea.'

'Eritrea? Interesting place. I've done some work in Oman and of course Dubai, but always thought the Art Deco capital – what's it called? – would be worth a look.'

'Asmara.' I wondered if I'd ever find a place he didn't know.

'You'll be going to the Islands, the Dahlak, I think. Marine park, near the main port, just your sort of thing.' These were the specs I had spotted on the chart close to the narrow southern entrance to the Red Sea, romantically named the Bab al-Mandab, *The Gate of Tears*. This was annoying. He even knew about 'my' archipelago.

'If you're going there,' he carried on blithely, 'you'll need company. It's not the place for a pretty girl on her own. How about I join you?' The train jolted, or maybe it was just my heart.

'Would you really come with me?' I asked. 'There'll be quite a lot of tiresome stuff to cover.' What could I do about Stuart, or whoever it was Michael had organised? HH would most certainly be a distraction, the recce could turn into a holiday. The sensible Amelia took over. 'I'd love that, it would be wonderful.' I wanted to make his company still sound a possibility, but that would not be fair. 'I'm afraid the office has lined someone up, an IT geek. Not my idea of support or even good company.' However much Michael might like him, Stuart would not match up to the thrill of HH.

'Pity. Get in touch when you're back. I'll be interested to hear about it. You'll end up the star of the travel world. Speak soon.' He was gone, he never wasted time chatting, his phone calls barely merited being called conversations. Disappointment flooded through me and I sagged into the dusty train seat.

We pulled into Kings Cross on time and as I made my way down the long platform there seemed to be even more couples than usual greeting each other with kisses and hugs. At the barrier stood a chunky figure in black Lycra. A reflective orange top and luminous stripes on his shorts marked him out as a hardcore cyclist.

'Hello, you must be Amelia.' Nice smile, 'I'm Stuart. Michael described you perfectly.'

'Hello, Stuart. Ok, so what did he say, then?'

'I'm not telling you that,' he laughed, adding, 'but it was Ok. How about a coffee? Is that little computer still working?' We walked across the station forecourt; his cycling shoes clicked on the shiny surface. Compact and muscular, he had the air of a taut professional athlete rather than a light-starved IT weed. Unnervingly he pronounced he was ready for Eritrea. I wondered what 'ready' meant; I felt far from ready.

Hills, arid and sandy, stepped into neat terraces, spread like corduroy below. As the landscape became mountainous and barren the Red Sea slid away behind. The plane banked and landed smoothly. Asmara. Using the experience gained in the Comoros, this time I had emailed the Director General of Tourism in advance. But, as I had feared, there was no friendly local holding a board with my name on, so we climbed into a battered taxi and headed for the hotel. The entrance was an unexpectedly modern façade of plate glass and steel. Stuart jumped out and grabbed the bags from the boot. Until now he had been absorbed by his headphones, preventing communication, but this was encouraging. I was already glad not to be alone.

The soaring façade belonged to the Intercontinental Hotel, built to provide Hillary Clinton, when she visited as Secretary of State, with the facilities she had specified. Everything was relentlessly modern. We could have been in any hotel in any developed country, but in Eritrea, a land of eight ethnic peoples with a history dating back to the twenty-fifth century BC, and part of the Land of Punt, this glossy hotel looked bizarrely out of place. Eritrea as an independent country was only ten years old by then and, as I had gathered when doing my reading up, was not for the faint hearted.

'I'd like to get into the town proper, if that's Ok with you? See the real bits – Liberation Avenue, the cathedral, or rather duomo! Some of the Art Deco architecture?'

'Pool first,' Stuart replied firmly. 'Meet here in forty-five?' Without waiting for an answer, he strode lightly across the polished marble floor. He was right, the pool turned out to be everything indoor pools rarely are. Warm, spanking clean and with no dripping humidity.

Reinvigorated, we set off to explore the capital.

Keen to engage Stuart's interest, I told him what I'd learned about Eritrea. Italy had been anxious not to miss out during the 'Scramble for Africa', so they developed the city and the country had become the jewel of their African colonies. There had been a long fight for independence from Ethiopia, over thirty years with Ethiopia backed by Russia, but Eritrea won its freedom eventually.

Liberation Avenue came as a surprise; it was thronged with people. Women, elegant in white embroidered robes, their heads a mass of tight plaits, sauntered arm in arm with their men. Also dressed in white, they had long skirt-like tunics and perfectly pressed shirts. The city's population was strolling and chatting, leaning towards each other to pass on the evening's gossip. It was a true Italian *passeggiata* with an African twist, taking place beneath arching jacaranda trees. We joined in, to stroll past the opera house where wide steps rose to a classical façade of Romanesque arches and columns flanked by tall palm trees. Bougainvillea romped over walls and railings in vibrant shades of magenta. Next, came the cathedral, built with encouragement from Mussolini. Inside the cool interior we were met by lingering scents of incense and wax. Columns, stripy like seaside rock in white marble and warm brick, soared towards a cupola patterned like a chessboard. In memory of Digby, I lit a tall thin candle and pushed it into the metal stand under a garish painting of the Madonna, thinking how much he would have liked the vivid reds and blues. In every church and cathedral I had been into throughout my travels for over three years, I had lit a candle for him, and it pleased me to think of the many, many places remote and lonely where a candle had burned in his memory, from Tromsø to Tana. Now Asmara was part of his trail.

'Come on, you must be starving,' I said not wishing to dwell on memories of Digby.

'You bet, what's the plan?'

'Is local Ok for you? There's a place described by the *Lonely Planet* as "the best restaurant in town", what do you think?' I asked, hoping he would not prefer the Pizzeria Hawashait visible ahead.

'Sounds good to me. So, what's local?'

'*Wat.*' I replied rather smugly.

'Sorry. I asked what we're going to eat, what's the local food?'

'W*at!*'

He looked at me quizzically. 'What do you mean, what?'

'*Wat* is a kind of meat stew eaten with a pancake called *'injera'*. The stew goes in the middle, you tear a piece of pancake off, wrap it round a chunk of meat and pop it in. Are you up for that?'

'Of course!' He sounded almost affronted that I might think otherwise. I was beginning to appreciate Michael's introduction; Stuart was easy to like.

'There'll be no cutlery, so don't forget you only use your right hand. Beer?' We were led to the back of the room to settle on the floor, leaning against giant stripy cushions. In the dim light, we peered at menus. *Injera* was the most expensive option. 'The local brew is a Bellotti. Apparently, if you drink much you'll get *"Bellotti botti!"* So maybe you'd prefer an Asmara Gin, I expect that's pretty good firewater too.'

Our alcove was tucked into the deepest recesses of the

restaurant. Deep crimson curtains generously swagged created a secluded, if rather gloomy, tent. Pushing aside a fold, a waiter appeared like a genie, the toes of his shoes curled with age rather than Aladdin style. With a flourish, he placed a small, highly carved table between us and disappeared. Reappearing a moment later, he set small dishes precisely round the edges of the table, each with a dollop of sauce and a small wooden spoon. Every bowl looked the same, a muddy brown, the only difference seemed to be the size of the lumps breaking the surface. The middle of the table remained empty, the *injera* slot.

'I have ordered what is supposedly the "top" injera.' I said, 'which is, naturally, the most expensive, but at six dollars we're not denting my allowance too much.'

'Did you understand what sort of meat it'll be?' asked Stuart.

'I think the top *'wat'* is lamb.'

'Wat Ho!'

We waited, beers rapidly diminishing. Eritrea's national dish was obviously not to be rushed. The curtains swished, the genie popped in again and simultaneously the table was flooded with light from a big sixties-style spotlight, tucked into a fold of the curtains. With due reverence, he placed a large basin on the table, clouds of steam billowed round our tent increasing the humidity and heat.

'Wat a surprise.'

'Difficult to see *wat* it looks like.' Giggling, I flapped at the clouds of steam for a proper look at the *injera*. It was reminiscent of the washing facilities at boarding school. There was a large bowl lined with *injera,* a pancake resembling grey flannel that flopped over the sides. The bright light revealed the *wat* in all its greasy glory. Grey lumps of meat were stranded like volcanic islands in an ocean of fatty liquid.

'Well, maybe it tastes better than it looks,' I said hopefully, tearing off a piece of the *injera*. The pancake was cold, its consistency an unhappy mix between sponge and flannel. Bravely, delving into the basin, I wrapped it round a chunk of meat. It tasted much, much worse than it looked. The meat was inedible, tough and fibrous. Stuart watched as I chewed and chewed.

He grinned. 'Looks good then.'

'Well,' I spat the piece into my hankie, 'it may be Eritrea's national dish, but it is, without doubt, the most disgusting thing I have ever eaten. You try.'

'No way! Your expression is enough for me.'

'Go on. You've got to. You can't come to Eritrea and not even try it.' Unwillingly he tore off a piece of flannel and chewed reluctantly, finally swallowing in a gulp.

We settled the bill and went for a pizza, followed by *gelato*, mine a crunchie *nocciola* and Stuart's a smooth *caffe;* both were delicious.

'What did you think of the Bellotti?' I asked, between licks.

'It's Ok, nothing remarkable, thirst quenching in this climate. Why?'

'I'm interested in the brewers, the Bellotti family. Apparently, they built a stunning villa on the coast, near Massawa, the port, that's where we're going tomorrow. One of the family's old Mammas lived there throughout the Russian bombing. It's all closed up of course, but I'd love to see it. An Art Deco gem.'

The next day's drive took us down from the two thousand metres of Asmara to the heat and humidity of the coast. It was an interesting drive, one moment typically African, the next an incongruous white Italianate church would be the focus of a straggling community. We drove past simple villages of mud houses, their corrugated iron roofs held in place by stones dangling on strings. Donkeys, goats, scruffy dogs and cows with wide-curving horns stood among the houses or ambled across the road. Children smiled and waved, kicking footballs and scampering in the dust. Women walked along the verges, elegant and upright, swathed in thick white cotton shawls despite the heat, water pots balanced on their heads.

'Is the road tarmacked all the way to Massawa?' I asked.

'Yes, it is a good road' replied Semhar, our guide. Semhar was a surprise. After escaping to avoid the worst of the fighting, she had spent several years in Belgium and when Eritrea achieved Independence, she had returned, feeling her country needed her skills. Smart, and with an appreciation of European ways, she spoke excellent English and was also very beautiful, her skin a delicate café au lait.

'Oh! They are lucky today. They have a little mist.'

'What's good about the mist? It just means we can't see,' asked Stuart grumpily.

'The valley traps the air coming up from the coast, look you can see how green it is here. This makes the village rich; they can grow good fruit, so their market is popular.'

'Semhar, what did you do in Brussels? You have such perfect English.' She smiled, saying nothing. Maybe she had been a spy.

The road wound on, twisting and turning in big loops as it wound down to the coastal plain. A viaduct loomed out of the mist, another relic of colonisation.

'Soon it will be working again,' Semhar pronounced

proudly. 'The government has promised to get the train going. When it transports goods up from the port it will make a big difference to our economy.'

Acacia scrub shared the foothills with small fields of maize, and we shared the road with camels, the ubiquitous goats and docile spotted cows. The road seemed to unravel like grey ribbon, spooling towards the coast across the harsh dry landscape. Spaced across the flat terrain white mounds began to appear. Each was dotted with brilliant bursts of colour.

'What's all this, Semhar?'

'Salt. Once,' she said, almost wistfully, 'the trade from Massawa was pearls, incense, myrrh, frankincense, ostriches and even giraffes, but now, now this salt is our major export. It has been collected here since ancient times, going mainly to Ethiopia but of course not now. The Italians really got the industry going again, and then it went as far away as Japan. But now only across the sea to the Yemen. The whole industry is trying to get back on its feet after the war.' As we passed one pile close to the road, the vivid splashes of colour were revealed as baskets. They were woven with zigzag patterns in vivid, almost clashing shades of orange, red and shocking pink, and were filled with heaps of harsh white salt.

'Is that Massawa ahead?' Through the shimmer of heat, a broken line of gappy white teeth, grinned along the horizon, a mirage, insubstantial and jagged.

'Yes, that's Massawa. It is a different world down here. Even the two islands that make up the town are not the same. One is Arabic and Turkish with bits of Portuguese and Egyptian – that's officially Massawa. The other, Taulud, is full of Italian villas.' She turned round from the front seat, adding with a smile, 'But there's hardly any sign of the British occupation.'

'Is the Villa Bellotti on Taulud, then?' I asked, hoping she might be interested in the villa too. 'I'd love to see it.'

'I'd like to see it as well,' she said, 'but I'm afraid that's impossible. It is fenced off. Even I have never been there.' We rattled over a causeway, the water of the port looked surprisingly clean, a still clear turquoise. 'Will you be Ok if I go and see my friends tonight?' she asked. 'I don't get down here very often so it's a great opportunity.'

'Of course,' I replied, happy to have freedom to explore. 'The minister has confirmed there will be no difficulties at the port, so shall we meet about seven-thirty tomorrow? You can show us the town, then. I would like to plan the route for a walking tour, maybe among the old Arab buildings.'

'Sure. Here's your hotel, see you tomorrow.'

The late afternoon sun emphasised the grubbiness in the lobby of the Dahlak Hotel. Large ugly chairs, with worn blue covers filled the whole dreary space. Not one of the sagging seats was occupied. From the array of keys hanging behind Reception, it seemed we were the only guests.

'You all right?' Stuart asked, appearing at a run down the stairs. 'Any water in your taps or the shower?'

'No, none. And the mosquitoes are like B52 bombers.' I hoped he was not regretting this unglamorous recce.

Stuart was more interested in exploring than moaning. 'Come on, let's get out of here and find a beer. I'm beginning to like Bellotti after all, botti or no botti.'

'It looks like a short walk to Massawa island, shall we go that way?'

Almost immediately we entered a maze of exhausted streets. Trees, collapsed furniture and broken-up concrete clogged the road. But even in the rapidly fading evening light and amidst the devastation inflicted by the bombardment, the air of elegance and grandeur remained tangible. Sweeping arcades with lattices and white stuccowork were all around. Ruined palaces with Ottoman windows and arched doorways slumbered in the heavy evening air. Above us hung ornate balconies of latticed wood, the *mashrabiya,* only partially attached to their houses, still clung on. The evening light softened the decay and quickly I became absorbed in taking photos, while Stuart slowly sauntered on, gazing at the buildings. Before long he was just a shadowy outline, waiting for me to catch up. As I drew near, a rich smell of cooking, spicy and fragrant, became stronger. Stuart stood beside a waist-high terracotta pot; a heat haze shimmered above the open top.

'What do you reckon?'

Squatting on his haunches in an arched doorway, steadily watching us, was an old man with a neatly clipped white moustache. On his head rolls of white fabric were wound into an oversized turban. The contrast of white turban, dark skin, deep hooded eyes and pale moustache were striking. Aromas of coffee and ginger mingled in the haze above the clay pot.

'*As-salaam alaykum,*' he greeted us, standing up and holding out a tin cup.

'*Wa alaykum as-salaam,*' I replied, taking the offered cup with my right hand, and hoping my reply was correct. Stuart, quick to catch on, bowed a little and took another proffered cup. He waved at the shimmering pot.

'I've been watching him. I think he just plasters a fish with spices and then slaps it onto the sides of the pot.' Stuart was intrigued. 'It's as hot as Hades, look at the charcoal in the bottom.' Heat buffeted my face as I tried to see inside. The old man shuffled forwards and slapped two large fish against the walls of the clay oven, quickly following with discs of white dough. The heat was so intense it was difficult to get anywhere near the oven, never mind plunge in your hands to slap both fish and bread inside. We smiled and grinned, pointing at the oven and then fanning our faces. He bowed slightly and thrust a hand into the searing heat. First the fish came out and then the chapatis. He presented them to us with a toothless grin.

Stuart pulled a fish bone out of his mouth. 'Asmara can keep its yuky *injera*. I could eat this every day. There is a problem, though, the beer's missing.'

18

Eritrea

Isles at the Gate of Tears

By contrast, breakfast was mostly disgusting. We gave the flabby slices of white bread a miss in favour of dark aromatic coffee and scented mango. Fortunately, the view from the harbour was wonderful: you could see the dhows manoeuvring, some without engines, just manpower and a sail.

Semhar appeared.

'Good morning, are you well? How do you like this room?' she asked politely, adding, 'It is round.' To be sure, we had noticed.

'Hi, Semhar.' Stuart appeared, pink and sweaty. 'Are we walking around the town this morning?' In the relative cool of the morning, he had been out for a run and Tigger-like was now bouncing, ready for the day.

'Yes, we go to see the buildings. Many are damaged from the bombardment, but they are still wonderful. It will be hot and dusty so please bring your hats.'

These were the days before bottled water when sunscreen and a hat were thought to be sufficient.

Our stroll the previous evening had revealed a city of glamorous faded elegance and exotic trade but this morning the scene had no soft light, gentle and mellow to flatter the ruins. The white sunlight was harsh on wrecked buildings, bomb craters, broken roofs and battered balconies. Everywhere was brutally damaged.

'Semhar, what are those there for?' I pointed towards three dark tanks. With gun barrels angled only just above the town, they loomed threateningly on black marble plinths.

'This is our Monument. It is very important to us. It marks the Struggle for Independence. They are polished every morning,'

'And that building?'

Two rows of blue-tiled columns, now battered and pock-marked, rose to a colonnade of arches, topped by a silver dome. Half of it was missing leaving a gaping hole. Open to the skies on one side it had the smashed appearance of a boiled breakfast egg.

'That was where he stayed, Emperor Haile Selassie. It was his winter palace,' Semhar said proudly. 'The building had the first elevator in the country.'

In searing edge-of-desert heat we strolled through the maze of streets. Whether Ottoman, Art Deco or Venetian, a palace, a bank, coral-block house or mosque, it was the most eclectic architectural confusion I had ever seen, though now tragically destroyed. We hardly saw a soul. Throughout this little island town, the buildings had finely detailed façades, deeply carved doors and shutters, but the morning light was harsh and the broken *mashrabiya* we had seen the previous evening, with its latticed woodwork permitting cooling air to flow into the house, looked even more distressed. It hung from the walls of the first floor, air free now to flow in anywhere. Once the typical Islamic windows had graced magnificent palazzi and rich merchant's houses, but all these stylish architectural features had been wrecked.

'Semhar, I think we're done for just now, thank you. What's the plan for the afternoon?' I asked at the end of the morning. 'Shall we visit Taulud?'

She scuffed her shoes in the dust, studying the toes. 'This afternoon, I leave you.' It was a statement, not a question. 'I have friends down here, in Massawa, I don't see them often, and I have shown you the port, so I am done.' This was annoying: after all, she had been employed as my guide and it was because of me that she was here at all.

Seeing my expression Stuart said, 'That's fine. You go and see your family. We're Ok, we'll go exploring, but what about the arrangements for tomorrow?'

'I have fixed the boat. It is ready. You must be at the harbour by seven o'clock in the morning.'

I fought back my annoyance. Would she not be with us? 'Does the captain speak English?' African laisse-faire was creeping into my carefully planned recce. I needed her help and local advice to work out how a ship over ninety metres long with eighty passengers would manage a programme at a barely heard of archipelago. It was by far the most complicated element of what I was doing down here in the southern part of the Red Sea. All the arrangements, whether Asmara, Massawa or the Dhalak Islands, must work, or there was no reason to be in her country.

'Yes, he speaks English. He says he has a good boat and knows where you want to go.' My hackles rose. How could he possibly know where I wanted to go? He had no knowledge of our passengers and knew nothing about the ship. Again, Stuart stepped in.

'Don't worry, I'm sure we can work it out. Will we see you again? Maybe this evening?'

'No, I will see my friends and then stay a few days with

my aunt. I've not seen her for many years.' She shrugged her shoulders. 'Now it is goodbye. Enjoy the boating tomorrow.'

I knew when I was beaten.

In the cool, early next morning, the taxi dropped us at the harbour. The quays were lined with small steel cargo boats, a shabby but serviceable fleet that traded along the coast to Djibouti, or across the waters to Mocha and Aden, perhaps even as far east as the island of Socotra. Among the battered jumble of steel struts, aerials and small cranes, were traditional wooden dhows. Their short masts angled at the cloudless sky, they varied in size from small, neat *sambuk* to the bigger *zeima*. Most lay in the deep water away from the quay's edge waiting for work. A figure waved from the deck of one. We were easy to spot.

'Good morning!' I shouted towards the elderly grizzled man standing beside the long boom as the boat drew near. Knowing who was the captain is simple anywhere in the world, an air of confidence and command no matter the size or sophistication, marks them out anywhere, on any vessel.

'*Marhaba, marhaba.*' He reached up a welcoming hand. Cautiously I stretched a leg down, putting one foot on the dhow's thin bulwark.

'This looks like fun, Amelia.' Stuart said. 'But will it get us out to the islands? The engine doesn't seem to have much power.'

'They'll put the sail up in a moment and then, you watch, she'll get going properly.'

I loved these boats, they were so perfectly designed for these waters, making use of the monsoon winds. But they were difficult to manoeuvre and being in a rush was futile. It was all about going with the prevailing winds, being part of the weather patterns, rather than engine power.

The bustle of leaving a harbour excited me as much as ever, a combination of the unknown ahead combined with that feeling of freedom. The crew untied faded strips of canvas all along the boom, shaking loose the fabric and heaving up the triangular lateen sail. The coir ropes made the wooden blocks squeak as the sail was stretched out over the side. Our boat was weather worn, bare-foot-polished, a practical trading craft, a typical vessel of the Indian Ocean and, I could see, with an experienced crew. It was totally appropriate for these waters and a romantic way to do my recce of a Red Sea archipelago.

The wide teak planks were warm and smooth underfoot as I walked towards the high stern edged with a carved balustrade. The captain gave the tiller a slight tweak and glanced up to check the sail. After my early days in Scotland, I had learned to bide my time, wait until the boat was in open water and clear of the harbour and other shipping before opening a conversation with the boss. The sail filled, ropes were adjusted until the boom and sail were at right angles across the hull and steadily, the port with its cranes, freighters and clanking activity fell astern. I knew exactly where I wanted to go, but this was Arabia, where a woman was not expected to give orders or directions.

'Where are we heading for, please?' I asked, wondering whether we would be able to communicate.

'I take you to the village.' Communication seemed all right, but the village was not where I wanted to go. I knew it was about thirty-five nautical miles to the village of Dahlak Kebir, and it would take most of a day to get there. Tight for time, as ever, two days had been my allocation for recceing these islands. The village was no good to the passengers either, it would necessitate transporting people to reach the area of interest. Nor, I felt, would it be appealing – no doubt the transport would be dodgy too. This was not at all what I wanted.

The archipelago had once been a major trading site for the Arabs and Turks. There were historic sites, ancient graves and water cisterns, which I hoped would hold sufficient interest to make these arid islands a good addition to Asmara. However, it would be more diplomatic to do what the captain had chosen, see what he wished to show me first, then I would get what I wanted. I hoped.

Predictably the fishing village was a collection of low, concrete huts separated by dusty tracks. Nets, with desiccated fish skeletons still caught in the mesh, were stretched on poles, drying in the heat. Scrawny mongrels, rib cages a rack of bones, lay baking in sandy hollows. I was impatient to get on with my plan. But dusk was quickly upon us and we had no choice but to stay in the village, at the Luul Hotel. Surprisingly, after Massawa, we seemed to have arrived at the Ritz. Floors were tiled, cool and clean, there were no droning mosquitoes, ironed cloths covered the tables and best of all the taps produced water and my bed had sheets, a pillow and even a mosquito net.

Pointing at the chart spread among the breakfast plates next morning, I explained what I wanted to Stuart. 'I need to get them to take us here. Look, that's deep water, there in that bay, right up to that cliff. I reckon that must be where the big dhows came to get fresh water on their way to Mecca. The crew wouldn't want to lug the water far, so the boats would need to get close alongside somewhere.'

'Shall I see if I can find some transport?' he asked.

'I'd prefer to go round there in the boat. See it from the sea if possible and then go ashore. It looks as if he could bring her in there. If those big dhows used that bay, our tenders could too and it doesn't look too far to walk the graves and cisterns, even in the heat.'

'Ok, you're the boss, but seems like a long shot to me.'

'Maybe, but please could you tell the boat fellow? He's far more likely to take instructions from you than me.'

The heat was like a solid wall as we came out of the hotel for the five minute walk to the harbour, but it was dry rather than humid. Stuart, still fulfilling his role as IT guru, had checked the compact little computer, the size of a paperback, which I had grown to appreciate. It was light to carry and easy to use. Now it was wrapped in a towel sheltering inside the Prada rucksack.

'Morning, Master,' Stuart greeted the captain. 'We'd like to go south.' Stuart was undaunted by the lack of response. 'Along the shore a bit before heading back to Massawa, if that's OK with you?'

'We go to Massawa, yes?'

I jumped up with my scrap of chart, knowing he had probably never seen such a thing before.

'I'd like to go here.' I pointed at the bay, down to the south. Without bothering to glance at it, he pushed the tiller and the dhow slowly turned as the inadequate engine brought the stem round, saying only, 'You have paid.'

Back-to-back, Stuart and I sat propping each other up, fanned by a breeze under the canvas awning rigged up over the deck for shade. I faced to port watching a low, rocky shore slide past. At first glance the landscape seemed feature-less and dull, but the birdlife was varied and surprisingly abundant. Grey herons waited patiently on the beach, terns swooped over the shallows, darting down suddenly for a fish disturbed by our passage across the still sea, and sandpipers scuttled along the water's edge, prodding the sand with narrow beaks. Occasionally a stunted tree sprouted up from the low coral cliffs. I felt increasingly determined to make this recce worthwhile. Pliny had known of these strategic isles and the Portuguese had paused, raiding here on their way further east. They must be worth it.

'We turn here. This is far enough. Now we go to Massawa.'

'Captain, just a little further, please. I would very much like to see the graves and cisterns.' I hoped I sounded firm but not too pushy.

'There is no port down here, nowhere to land.'

Stuart, more patient than me, added, 'Well, I am sure you are right, Captain, but we'd like to have a look anyway. So, let's just carry on, round that headland would be good.' A male command carried the necessary weight, the blocks creaked and slowly we sailed further south, creeping along the shore.

There were no mountains, no hills in the distance and none of the islands had any height. The whole archipelago was simply a series of low coral plateaux with a few villages trading in sea cucumber and dried fish. Turning the corner, the dhow entered a bay where the dark blue of deep water changed to turquoise, and before long it was possible to see the sandy bottom. The captain shouted a command. The lateen sail fell and the lad in the bow threw an anchor over the stem. Gently the boat came to rest over a mile offshore in deep water.

'Captain, any chance we might get a bit closer in, please?' There was not a flicker of recognition that I had spoken. I tried again. 'Could we get up to those dhows just ahead? I expect you know how much water they draw.' I was trying not to sound exasperated. He would know perfectly well how much water they needed to float.

'She's right you know,' Stuart said, grinning at him almost apologetically, 'Let's just get up to those boats, then we'll jump over the side and wade ashore.' Reluctantly the anchor was retrieved. Little rivulets of water, drying as they went, ran down the deck as the *zeima* crept nearer to the shore. It was simple, the soft sandy bottom barely shelved, so he could easily judge the depth in the clear unruffled water.

'I go no further. Here we stop.' Another loud splash and the anchor plunged back over the side, but far less rope disappeared this time.

I gave him my sweetest smile. 'This is fine, thank you.'

Stuart crammed on his baseball cap and leapt over the side. 'It's fabulous, come on in!'

'It's the depth I'm interested in. Stop swimming and stand up!'

He stood upright and the water came up to his chest. I lowered myself over the side. Water tickled my armpits. Reaching behind me over the gunwale, I grabbed hold of my rucksack. Balancing it on my head, I began to push my way through the tepid water towards the beach.

Stuart took my hand and we waded towards the shore, Prada safely lodged above the salt waters. Thinking I was now in the shallows, I relaxed my grip and stumbled into a hole, but Stuart held on and my beloved rucksack remained dry. The beach was hard and white. It was easier to walk on than the soft beaches of Madagascar. There were no spiky bits of broken coral underfoot, no flotsam, merely a few thin bleached and broken shells scattered in a curving line. A beach landing here would be easy, the passengers would manage this. Part One would work.

Backing the beach was a low rock face, conveniently eroded into steps. We made our way to the top, clothes quickly drying in the strong sun. We were greeted by an undulating limestone plateau stretching for miles, harsh and barren. Surprisingly, in the distance the figure of a man appeared, hazy in the mirage of heat. He came towards us, inevitably a goat at his side on a piece of string. I was relieved my clothes had dried so quickly and were no longer plastered to my body. He stopped a few feet away and stared so, pulling out paper and pencil from my rucksack, I sketched what I hoped a cistern might look like. Without a word, he turned, released the goat and waved, indicating we should follow. The goat, freed from its string, trotted off, pausing for an occasional nibble at the sparse bushes with lemon-green leaves. Only a goat would find something to eat in such an arid place. We too trotted along, following our new guide.

The cavernous cisterns were the reason the archipelago had drawn people throughout centuries of trade and had fascinated me as tangible links to the seventh century. Massawa, while a port, had virtually no fresh water, but here the islanders had burrowed into the coral and limestone to carve huge underground chambers. The natural dips and hollows of the surface rock had been increased so when the rare rains came, water was channelled to collect deep underground. None would be lost through evaporation. The huge *zaroug* dhows carrying hundreds of pilgrims to Mecca, that had come across the Arabian Sea from India's ancient ports of Mandvi, Cannanore and Cochin, and made the Dhalak Isles a regular call. The islands were known as a reliable watering place.

Following the goat, which knew exactly where to get a drink, we came to a circle of concrete barely ten inches high surrounding a hole. It lay like an abandoned child's swimming ring, smooth and incongruous on the broken ground.

Beside the ring was a young girl, her shawl wrapped over her head. At her feet was a battered jerrycan, while a donkey, harnessed with canvas panniers, waited patiently, head down, ears drooping, resigned to the burning sun. Our goat-herd guide pointed at the hole and I stuck my arm through the opening into the darkness below. Instantly I could feel the change in temperature and the slight breath of air in my face was cool and fresh.

We moved aside and the girl moved closer to lower her can into the darkness. Green plastic rope slipped through her hands until there was a soft splash. Taking the rope from her, Stuart hauled up the heavy can. She covered her mouth with a little brown hand, giggling and looking at him coyly. He stood the jerry can carefully on the ground at her feet, where she gave it a gentle push so that water slopped out, filling the nearby rocky hollows. The goat and donkey knew the drill and ambled up for their drink before it had time to evaporate.

I waved my camera at our guide, wanting to capture such a picturesque scene, but he shook his head, so I had to make do with photos of the cistern, the wide landscape and Stuart peering into the hole. No little girl with flashing dark eyes, robes and jingling jewellery, just a goat and donkey.

Our guide ambled off, walking slowly towards a patch of low, scrubby trees. Maybe this was the graveyard. The acacias grew more densely by comparison with the surrounding landscape and many were in flower. Fluffy pompoms were clustered among tiny fronds of green leaves, little bursts of acid yellow. In amongst the trees were black basalt tablets in sharp contrast to the white limestone. Tightly bunched, these slabs protruded from the rocky surface; each was nearly a foot high and marked an ancient tomb. Many were carved with ornate script and some had arabesques and curls embellishing the tops. In London, I had struggled to visualise this first century AD necropolis and it would need an inspirational description, but I now felt sure the cistern and these ancient tombstones would provide a curious and memorable morning's visit. No one would ever experience these islands if they were not taken by an adventurous expedition vessel. It would be another visit worth the complicated logistics.

As with a horse returning to its stable at the end of the day, our voyage back to the mainland across the Mits'iwa Channel was curiously much quicker than the outbound one. We returned to the hotel weary and so crusty with salt that even the featureless grubby foyer felt welcoming.

'Hello, here we are again. Is there water today? Any chance of a shower, please?' I asked, ever hopeful.

'Yes, of course we have water. Why do you ask?' The fellow chewing noisily at Reception, unwillingly took his feet down from the desk. Stuart shouted over his shoulder as he bounded up the stairs, three at a time.

'See you here in thirty and get me a Bellotti if you're down first.'

I followed quickly, anxious to get my share of water.

'Ok, so what's the plan for tomorrow?' Stuart asked. 'What about the beer villa?'

'It's officially out of bounds, but I know where it is.'

'Of course you do!' he grinned at me. 'Let's go early, before anyone else is about, I'll see if someone from the hotel can come with us.'

It was pleasantly cool and fresh when the three of us set off next morning, walking quietly through the still sleeping houses. Dogs searched for scraps among the broken masonry piled at the feet of the battered doum palms. Jemal, who had said he was delighted to be out of the humid kitchen, led us to a chain-link fence. Over six-foot-high, it barred the road. Without the slightest pause, he turned right, walked another ten feet or so and, stooping, he pulled the mesh apart, holding the links open for us. Quickly, we squeezed through the gap. Ahead was the most perfect Art Deco villa. We could have been among the glamour of the Cote D'Azur were it not for the pockmarks and bullet holes spattered across the white walls, a frightening reminder of Signora Bellotti's predilection for hiding infiltrators and also of her determined resistance.

A wide terrace ran round the entire building with wide, shallow steps leading to the entrance. The air of abandonment was increased by the bougainvillea, arching over terracotta roof tiles and windows, it grew unchecked and exuberant. Jemal had disappeared, there was just Stuart and me. Feeling more like a spy than an expedition ship planner, I followed Stuart up the front steps and into the villa. Strong clear light filled the house, emphasising the architecture. Rooms had high ceilings, well-placed windows let in a breeze from the sea, the staircase had a sweeping banister, the chrome no longer shiny. Metal-framed chairs clustered in groups, ready for occupants, but their seats sagged and the scarlet cushions, once chic with white piping, were now mouldy and grub-chewed. Walking on into the house, beyond the staircase vaulted arches led to an empty swimming pool. Light bounced off the walls and curled round pillars bathing the pool in warm sunshine. Signora Bellotti and her friends would have been able to slip into the pool from a lounger indoors, glide through the pillars and interlinked basins to swim through the outer walls and into the garden beyond.

Now, cool, deserted but not quite derelict, the whole villa still held a frisson of thirties glamour.

'Martini, darling?'

I jumped. Stuart bent over a chrome and glass-wheeled drinks trolley, lifting the lid of an ice bucket. The little carriage, waited in perfect condition, ready to produce the next cocktail.

'No, thanks. I'm hoping Noel Coward swathed in a silk dressing-gown and brandishing a cigarette holder will appear in a moment. You know how he described a martini, don't you?' I asked, trying a languid imitation: 'My dear, a perfect martini should be made by filling a glass with gin then waving it in the general direction of Italy.'

19

Greece

Chôras and A Knight

I walked down the metal steps, descending from the ship's top deck. In two hours' time, following the Naming Ceremony here in Leith, my responsibilities for the passenger visits and carefully drafted itineraries would be put to the test. After years of coaxing to get my way, of adventures, scorpion stings, dodgy agents, one-engine planes and abandonment on uninhabited islands, the recces, inspections and planning were about to become real.

Only I knew the schedules were inoperable.

The visits to inaccessible islands, specially designed for our loyal passengers, were impossible. The tenders had not arrived from Orkney.

They were over a month late. Now, not only was there no time for practice, but more importantly, without them there was no means to transfer passengers from the ship ashore. It was irrelevant how magical, curious or mysterious the islands were. It would be impossible to reach them.

My phone buzzed and I moved around to get a better signal. 'Hello? Hello? Yes, this is Amelia, but I'm afraid I can't hear you.'

'Don't you recognise my voice?'

It was months since HH had failed to appear in the Maldives. How dare he ring so casually after all this time with his smooth, man-of-the-world air? I was annoyed and impatient. I had enough to deal with right now.

'Where have you been? Your phone's been off for so long.'

'I've been travelling, now I'm on the ship. We've been sailing round from Oban.' I knew I sounded irritated. 'Didn't you feel my presence as I went past Ocean Village?'

'My dear girl, I haven't been there for ages, I sent the boat to the Med months ago. Do keep up.' I bit back a retort on the values of communication. 'Where are you now?' he asked.

'Leith, the Naming Ceremony is in a couple of hours. Everything perfect, even the weather.' Loyally, I didn't mention the Marigold action, the blocked heads or my worries over the absence of tenders.

'Who's doing the Naming?' he asked, 'Someone international?'

'Yes, assuming you call Princess Anne international!' I replied tartly. I needed to establish I was not at his beck and call. 'I must go – put on my glad rags. Should be fun.' Now I wished I sounded more relaxed and friendly.

'Why didn't you invite me? Sounds a splendid occasion.' I had considered this. I knew he would dress smartly, with old-school style, probably in a well-cut dark suit, with maybe a yellow tie, possibly a slightly OTT gold watch chain and good shoes. He would do wonders for my image and would definitely be noticed. But his presence would give rise to endless questions and after all this time, I still had no answers. Anyway, he didn't deserve to be asked, after letting me down so casually.

'I would have loved you to be here, but it's supposed to be family only, and you don't exactly behave like family.'

'Pity, sounds just my sort of event. How long before you're free? Be good to see you.' Annoyingly my heart gave a little flutter.

'I was supposed to sail with the ship to Norway, but sadly I have to go to Greece tonight. I covered the Peloponnese last time but in three months she'll go through Suez, and I must establish the programme for the Greek islands.'

'Ah, so I conclude you don't want to have dinner with me?' He was exasperating. Why did he make my heart sing? And it was irritating that he never gave me any warning of his plans, keeping his cards so close to his chest.

'Of course, I'd love to, but I'm flying from Edinburgh tonight. I really don't want to go. Greece was bad enough last time. No choice, I'm afraid.'

'Keep smiling, and I'm sure it'll be better this time.' Despite everything, I was still glad of his encouragement. 'I'll just have to amuse myself without you, I'm due a visit to Delilah anyway. I've abandoned her for far too long. Ignored her seductive charms.'

Who was Delilah, I wondered jealously? Greece was dispiriting enough, without this.

'Yes, it's been ages.' His voice was as attractively mischievous as ever. 'You met her way back, when she was having her bottom cleaned.'

Bottom cleaned? Of course, his elegant yacht, all fitted cushions, teak and polished brass.

'I'll give you a shout in a couple of weeks,' he said. 'But don't forget to send me some photos of the ceremony. One of you wearing a hat, in your finery.'

'Don't be silly. I won't be wearing a hat. Might blow off! This is Scotland.'

'Pity, you'd look good in a little pillbox number. Anyway,

have fun, hope it goes off smoothly, and watch out for those wily Greeks. Untrustworthy lot.'

Yellow Mercedes taxis jostled for custom, emitting clouds of exhaust fumes. I rather wished it was impossible for me to recognise Nikos, but his stocky figure was unmistakable among the throng. Greece, again. My heart sank.

'Hi Nikos. Hello Yannis, good to see you,' I lied. Once again, as we drew away from the airport, clouds of cigarette smoke blew between the front seats, joining me in the back.

'How are things in Athens? What time are the boat inspections?'

'I have chosen a boat for you. Don't worry, nothing for you to do. All is ready at the marina in Glyfada.' My hackles, already up at the sight of them, rose further.

'Interesting.' I tried to sound casual. 'What kind of boat?' He didn't even bother to turn round to speak to me, simply waved a tobacco-stained hand, his heavy gold ring caching the headlights.

'It is a good boat. It will be fine. Just what you need, and I will come with you. Yannis too naturally.' This was outrageous. How on earth could an Athens taxi driver be necessary for a recce of the scattered isles of the Cyclades?

'Nikos, I know there's a holiday in a couple of days, so surely you'll want to be with your family, not working? And Yannis too.'

'No, no, it's fine, you will need us. We collect you in the morning. Bring all your things, then we leave, straight to Aegina island. Everything is ready.'

'Sorry, but Aegina is not on my list. I'd like to start with Kea. There's time to see the boat now, even in the dark. No doubt the marina is well lit.' I could tell from the back of his neck the answer would be unhelpful.

'That is not possible. The captain has gone home. It is a good boat. You will like it.'

'What is it called? Have you faxed all the paperwork to the office? They are really busy with the first cruise, but they must have all the details of the charter before I set off.' I wanted to remind him it was not only me he was dealing with.

'It is called *Argo*.' I suppressed a giggle feeling confident neither Nikos nor Yannis had special protection from Athena. Immediately they left me at the hotel, I called the office at the marina. Thanks to the Greek love of late hours, the boat charter office was still open.

'Good evening, I'm interested in a boat called *Argo*.' I hoped I sounded professional. I could hear the girl flicking through her papers.

'It's here.' Bracelets jangled. 'You can come and see it any time, it is by the first pontoon.'

Ten minutes later another yellow Mercedes taxi dropped me by the gates. Alone.

'Hi, Nikos. Apologies for disturbing your evening, it's Amelia.'

'Who?' The babble of restaurant chatter came loudly over the air.

'Nikos, it's *Amelia*. I'm at the marina. I am afraid to say the boat won't do. There is far too much weed on the hull.'

'Weed? What do you mean weed?'

'There's about a metre of weed hanging off the bottom. Our recce will be about two hundred miles around the islands and weed will slow the boat down, as well as cost more in fuel.'

'No problem, we will see tomorrow.'

'I want to see her out of the water early in the morning.'

'You can't. You cannot see the boat out of the water...
Women not allowed in shipyards,' he ended triumphantly. I
was tired, it had been a long day, a day of curtsying to HRH,
worrying how my itineraries would be received, and still
there was no news about the tenders.

I paused, thinking. Would I regret this? Too bad, he was
more than simply slippery and by now it was clear he always
had to get one over on me. He simply preferred to tell me a
lie than the truth.

'Don't you worry, I will find a boat myself. Goodbye and
thanks for your help.'

With me went his commission, his lucrative percentage
for every time the ship stopped, every call she made and each
time a passenger set foot on shore.

'No, no. I find another boat for you.'

'Too late, Nikos.' I hoped I had not made too much of an
enemy.

Two days later, in a flurry of fumes, I left the marina. Kea,
my first island in the Cyclades was a dark shape about ten
miles ahead. I felt more at home among the swells and vast-
ness of the northern Atlantic, but simply being on the water
was relaxing and created that same sense of freedom. The
cloud of Nikos fell astern, mingling with the dark haze of
exhaust fumes, and I could feel myself unwinding. Michael
had come up with a new shipping agent, who was far more
willing and, quickly assessing the value of a small vessel
with passengers visiting spring and autumn, had produced
this functional fibreglass motorboat. The *Poseidon* had two
cabins, one for me with tiny separate hand-pumped loo
and shower, and another for Nafalei, my translator. It was

perfectly suitable, if charmless. The captain, Leonidas, was appropriately sized for his craft; diminutive and swarthy, he bore no resemblance to a lion. He had been briefed to follow my itinerary south through the chain of the Cyclades and with nine islands to visit, there would be none of the usual lazy afternoon swimming, beach time or long barbecue lunches. This was purely work, and I had chosen the best route in advance, fuel calculated and at the end, assuming all went well, he would receive a healthy bonus.

Kea was a charming island. Walking in the hills, chamomile sprouted from gaps between square marble slabs releasing a fresh green scent. Ragged clumps of big yellow daisies jostled with the spikes of yellow mullen flowers. On the steep terraces below were pomegranate, olive and judas trees, their crowns at waist height buzzing loudly with bees enjoying the hot sunshine. Curling ahead of me, following the contour of the hill, wound the Byzantine road, smooth and polished by countless feet and sandals walking this charming track. This was what I had come to see and strolling downhill in the scented air was a joy. I was thankful Nafalei kept to translating rather than chattering.

Each day we landed on another island, exploring another village chóra, perched high above the sea, safe from marauding pirates and the buccaneering Ottomans. Each was a maze of buildings, tightly packed together to channel cooling sea breezes or deflect a chilling winter blast. Buildings were stark white, sunshine bounced off white walls. Doors and windows were painted lapis blue, terracotta pots, bright with scarlet geraniums, marched up steps and clustered in doorways. Every little village was charming and each the same as the next, so it became difficult to distinguish one from another. All went smoothly until, returning to *Poseidon* from checking another tiny chóra, we found Leonidas hanging over the stern, his arm buried up the elbow in the sea.

'What's the problem, Nafalei? What is Leonidas saying?'

'He says you must ring the office. Georg wants to speak to you.'

'I'll do that now, but please ask him to fire up, so we can get to Paros tonight.' Leonidas, hearing 'Paros', again launched into a tirade.

'He says he cannot leave. There's a problem with the gear box.'

I called Georg. 'Nafaleei said you wanted to speak to me. Yes, we're in Serifos, pretty little place. So, all is good, and I loved the Byzantine road on Kea.' I rambled on, wondering why I was telling all this to Georg.

'Good, I am glad all goes well,' he said politely. 'From our end there is a problem. We have not received the money from your office. No payment has arrived in the bank account.'

I apologised and said I'd call the office immediately.

Skipton could have been as close as the nearby chóra; the reception was crackle free.

When I asked Roger if the money had been sent, his indignation was clear. I rang Georg again to reassure him.

'Georg, I'm really sorry, this is hugely embarrassing, but the office has definitely sent it. I would like to keep up to the schedule, if that is Ok? Paros now. Yes, we can speak tomorrow. I'll give you a call about midday, is that Ok?'

A moment later Nafalei's phone pinged into life, she relayed something to Leonidas and miraculously the gear box was no longer out of action. In our now-familiar cloud of diesel fumes, *Poseidon* set off to Paros as the afternoon wind dropped and the evening sun sank a little lower.

Next morning, the Paros harbour thrummed with

motorbikes, dogs, delivery vans and elderly, black-clad women walking to the market. It seemed a metropolis after the quiet of the previous islands. I told Nafalei I wanted to look at the castle and the church in the village of Parikia.

'I have never been here before,' came her rather grumpy reply. 'This island is new for me. I will stay here and watch the boats.' Was she going on strike like the gear box, I wondered?

I set off away from the waterfront walking uphill towards the Kastro, climbing the shallow steps constructed from the island's famous white marble. Light reflected from the smooth, cool stone. Vines cascaded over courtyard walls to hang in curtains of green, and the morning air was already heady with the fragrance of orange blossom and hot bread. In front of me, the castle wall looked like a giant piece of meat pie. Huge slabs of stone, varying in size, were stacked on top of each other in layers, each layer resembling a different type of meat, pressed together to make a tempting pie. Among these were rounds like slices of hardboiled egg. Once these had been columns. The stone for the layers had been looted long ago from the nearby temple of Apollo and used to create this curious wall for the castle. Outside some of the houses were more chunks of columns, acting as perfect plinths for pots of vivid geraniums. To my surprise my mobile vibrated, catching a signal from between the buildings. I had missed a call from Michael, but he had left a message.

'Hope all's going well. A quick call to let you know you've won. Keep going and give me a ring when you can.' That was it. Won what? He had sounded less harassed but there was no mention of the money, the tenders, or of how the cruises were going in Norway. Had Gunna sorted out the problem of transferring the passengers ashore? In dealing with Nikos and Leonidas I had almost forgotten.

I called him back and asked first about the tenders.

'I left a message, didn't you get it? The low loader appeared just as we were about to cast off. Thank Goodness. HRH had gone or security might have been a problem. The lorry might have been stopped.' I fought back tears of relief. 'We were a bit late into Bergen, but no big issue. Gunna's doing well too. Oh, and you've won.'

'What do you mean *won*?' standing in the sun surrounded by ancient marble columns, I couldn't think what he was talking about.

'The competition, of course. It seemed only right, you deserve it, so they are called *Ardbeg* and *Talisker*.' Michael had wanted everyone in the office to suggest names for the tenders, and I had been determined to win: it seemed my suggestion of island distilleries with easy phonetic names to be called over the VHF from Copenhagen to Cochin had succeeded. I bounced back on-board *Poseidon,* relieved and happy.

Leonidas and Nafalei nursed mugs of coffee; their expressions were far from friendly.

'Georg wants to speak to you.'

Georg was barely polite, and I couldn't blame him. I had been allowed to take the boat on simply a promise, and it looked as if my promise of a transfer of the fifteen thousand pounds was a sham. I rang Yorkshire again. Again, Roger told me the money had been transferred. I asked him to check once more, then, disheartened by the lack of a result, I tried to mollify Georg.

'It's Amelia here. I've just spoken to the office and the Financial Director assures me he transferred fifteen thousand pounds, two days ago. It should come through today, or tomorrow, at the latest.' Hoping this would appease him, I carried on quickly. 'If I can keep to the programme, that would be really helpful. I'll miss out Ios, too popular for us. Sifnos next, then Folegandros. I should then be on schedule to finish in Santorini. Thank you, that's really helpful. Have a good holiday weekend.'

My crew of two had almost given up being polite, so silence ruled the waves as we left the harbour in the evening sun. I settled down in the saloon to write up my notes, file photos and bring everything up to date, each island was blurring more and more quickly into the next. The crackling of the VHF was irritating and I almost missed it, but through the interference came faintly:

'This is Delilah. This is Delilah.'

Could it be? My heart thumped.

'Leonidas, please could I use the VHF?' I tried to sound casual, but he looked at me suspiciously. 'Please, Leonidas?' He understood me perfectly well, but he went on gripping the receiver.

'This is Delilah, this is Delilah,' crackled again through the cabin. 'Amelia if you're there, Channel 77.'

'Nafalei, please could you explain to Leonidas? I think you can hear someone is trying to contact me. I only want to use the VHF.' She muttered and reluctantly he passed the handset over.

'Delilah, Delilah, this is Amelia. Channel 77.' I stretched past Leonidas to twirl the dial. 'Excuse me.' His jaw dropped.

'My dear girl, where are you? I've been shouting you up for days.'

'In the Cyclades, where are you?'

'Peloponnese. Monemvasia tonight.' No wonder it was crackly, he was nearly seventy miles away but of course HH did have a big aerial.

'I love Monemvasia, one of my favourite places. I have a

couple more islands to do before I finish in Santorini. Maybe two days' time.' I enunciated each word carefully, wondering how much he could hear.

'Right.' The interference grew louder. 'Give you a shout— mobile, not VHF.' So quickly the communication was over.

Sifnos, with its capital, Apollonia backed by high hills, had beaches, better ones than the other islands. The small museum of local life with the inevitable pottery and shards failed to capture my flagging interest. Again, there was another charming chóra, with dovecotes and fig trees shading the houses, but my enthusiasm had waned. We moved on to Folegandros.

From the moment I jumped off *Poseidon,* bouncing in the motion beside the jetty, I was aware of stillness and peace blanketing the neglected terraces and their retaining walls. The island's barren slopes were deserted and going wild, being too arid for olives or figs. There was only thin grass, sun-dried to wispy ochre. A donkey stood in a tiny patch of shade, motionless in a dry ravine. Blending with the brown surroundings, he waited, head down, waiting for what? Nothing else seemed to have life, only the ubiquitous yellow daisies frothing over walls. But there was something bewitching about the island. I pushed on up the steep road climbing higher away from the harbour. Here the chóra clung to the cliff edge, the flat-roofed houses gazing over the Aegean. A track edged by white walls zigzagged uphill to a tiny church, its dome brilliant white. More daisies danced beside the surrounding walls. Why was the island so bewitching? Maybe the lonely emptiness was appealing, maybe the power of the stark barren hills, maybe the wide, unimpeded views of the sea all around. But probably it was purely because I felt excited.

Out there on the azure Aegean, not far west, was Delilah.

The wind, whipping up the sea, blew straight into the harbour, so the moment I clambered back on board, Leonidas manoeuvred *Poseidon* smartly away from the quay. He had not acknowledged my return, but I was on time, so we were well clear when the white ferry appeared round the headland and entered the bay. Her bow thrusters churned, pushing her round to line up, stern to, on the quay. As Leonidas spun the wheel, the little boat left the shelter of the island and began bouncing and bumping through the waves. His mobile began to ring. An animated conversation ensued. I understood not a word, but even in Greek I could get the drift and his body language was a give-away.

Time to try the office again.

Roger's phone went straight to voicemail. 'I realise it's a Sunday but please call me. It's urgent. Have you managed to check the money has gone through? I'll have no mobile coverage now until we get to Santorini. That's where I get off. Please could you leave me a message?' I finished urgently. I suspected he had no idea where Santorini was, not that it mattered. I smiled sweetly at Leonidas.

After a couple of hours, to my surprise, the Nokia burst into life. I had two messages.

'This is Roger. Sorry to miss your call, I'll try again later.' The other was far more encouraging.

'I've missed you again. You are elusive. Brief signal here off Milos. Let me know where to find you.'

I tried Roger again, but again the call went to answerphone. I tried to look unconcerned, but judging by Leonidas's expression, he had a better grasp of English than he cared to divulge.

Ahead rose stripy Santorini. Each horizontal deposit

of volcanic ash was a different shade. Dark brown, burnt umber, grey and rich ochre, the island rose in horizontal banded layers, sheer from the sea. Along the crest, the cubist structures of Oia came into view. Like a capping of snow, the village ran along the ridge looking out to sea. This famous island caldera was my voyage's end, and I was longing to escape the atmosphere and confines of this horrible plastic boat. Leonidas, phone again pressed into his ear, eased back the throttle as he spoke steadily to someone. Gazing at the cliffs ahead, I noticed a white streak separate itself from the shore. Drawing nearer, the streak materialised into a grey speed boat. It headed unerringly towards us until I could read the tall white letters painted along the hull. 'Hellenic Coast Guard'. The boat turned and drew abeam, leaving a few feet between us. Standing by a life raft was a man in uniform. He raised a loud hailer.

'Mrs Dalton?' Surprised he knew my name, I waved.

'Mrs Dalton, you are under arrest. We will escort you in.'

The police truck ground up the precipitous road, blaring its horn, blasting at tourists and donkeys that blocked the way. Slowly it churned round each zigzag until I realised the sea must be far below. The road was so steep I had to brace my legs to prevent myself from slipping off the metal bench seat and onto the floor. It was difficult to balance with my arms behind my back, my wrists already rubbed by the handcuffs. My Prada friend, bulging with laptop and Nokia, slipped noisily across the floor, sliding from side to side as we rounded each corner. Opposite, not taking his eyes off me, sat an officer, expressionless and still, gun across his knees. Dark patches of sweat spread under the armpits of his shirt. The padded vest must be hot. Was I really so threatening that he needed a gun and bullet-proof vest? They were taking no chances.

At the hilltop station, the officer took my fingerprints and all my possessions. Everything apart from my clothes. They put the handcuffs back on and led me along a corridor. A grey steel door marked No.2 clanged shut behind me. There was only a bed with a filthy blanket. Rough and scratchy, it gave off a powerful stench of pee and vomit. The late afternoon sunlight lit a golden square of hope on the wall. It was the only thing that was not grey.

What now? I tried to think rationally, not let myself be overcome by a rising sense of panic. What should I do? What could I do? Today was Sunday and it was almost over, tomorrow was a holiday in Greece. Even if I were allowed to phone who would I ring in Greece? Would I be allowed an international call? Probably not. If they needed guns and padded vests to arrest me, it was unlikely I would be allowed to use my own mobile and an international call would be beyond their budget.

Weary after the past days of island recces and broken nights in *Poseidon's* cramped, airless cabin, I lay down and fell asleep. When I woke, I was stiff, the sunlight had gone, and the cell was no more than an imprisoning dark box. I had drunk my allowance of water earlier and I was hungry and chilly. Walking up the steep slopes of Folegandros seemed a long time ago. How did prison work? Did someone appear with food or should I rattle the door? That would probably annoy the guards. It felt like a mixture of boarding school and a horror movie. But much more frightening.

They had taken my watch, but I reckoned it must be about ten by now. I lay on the narrow canvas bed, trying not to think too much about the reality of being imprisoned in a Greek jail, fighting my rising fear that I might be locked in here for several days. I dozed again, waking, damp and cold.

Something had roused me. A noise in the solitary, echoing silence. Boots were coming along the corridor. Keys jangled. More and more like a movie, I thought hysterically.

A key jiggled in the lock and the metal door swung open.

I tried to jump up, tried to get my legs just to move, but they had gone to sleep. Pins and needles fizzed up my shins and my feet were numb.

'Come. You follow me.' I stumbled after him, afraid he would change his mind, reaching out as I went to prop myself up on the grey walls. Silhouetted at the end of the corridor stood Helly Handsome.

'My dear girl, you look as if you could do with a drink.'

He held my hand in a warm reassuring grip, as the taxi whizzed downhill swerving round the zigzags at speed, throwing me against him.

'How did you know where to find me?'

'Well, there are not too many red heads in this place.' He grinned. 'A fellow in the café on the quay has a cousin who's one of the crew on the patrol boat. Mind you, it was expensive.'

'What do you mean *expensive*?'

'I had to loosen him up to get the information. The bottle of ouzo cost me twenty-five euros.' He sounded offended.

'Twenty-five euros, is that all I'm worth?'

'Possibly. That and the other fifteen thousand.'

'Ah! So, the money had not gone through, then.' I said slowly, leaning over to kiss his cheek.

'That was nice. More please.'

'How did you get hold of the agent at this time of night?'

'I didn't even try. The police seemed perfectly happy with a credit card.'

The taxi drew up inches from the edge of the quay, where

a square of blue carpet had been carefully placed at the foot of a teak gangway. HH jumped out and held out his hand to me.

'Here we are. Welcome, welcome again to Delilah,' I swayed a little and clutched his hand. 'She's pleased to see you. It's years since you were on board, and possibly years too since you were on a *decent* boat.'

'Thank you,' was all I could manage as he led me up the carpeted gangway.

'Shower' he said firmly, 'and then a Margarita, I think.'